Windows on Jesus

Windows on Jesus

Methods in Gospel Exegesis

Wim Weren

Trinity Press International
Harrisburg, Pennsylvania

Translated by John Bowden from the Dutch *Vensters op Jezus: Methoden in de uitleg van de evangeliën*, published 1998 by Uitgeverij Meinema, Zoetermeer, The Netherlands.

© Uitgeverij Meinema, Zoetermeer 1998

Translation © John Bowden 1999

First North American Edition 1999
by Trinity Press International,
P.O. Box 1321, Harrisburg. PA 17105

Trinity Press International is a division of the Morehouse Group.

Cover art: *Red Alert* by Harvey Sibley, Gallery Contemporanea, Jacksonville, Florida/SuperStock

Cover design: Corey Kent

Library of Congress Cataloging-in-Publication Data

Weren, Wilhelmus Johannes Cornelis.
[Vensters op Jezus.   English]
Windows on Jesus : methods in Gospel exegesis / Wim Weren. —
1st North American ed.
p. cm.
Translated by John Bowden.
Includes bibliographical references.
ISBN 1–56338–282–2 (pbk.)
1. Bible.   N.T.   Gospels—Criticism, interpretation, etc.
I. Title.
BS2555.2.W3713   1999
226'.06'01—dc21   99–34676
CIP

Printed in Great Britain by
Biddles Ltd, Guildford and King's Lynn

Contents

Preface

Windows on Jesus has grown out of a passion for teaching. The shape and content of the book have gradually developed in my introductory courses for theological students, first in Amsterdam and later in Tilburg. The book offers an introduction to the exegesis of the Gospels. The fact that the New Testament contains four writings which fall under the literary genre 'Gospel' opens up special possibilities for their exegesis. They can be read one by one as independent and rounded stories but of course they can also be compared with one another. Moreover they form a link in a long intertextual chain which extends from the Old Testament to modern novels and poems. Finally, they are renowned as sources for our knowledge of the historical activity of Jesus. So there are many lines of approach. In this book we shall be looking through four different windows, which together give a representative picture of present-day exegetical methods and approaches. Theory is always at the service of practice. This book contains a selection of worked-out examples, for how a method works can best be seen from the results which it gives. After all, no one learns to swim by sitting at the edge of the pool.

Windows on Jesus is primarily meant for students of theology and literature in universities and colleges. Its surveys of new approaches in exegesis will also be found informative by professional theologians, pastors and catechists and will help those who attend Bible groups and schools to understand the Gospels better. A knowledge of the original languages of the Bible is not presupposed. My analyses are based on my own translations. To stimulate users to explore the Gospels on their own, some exercises are included at the end of the book and there is a list of books for further study.

Previous drafts of this book were read by Marleen Verschoren of the Catholic University of Leuven and Ron Pirson, assistant at the Theological Faculty of Tilburg. I am very grateful for their stimulating criticism.

Wim Weren

Introduction

A house with many windows

The title of this book, *Windows on Jesus*, has two meanings. First, the title refers to the extended stories about Jesus which are known as the Gospels.[1] In these writings, the Word that has become flesh (John 1.14) is expressed in language and text. The canonical Gospels are four windows on Jesus. Each evangelist gives his own view of him. The portraits are similar, but deep differences are often concealed in this very similarity.

By 'windows on Jesus' I also and above all mean the methods and approaches in present-day exegesis of the Gospels. More than ever we are aware that a reliable exegesis is not bound to one method. There are different perspectives. To a great extent the perspective chosen determines what the exegete sees. It's as if we were standing before a house with closed doors. But we can discover a lot about the interior, since the house has a number of windows. Looking through one window we see part of the lay-out and what is going on in the house. The scene that unfolds appears in a particular light, also because the window is made of a particular kind of glass. The second window shows us things that we didn't yet perceive when we had taken up a position before the first frame. Or perhaps we do see the same thing, but from another perspective. This is again true of the third or fourth windows.

The windows supplement each other. It is not a matter of playing one perspective off against another. Certainly the exegete will regularly investigate the existing windows to see how useful they are. The ways of reading employed need to be the subject of ongoing reflection. What are their strong points and weak points?

Which window needs to be repaired? By regularly renovating the windows we can substantially modify the view of the interior of the house.

Today we still make full use of methods which were developed a long time ago and which have meanwhile amply proved their use. At the same time we are eagerly in search of new windows. The present-day situation is so variegated that even specialists are not equally at home on all parts of the terrain. For lay people in the discipline it is almost impossible to get an overall view.[2] Which approaches belong to the same cluster and what is the relationship between the different clusters? In this book I try to offer a harmonious and thorough survey. The survey does not have the character of an encyclopaedia. I shall limit myself to a representative selection. Here I shall allow myself to be guided by the possible applications to the literary corpus of the four canonical Gospels. Hence there will be no discussion here, for example, of rhetorical analysis, which is useful for the exegesis of the letters of Paul.

As I have said, how the approaches selected relate to one another is an important question. An often-used but somewhat naïve procedure is to present the methods in the order in which they came into being. The line then runs from old to new. Another option – in my view just as untenable – is to attach all the different perspectives to one particular method. The trouble is that this grows out of itself, loses its own contours and assumes the function of a kind of queen mother who still governs the whole realm behind the scenes. In order to bring out the connection and the differences in this book I have chosen four large windows, each of which in turn consists of different panes. I shall present them here in a short survey, in a way which at the same time makes it clear why I recommend a particular order.

The window of synchrony

In ordinary terminology synchrony means contemporaneity. Synchronous or synchronic means coinciding in time, occurring side by side at the same time.

Synchrony also functions as a technical term in linguistics;[3] it then relates to the standpoint that the investigator adopts towards the linguistic phenomena which are being studied. What is meant is a linguistic study of the construction of a language at a particular moment of its existence, without taking historical evolution into account.

The same technical term is used in literary theory. Here the term synchronic approach is used when the relations between the constituent elements in a text are investigated. We then concentrate on the text as we have it before us, without investigating the question whether the text is composed of earlier and later layers. In a synchronic reading we try to uncover patterns of organization and make lines of meaning visible. In this connection it is illuminating that through the Latin word *textus*, 'text' is connected with 'weave' (cf. 'textile'). In a synchronic approach a text is regarded as a colourful whole in which different threads are woven together. In all this the reader performs an active role. An important activity of readers is for them to relate the component parts of the text to one another. From the component parts we gain insight into the text as a whole, while conversely the whole again sheds its own light on the different components.

The purpose of Part I

In the first part of this book I present some ways of reading which fall under the synchronic approach. I begin at the simplest level. First the boundaries of a text must be established (Chapter 1). The techniques needed to do this also play a role in the next step, the study of the structure or the construction of a text (Chapter 2). Chapter 3 is devoted to narrative analysis. The term already indicates that this is about characteristics of a particular kind of text, namely narratives. A large part of the material in the Gospels falls within this category. Chapter 4 contains an introduction to semantics. Here we consider the aspects of the meaning of a text. Within a synchronic perspective the question is one of meaning in context. Hence the title of Chapter 4.

In this book I give priority to synchrony above other

approaches. I am convinced that we must first steep ourselves in the literary aspects of a text. Only after that do other approaches to the text arise. For a number of exegetes the order chosen here is less obvious. That is because the application of synchronic ways of reading is relatively new in exegesis, and how these new models relate to other, more proven methods has still not been settled precisely.

The window of diachrony

Diachrony ('through time') is the twin sister of the term 'synchrony'. Diachronous or diachronic refers to historical development; here uncontemporaneity comes to the fore.

In linguistics a diachronic study means an investigation of the developments which a language has undergone in the course of its history. The term 'diachronic' is also used in literary theory. Then a diachronic approach means that attention is paid to the way in which traditions and texts have developed over time. Different phases can be distinguished in that process. To a certain degree the traces of the process of development can still be discovered in the text we have before us. In a text which is the result of a long process of maturing, earlier and later layers have been fused together. We can sometimes still detect that the constituent elements did not originally belong together from the fact that they are not seamlessly attached to one another, that they show a certain tension between one another or even directly contradict one another. The literary inconsistencies and tensions form the point of departure for a reconstruction of the history of the coming into being of the text. The text in its present form then functions as a springboard for statements about preceding stages in the process of literary production. The text is thus situated on a historical axis. The presupposition is that the study of the origin of a text is of great importance for understanding it. During its formation the text can be enriched with new meanings, while older layers of meaning disappear into the background or are even completely snowed under. Here one could speak of meaning-in-the-making, or of a progression of meaning.

What is said here about a text perhaps sounds somewhat strange. That is because we are mainly familiar with texts with a short life-span. In our culture of instant communication many texts seem like a plant which shoots up one day and withers the next. Only the definitive version appears in print, and in reading a text no one bothers about the rough drafts which landed in the writer's waste-paper basket. Present-day texts usually came from the brain of one writer, and originality is a lofty ideal.

But we are also familiar with texts of another type. Reports and notes go from one office to the next before they are released for publication. A large-scale work like a translation of the Bible is rarely still the work of one person. Often the work goes on over years, involving Hebrew and Greek scholars and linguists; in the definitive edition it is no longer possible to identify the contri-bution of each individual precisely. In its present form a legal text is strongly influenced by amendments called for by members of parliament, which in turn are modified by lawyers and other experts. A study of the history of the coming into being of such a document can make a substantial contribution to a better under-standing of the end-product.

For texts from a distant past a diachronic investigation is almost a must. They obey different literary conventions from those which we now observe. Many ancient texts go back to oral traditions. In a literary text the author did not so much express his own individual thoughts and emotions; the writer gave voice to what he experi-enced in the community. Earlier presentations of the same material were regarded as models worth following. Imitation was an ideal. At most an author tried to surpass the old models by putting the same thing into words even better or more attractively.[4] Nor did it matter very much in whose name a text or a tradition was handed down. Sometimes texts and traditions are even presented in the name of an authoritative figure from a distant past (like Enoch or Solomon).

Diachronic analysis is extremely meaningful in the case of texts with a long period of incubation, in texts which have functioned in different versions in different communities, in different places and in different times. The situation of the users may have determined

the form, the meaning and the function of the text to a considerable degree.

The purpose of Part II

In past centuries the mainstream of biblical exegesis had a markedly diachronic character. Even now this approach still has an
important place. Most exegetical studies and Bible commentaries
are unreadable to those who are unfamiliar with the basic principles of this model of approach. Therefore full attention is paid
in this book to diachronic approaches. The whole of Part II is
devoted to this trail in exegesis.

In Part II I first give a theoretical description of the diachronic
methods which prove to be particularly fruitful when applied to
the Gospels (Chapter 5). After that come a number of examples.
Here I concentrate first on texts from the Synoptic Gospels. In
Chapter 6 I discuss some passages which Matthew, Mark and Luke
have in common. In Chapter 7 there follows an extended analysis
of a text which appears only in Matthew and Luke, a so-called
Q-text. In Chapter 8 I put the spotlight on connections between
texts from John and passages from the Synoptic Gospels.

The window of intertextuality

The word 'intertextuality' already indicates that the primary concern here is with relations between texts. There is nothing new
about comparing texts with one another. That has happened as
long as there have been texts. The basic idea of an intertextual
study is that a text is interwoven with other texts and that its form,
meaning and function are defined by these connections. This can
be clarified as follows. If we imagine the writing or reading of a text
as a linear process, then we could say that in writing or reading it,
time and again words and sentences from other texts go through
our heads. These other texts form vertical lines which time and
again cross the horizontal line of the text. We can relate a brand
new text only to texts composed earlier, since the text has not yet
made any contribution to texts which have come into being later.

However, texts from the past can be connected with both earlier and later texts. In reaching such a text A (for example from the Gospels) we can note both earlier texts B, C, D and E, which have played a role in the composition of A, and later texts F,G, H and I, which have seen the light under the influence of A.

Here we encounter a way of looking at a text in which synchrony and diachrony coincide in a certain way. So I am putting the window of intertextuality in third place. It does not make sense to approach relations between texts purely from a synchronic perspective. Although the texts are before me on my desk at one and the same moment, I am not completely free in making connections. A text from Isaiah cannot be influenced by a text from Matthew, whereas the reverse can be the case. The chronological sequence is of great importance. But why don't I put intertextuality within the window of diachrony, which has been argued for by many other exegetes? For the following reasons. Intertextuality is interested in the relationship between rounded texts which really exist, whereas the diachronic methods are primarily concerned with the history of literary development, and in looking for relationships between texts are fond of considering hypothetical stages of development. Furthermore, in a diachronic approach attention is paid one-sidedly to what came earlier; for the most part it is beyond the scope of this approach to listen to echoes of a text in later texts, possibly even texts from our own time. So for the sake of clarity I shall present intertextuality as a separate approach, alongside synchrony and diachrony.

The purpose of Part III

In Chapter 9 I begin with a short presentation of the modern theory of intertextuality. I also illustrate its possibilities and limitations by means of four short examples which refer to relations between texts from the Gospels and the Old Testament. Chapter 10 continues in this perspective. This chapter discusses how the genealogy of Jesus at the beginning of Matthew is crossed through with Old Testament narratives. In Chapter 11 we see how the Gospels have left a colourful trail in modern artistic texts.

The window of history

Only last do I introduce the window of history: how far and on what conditions can the canonical Gospels be used in a reconstruction of the life of Jesus? Usually readers of the Bible are inclined to begin with this question ('Did this story really happen?') or perhaps even to pass over it completely, with the idea that of course everything that is written in the Bible really took place.

For our knowledge of the past, among other things we are dependent on written sources. In the case of historical investigation of Jesus, the canonical Gospels are of great importance. However, the question of the history behind the text must not be raised too early. It is certainly not the first question. Much critical acumen is needed to be able to make the leap from literary phenomena to history.

At this level the window of synchrony does not offer any support. Looking through this window we perceive Jesus as a literary character, in his interaction with other 'paper people'. But a synchronic reading can arouse curiosity about the question of the historical Jesus: how does the person depicted in the text relate to the man from Nazareth, who at the beginning of our era gave the starting signal for a renewal movement which is still active today?

Diachrony does open a window on history. Initially people even thought that this approach was the royal way which – starting from the Gospels – would give us direct access to the inspirer of Christianity. In the twentieth century this notion has been virtually dropped. The Gospels give us a view of the time of their definitive redaction (between 70 and 100) and also of the life and faith of the earliest Christian faith communities in the period between 30 and 70, but it is extremely difficult to go further back into the past. So diachronic studies do not themselves provide the solution. But they are absolutely indispensable for any attempt to reconstruct the portrait of the historical Jesus.

I am keeping the window of history separate, because while the diachronic perspective is necessary, it is not sufficient. A diachronic approach can easily get entangled in circular arguments in the search for the history behind the story: we begin from the text, argue from that to a particular historical development, and in turn allow this reconstruction to influence our reading of the textual material. The quest for the historical Jesus calls for considerable knowledge of the socio-political and religious conditions of the time in which he appeared. To get a view of this complex whole the collaboration of many disciplines is needed: historical, archaeological and sociological investigation of Judaism at the beginning of our era.

The purpose of Part IV

The concluding part of this book is only a single chapter. Here I give a bird's eye view of the course of modern investigation into Jesus. Its history is particularly instructive. The pitfalls and snags in the quest of the 'authentic' Jesus stand out clearly. In connection with that I describe the criteria by which the investigation is determined, what we (can) know about Jesus and how far the question of the historical Jesus is important for the believer.

I end this introduction with a poem which shows in a splendid way how Jesus is not imprisoned in the paper on which the stories about his person are set down. In writing this book I have been inspired by this poetic voice.

JESUS

You last a human life,
I can read you and reread you,
I pick you up and put you down,
I turn the pages forward and back,
you are patient and at my disposal.

But not so lowly that
words do not put down roots,
fill my landscape,
have their tops in heaven,
stand up to storms.

It takes something
to cap them, and yet,
the trunk is deeper in my earth
than I thought, it buds, a twig –
O Jesus, before I keep silent about you.

Jaap Zijlstra[5]

Part I The window of synchrony

The limits of a text

Demarcation

Any textual analysis begins with a survey of the limits of a text: where does it begin and where does it end? These questions relate to demarcation. A well-demarcated text is a linguistic unit, a rounded and meaningful whole which can more or less stand on its own feet.

The problem is that these units can be of very different length. When do we really speak of a text? In the case of the Bible we can distinguish five levels. 1. Sometimes a detached sentence is called a text, for example when someone says: 'The sermon was on the text "You shall love your neighbour as yourself"'. 2. A short, rounded unit (pericope) is regarded as a text. 3. Two or three pericopes together form a text: the Sermon on the Mount is an example of this (Matthew 5.1–8.1). 4. Sometimes we reserve the word text for a whole book of the Bible (for example the text of John). 5. Finally text can relate to the Bible as a whole.

In this book I address primarily the second and third levels. By 'text' I understand a small or larger unit from a particular book. In these particular cases it is not immediately clear how the text can be demarcated in a meaningful way. In a detached sentence, a complete book of the Bible or the whole Bible the question of demarcation is really completely superfluous: the limits of that kind of text are established.

The question of demarcation must be answered with the help of arguments relating to form and content, which as far as possible have been derived from the text itself. General rules are difficult to establish, since texts differ. Here I shall formulate a few points which are useful in demarcating a particular kind of text, namely narratives. A narrative is a world in words, which does not coincide with the real world in which we live but does have particular characteristics in common with it. Our world is fundamentally determined by space and time and populated by people of flesh and blood. In a rounded story, however small, we also have to do with space and time, and with people, but now paper people, characters.

So to define the extent of the narrative we have to note indications of time and place. A coherent and well-rounded whole has a unity of place and time. Changes at that level can indicate the beginning of a new textual unit. The characters are also important. Usually one of them plays the main role. That character is present in almost every sub-division. In the Gospels the main role is played by Jesus. Because he is so continuously present, he need not be mentioned by name each time: the narrator can simply be content with 'he'. The other characters present a more fluctuating picture. Often new characters appear on the scene, whereas actors who were present earlier disappear. Such changes can also indicate the start of a new sub-division. The characters are usually active when they appear: at least for a moment they make a contribution to the course of action which can mainly be recognized from the verbs used.

Stylistic features also provide some support in looking for the limits of a text. Biblical texts often display a parallelism (A//A'), a chiastic pattern (AB B'A') or a concentric order (AB C B'A'). A stylistic feature which is very important for demarcation is the inclusion (literally framework, frame). This stylistic device was often used in antiquity. A writer often marked the beginning and end of a text by repeating a particular word, expression or complete sentence. Here are three examples:

- Psalm 8 is framed by the sentence 'O Lord, our Lord, how majestic is your name in all the earth.'
- The creation poem with which the Bible begins (Genesis 1.1–2.4a) is framed as follows:
    1.1 In the beginning God created heaven and earth.

2.4a This is the history of the origin of heaven and earth as they were created.

* In Matthew 15.20 Jesus says: 'eating with unwashed hands does not make a person unclean'. This statement concludes a long narrative unit which began in 15.1–2 with the Pharisees' accusation to Jesus that his disciples did not wash their hands before eating.

The reader can also regard a text as a coherent whole because a particular word is repeated a number of times and thus functions as a motif. In the book of Jonah we find the word 'go down' appearing with some degree of regularity in the first two chapters. The term shows how the disobedient prophet manoeuvres himself step by step into an untenable situation: first he goes down to Joppa (1.3), then he goes down into a ship (1.3), then he goes down into the hold of the ship (1.5), and after he has been thrown overboard and swallowed by a big fish he says that he has gone down into the realm of the dead (2.6). This repetition provides a Leitmotif in the narrative. Jonah is fleeing from God. He leaves Israel via the port of Joppa (near present-day Tel Aviv) and tries to reach Tarshish, probably a place on the east coast of Spain. The route of his flight is given a particular colour by the verb 'go down', which is repeated time and again: really Jonah has landed in a spiral movement which ends up with death.[1]

Often a text contains words which differ from one another but which nevertheless belong together, because they have a particular element of meaning in common. Together they form a cluster which is important for the demarcation and unity of a passage. Luke 22.14–38 is an example of this.[2] At first sight this is a collection of fragments, consisting of six blocks which follow one another quite loosely (22.14–20; 22.21–23; 22.24–27; 22.28–30; 22.31–34; 22.35–38). However, on closer inspection it proves that the text contains two groups of words which provide the necessary coherence. The first group relates to the holding of a meal, the second is connected with the suffering and the death of Jesus.[3]

Despite all these rules, in practice it is not always possible to draw sharp lines between textual units. The transitions are often fluid. The evangelists have avoided breaks which are too harsh, since excessive use of them would break up their narrative about Jesus into static pieces standing side by side. The following examples show that there are limits, but at the same time how relative they are.

Mark 3.1–6: a discussion of the sabbath

1 He entered the synagogue again. There was someone with a withered hand. 2 They watched him, to see whether he would heal him on the sabbath, so that they might accuse him. 3 He said to the man with the withered hand, 'Come and stand in the centre.' 4 He said to them, 'May one do good on the sabbath or do evil, save a life or kill?' But they kept silent. 5 He looked around at them, angry, and grieved at their hardness of heart, and said to the man, 'Stretch out your hand.' He did so, and his hand was restored. 6 The Pharisees went out and immediately held counsel with the Herodians against him, how to do away with him.

Demarcation and unity

This short narrative has a unity of place and time: it takes place in a synagogue, on a sabbath. Three characters are mentioned: 1. A man with a withered hand, 2. a certain 'he', and 3. an opposing party, indicated by 'they'. Only at the last moment, in v.6, does it prove that the opposing party is made up of the Pharisees. The text does not say who is meant by 'he'. For that we must look beyond the margins of the text. From the direct context it proves that this character is Jesus.

The unity of the text is confirmed by an inclusion: in v.1 Jesus enters the synagogue, in v.6 the Pharisees go out of it. A little drama takes place between the beginning and the end of the narrative. According to v.2 the opposing party is out to accuse Jesus. In a moment of time a clear escalation takes place: in v.6 the Pharisees already plan to do away with Jesus and make a pact with the Herodians to achieve their aim.

Jesus, the main figure, formulates a question in v.4 with which he expresses a dilemma: is the sabbath meant for doing good or for doing evil? He gives 'doing good' the content 'saving a life' and 'doing evil' the content 'killing'. Within the total text, doing good and saving are connected with the activity of Jesus: he heals the sick. The other option, doing evil and killing, is chosen by the opposing party: they want to do away with Jesus. So two lines of force run through the text, which are fiercely opposed. As so often, life and death are here arch-enemies.

Mark 3.1–6: finale of a longer whole

The unity of Mark 3.1–6 is confirmed by what follows. There is quite a deep break between 3.6 and 3.7. In 3.7 Jesus departs in the direction of the sea. So there is a change of place. He is accompanied by his disciples and a great crowd follows him. So there are different characters from 3.1–6. For the moment we hear no more of the Pharisees; only in 7.1 do they come on the scene again.

The break between 3.1–6 and what goes before (2.23–28) is much less deep. Here there is only a wafer-thin boundary. We are even surprised by the many agreements. In both texts it is the sabbath. In both cases Jesus gets involved in a dispute with the Pharisees. In 2.23–28, too, the difference turns on the question what one may and may not do on the sabbath. But there are also things which justify a slight break. Mark 2.23–28 takes place in the open air, in the cornfields, while the following block is situated in a synagogue. In 2.23–28 the disciples are mentioned, but not in 3.1–6. The Pharisees criticize the behaviour of the disciples; in 3.1–6 they are mesmerized by Jesus' behaviour. We can best do justice to these facts if we regard the two pericopes as a close pair.

The limit can be moved even further forward. The opposition to Jesus already begins in 2.1. That means that 2.1–3.6 is a long, consecutive whole. This meso-unit consist of five micro-units (or pericopes):

2.1–12	2.13–17	2.18–22	2.23–28	3.1–6

It is interesting that this series begins and ends with a healing. That is a form of inclusion. It is also striking that all these parts have some subjects in common. Each time, there is mention of an

opposing party which criticizes the behaviour of Jesus or his disciples. The opponents talk to the disciples about their master's
behaviour and conversely they put questions to Jesus about the
behaviour of his companions. The occasional shifts which become
evident in this whole can easily be read off Table 1.

	Who are the opponents?	*What is their criticism?*	*Whom do they address?*
2.1–12	a couple of scribes	Jesus forgives sins	the scribes express their objections to one another
2.13–17	the scribes of the Pharisees	Jesus eats with toll collectors and sinners	the disciples are addressed about the behaviour of Jesus
2.18–22	the disciples of John and of the Pharisees	the disciples do not fast	Jesus is addressed about the behaviour of his disciples
2.23–28	the Pharisees	the disciples pluck ears of corn on the sabbath	here too Jesus must defend his disciples
3.1–6	the Pharisees and the Herodians	Jesus heals someone on the sabbath	the criticism is not expressed

Table 1: Shifts in Mark 2.1–3.6

We began with the short narrative in 3.1–6. The question of
demarcation took us much further forward. The fragment from
3.1–6 proved to be a last link in a longer chain. That last part forms
a dramatic climax. The opposition which is initially still slumber-
ing comes to light increasingly clearly. Gradually it proves that the
opposition comes above all from the side of the Pharisees. In the
end the dispute has escalated to such a degree that the opposing
party comes to the conclusion that Jesus must be liquidated. At
that moment in the narrative the Pharisees conclude a monstrous
alliance with the Herodians. The latter are supporters of Herod
allied with the Romans. These were the natural opponents of the
Pharisees, for the latter had a real horror of the desecration of the
land by the Roman occupying forces. That the Pharisees do
conclude an alliance with the Herodians is part of the drama of the
narration.

John 9.39–10.21: the good shepherd

Fragmentation of texts

That first example was instructive for two reasons. We saw that a short and rounded pericope has been taken up into a large whole. It also proved that the small piece became more meaningful by being read within that greater whole.

For many readers of the Bible there is a whole world to be discovered here. From childhood upwards, above all in worship and catechesis, they have been made familiar with short, isolated pericopes. Exegesis has made a little contribution towards this custom of reading. In the first half of the twentieth century form criticism shot up like a rocket. This approach put the emphasis on the small, indeed the smallest, units of which the Gospels have been constructed. Texts were distinguished on the basis of their literary form. Thus a healing narrative has its own characteristics which we do not find in a parable or a dispute. This meant that far less attention was paid to the relations between the different kinds of texts. This approach made an impact on the presentation of the text in editions of the Bible. In them the Gospels are often split up into mini-subdivisions separated from one another on the basis of quite external criteria. Over recent years the tide has turned. The tendency to break up a text unnecessarily has considerably declined, and more attention has been paid to larger interconnected wholes.[4]

John 9.39–10.21

I shall illustrate this shift by means of John 9.39–10.21. The text of this long passage is printed below. I have made a visual distinction between narrative sentences and direct discourse. Direct discourse is the term used for sentences which are spoken by a character in the narrative. Each time I have indented these sentences.

9.39 Jesus said,
> 'I came into this world to bring a clear division: those who do not see shall see, and those who see shall become blind.'

40 Some Pharisees who were near him heard this and asked:
> 'Are we also blind?'

41 Jesus said to them:

> 'If you were blind, you would have no sin. But now that you say, "We can see," you are stuck in your sin. 10.1 Truly, I assure you; whoever does not enter the sheepfold by the door but climbs in by another way, can only be a thief and a robber. 2 But whoever enters by the door is the shepherd of the sheep. 3 To him the gate-keeper opens and the sheep hear his voice. He calls each of his sheep by name and leads them out. 4 When he has brought out all his sheep, he goes before them, and the sheep follow him because they know his voice. 5 However, a stranger they will not follow; on the contrary, they flee from him, because they do not know the voice of strangers.'

6 In this veiled language Jesus spoke with them, but they did not understand what he was saying to them. 7 So Jesus went on:

> 'Truly, I assure you: I am the door for the sheep. 8 All those who came before me are thieves and robbers; but the sheep did not listen to them. 9 I am the door; if anyone enters by me, he will be saved, and will go in and out and find pasture. 10 A thief comes only to steal and kill and destroy; I have come that they may have life, and have it abundantly. 11 I am the good shepherd. A good shepherd lays down his life for the sheep. 12 But a hireling, and not a real shepherd, when he sees a wolf coming, abandons the sheep and flees – they are not his sheep – and the wolf falls on them and scatters them. 13 He is a hireling and does not care for the sheep. 14 I am the good shepherd; I know my sheep and my sheep know me, 15 just as the Father knows me and I know the Father; and I lay down my life for my sheep. 16 I have yet other sheep than those of this fold. I must also be a shepherd to them, and they will listen to my voice. So there shall be one flock with one shepherd. 17 For this reason the Father loves me, because I give my life, in order that I may take it back. 18 No one takes it from me; I give it of my own free will. I have the power to give it and I have the power to take it back. That is the charge I have received from my Father.'

19 There was again a division among the Jews because of these words. 20 Many said,

> 'He is possessed, he is mad; why do you still listen to him?'

21. But others said,

> 'This is not the language of one who is possessed. Can one who is possessed open the eyes of the blind?'

Demarcation and unity

In editions of the Bible, John 10.1–21 are usually printed as a unit – in contrast to what has been done here.[5] The revised edition of the Dutch *Good News Bible* puts the heading 'Jesus is the Good Shepherd' above 10.1–21. Granted, the image of the shepherd and the sheep appears only from 10.1, but it also plays a role after 10.21, namely in 10.26–28. The German ecumenical translation of the Bible wanted to respect this by giving the whole of 10.1–39 the heading 'The parables of the shepherd and the sheep'.[6] However, this solution comes up against yet another objection. There is an interval in time between 10.1–21 and 10.22–39. The first part takes place in the autumn, on the last day of the Feast of Booths (cf. 7.37). The second passage begins with a new indication of time: 'At that time the feast of the dedication of the temple was celebrated in Jerusalem. It was winter...'

The problem is not so much where the text ends (10.21 is a meaningful conclusion) as where it begins. I would want to move the beginning forward. In my view the break does not lie precisely between chapters 9 and 10. Jesus is speaking in the first verse of John 10, but that is also the case in the last verse of John 9. The direct speech continues without any interruption. We interrupt the speaker if we detach 10.1 from 9.41. But 9.41 is not a satisfactory starting-point either, for that verse does not indicate to whom Jesus' words are addressed. That information is given in 9.40. Some Pharisees ask a question there, with which they react to what Jesus says in 9.39: 'I came into this world to bring a clear division: those who do not see shall see, and those who see shall become blind.' This sentence forms the starting point of a discussion which goes on until 10.21.

John 9.39–10.21 consists of two stages. The first round in the discussion comprises 9.41–10.5; after that Jesus goes on speaking in 10.7–18. The first round is followed in 10.6 by a report from the narrator. He tells the reader that the Pharisees had not understood what Jesus had to say to them, since he had used veiled language. Therefore the image of the shepherd and the sheep is not clear to them. In 10.7–18 Jesus lifts a corner of the veil. He now gives himself a place within the figurative language that he had used earlier: *I* am the door, *I* am the good shepherd. He does not say explicitly who is meant by the thieves and robbers and the hireling, but there is a good chance that here he has the Pharisees in mind. In 10.19–21 the narrator concludes the whole passage as follows: 'There was again a division among the Jews because of these words.' The narrator makes the hearers express their divided reaction themselves. Some react in a markedly negative way; others have gradually gained a positive picture of Jesus.

The divided reaction at the end relates to the statement with which Jesus began in 9.39 (we have a clear example of an inclusion here). In 9.39 Jesus announced that he came to bring a clear division. Now at the end a division has really come about: there are those who receive Jesus' words positively, but there are also those who now become fiercely opposed to him. This connection is visible only if we mark out the text in a different way from usual: it comes to light only if we shift the beginning to 9.39.

Evaluation

This chapter began with the statement that every analysis of the text needs to begin with a survey of the limits of the text. The way in which the question of demarcation is solved has consequences for all further steps in the investigation, no matter what method we use. We must be aware that at this point certain choices have already been made in every edition of the Bible. The text is divided into manageable sub-divisions which are given a heading indicating the content of the passage in question with a few key words. In the Gospels the chosen units are often very short. A factor here is that they have much material in common with one another. The extent of these parallels is usually kept the same, though there are literary arguments against this. At any rate it is advisable to look with an eagle eye at the divisions offered. The traditional splitting up of books of the Bible into chapters is also by no means sacrosanct;[7] it is naive to think that there is always a deep break between two chapters.

In this chapter I have also argued for a reading in which the level of the separate pericope is transcended. The micro-units are bound up with the text that surrounds them with all kinds of threads. Not every break is as deep, and the transitions between the separate pericopes are fluid. The important thing is thus that we do not from the start approach the Gospels as a sum total of small fragments isolated from one another. In our attempt to mark out the various sub-divisions from one another, time and again we encounter phenomena which indicate that the separate passages are integrated into a larger dynamic network.

2

Structural analysis

Patterns in a text

For Luke, the structure of his text is very important. In the prologue to his Gospel he says that he has done his best to write an orderly account (1.3). He is not the only author who makes high aesthetic demands on the product of his pen. In the epilogue of II Maccabees (15.38–39), the author says: 'If it is well told and to the point, that is what I myself desired; if it is poorly done and mediocre, that was the best I could do... the style of the story delights the ears of those who read the work.' Note that the writer wants to gratify the ears of the readers, not their eyes. Here we get a glimpse of the old custom of presenting a text aloud (compare Acts 8.30). It can also be useful to us to note the sound of the text written in Hebrew or Greek, the acoustic effects.[1]

The ordering of the material, the construction or structure of a text, is the subject of this chapter. A structural analysis consists of two steps: (a) first the text is divided into small units (sections or sequences); (b) next we investigate what relations there are between the sub-divisions of the text and their function within the whole.

The first step follows the demarcation of the textual units closely. After it has been determined where the limits of the text lie on the basis of arguments from form and content, the question arises how the text is articulated. In tracing articulations internal to the text, for the most part we base ourselves on the same phenomena as in the demarcation: changes in the characters, changes at the level of place and time, agreements and differences in the vocabulary used, contrasts and oppositions. The sub-divisions marked out in this way are not totally disconnected. Otherwise a structural analysis would simply split up the text. The real structural analysis begins with the second step, which is directed towards getting a view of the dynamic interplay between the sub-divisions of the text.

The lines and patterns change when we move the limits of the text. If the elements A and B belong to the same textual unit, their relationship is not the same as if they belong to two different units. Thus reducing or enlarging the units changes the interplay. This problem returns when we bring small units together in a medium-sized text. The limits of this determine the network that is marked out within such a meso-unit. Investigation of the composition of a complete book is the most complicated. At that level we must find an answer to the question of the relations between middle-sized units.

A structural analysis must be judged in the light of facts that can be shown from the text. No single proposal can claim to do justice to all that a text has to offer. The preference will be for the proposal that does justice to the largest possible number of facts. Which literary and rhetorical techniques must we note in a structural analysis? No single recipe can be given for this. But we can formulate some rules of thumb, which I shall illustrate with examples from Matthew:[2]

- The theme or motif of a rounded whole can be expressed at the beginning. Thus Matthew 6.1–18 is dominated by the general admonition to righteousness in 6.1. Matthew 13.1–52 contains various examples of 'speaking in parables' (13.3).
- Sometimes such a link sentence stands only at the end. For example, Matthew five times concludes long discourses of Jesus with a stereotyped formula (7.28–29; 11.1; 13.53; 19.1; 26.1).
- How a text is articulated emerges from words or sentences recurring regularly; these function as a refrain (see Matthew 6.4, 16, 18).
- The internal ordering of a textual unit can be based on divergent principles. Here I am referring to the occurrence of alternating patterns (ABAB or ABC ABC), to parallelisms (AA' BB'), to

chiastic structures (repetitions of words and sentences in a reverse order: ABB'A'), and to the phenomenon of one narrative being interrupted by another (ABA; also called a sandwich construction).

- Several techniques can be pointed out in the way in which textual units are related. One pattern which occurs often is a concentric order (AB C B'A'): in such a construction the emphasis falls on the central sub-division. A long text can be enclosed within two related passages. One example of this is the parable discourse (Matthew 13.1–52); this address is preceded by a short passage about Jesus' kinsfolk (12.46–30) and followed by an account of his activity in his ancestral town (13.53–58). Another phenomenon which occurs regularly is that a text is bound both to the one that precedes it and to the one that follows it. Such a text functions as a hinge. Matthew 16.13–28 refers back to views of Jesus mentioned earlier[3] and anticipates the approaching end of his life. Another example is Matthew 4.12–17. This short fragment is coupled on one side to 1.1–4.11 and on the other to 4.18–16.12.
- In practice, it will prove that sometimes various patterns have been woven together, that a text shows overlapping structures. We shall also see this phenomenon whenever we survey a larger number of units from the same book. So we shall not always be able to arrive at a solution that is shared by all, certainly not as far as the macro-structure of a literary work is concerned.

Here now are some developed examples to make these theoretical considerations concrete. They show how skilfully texts from the Gospels have been constructed. What attracts me even more is that attention to the form already puts us on the track of the train of thought or the meaning of the text: structural analysis is the lobby to exegesis or interpretation.

A concentric pattern in Mark 3.1–6

In demarcating Mark 3.1–6 we were struck by the fact that the beginning and the end of this text are closely connected. At the beginning Jesus enters a synagogue and at the end the Pharisees leave it. This raises the question whether there are more such matches. Table 2 shows that this is indeed the case.

```
A Jesus enters a synagogue
     B Someone has a withered hand
          C The opposing party notes Jesus
               D Jesus speaks
                    E 'May one do good on the sab-
                      bath or do evil, save a life or kill?'
               D' The opponents keep silent
          C' Jesus looks around at them
     B' The hand is restored
A' The Pharisees go out
```

Table 2: Concentric structure of Mark 3.1–6

We cannot discover this concentric pattern on a first reading. It emerges only if we go through the text repeatedly, noting the internal correspondences or oppositions. A stands over against A'; the situation of need which is expressed in B is removed in B'; the action in C is similar to that in C'; the words of Jesus in D are opposed by the silence of the opposing party in D'. Within this total pattern the emphasis on E is striking. This sentence stands at the centre. Attention is drawn to this point by the text itself. It is so to speak the centre of a vortex. The dilemma formulated in E pervades the whole text. Here Jesus appears as the one who regards the sabbath as a day chosen for doing good. And that when he is suspected of violating the sabbath! The opposing party, on the other hand, begins to make plans to kill someone on the sabbath of all days. Here the text is extremely ironical: the reader can only come to the conclusion that it is precisely the Pharisees, loyal to the law, who rob the sabbath of its holiness.

Matthew 18.23–35: a parable in three scenes

Text

In Matthew 18.23–35 we find the parable of the unmerciful servant. This narrative has a crystal-clear structure which is already indicated in the rendering of the text that now follows:[4]

23 In this respect the kingdom of heaven is like a king who wanted to settle accounts with his servants.

I 24 When he began the reckoning, someone was brought to him who owed him ten thousand talents. 25 Because he could not pay, the lord ordered him to be sold, with his wife and children and all that he had, so that he could pay. 26 Thereupon the servant prostrated himself before him and asked:
>   'Have patience with me, and I will pay you everything.'
27 The lord had pity on this servant, released him and forgave him the debt.

II 28 When this servant was going out, he met one of his fellow servants who owed him a hundred denarii; he seized him by the throat and said:
>   'Pay me what you owe me.'
29 Thereupon his fellow servant prostrated himself before him and besought him:
>   'Have patience with me, and I will pay you.'
30 But he refused and had him put in prison until he had paid back his debt.

III 31 When his fellow servants saw what had happened, they were greatly distressed, and they went and told their lord all that had happened. 32 Then his lord summoned him and said to him:
>   'You wicked servant! I forgave you all that debt when you begged me to. 33 Should you not have had compassion on your fellow servant, as I had compassion on you?'
>   34 And his lord was so angry that he delivered him to the gaolers, until he had paid back all his debt.

35 So also my heavenly Father will do to you, if you do not each of you forgive your brother with all your heart.

Structural analysis

The parable of the unmerciful servant stands in the context of a conversation between Jesus and his followers about forgiveness. That is visible above all in the concluding verse (v.35). This verse gives the parable an appropriate conclusion: 'So also my heavenly

Father will do to you, if you do not each of you forgive your brother with all your heart.' In the original text this connection is even clearer than in translation, since in Greek the same term is used both for paying off a financial debt (vv.27,32) and for forgiving (*aphiēmi*). The king of the parable is transformed into God in v.35; so there is also a connection between the 'brother' in v.35 and the 'fellow servant' of the parable. The two verses which precede the parable also relate to forgiveness. Peter asks how often he must forgive his brother if the latter wrongs him. The introductory sentence of the parable takes this up ('in this respect', v.23).

The parable itself is composed cleverly. The narrative consists of an introduction (v.23) which is followed by three scenes:

vv.24–27	scene 1	the lord and his servant
vv.28–30	scene 2	the servant and his fellow-servant
vv.31–34	scene 3	the lord and his servant

The introductory verse announces that the narrative which follows clarifies how things are in the kingdom of heaven. It is a narrative about 'a king who wanted to settle accounts with his servants'. These words form as it were the title of the parable. The division into three scenes is based on the characters who play a role in the story; here it is striking that the same characters appear in the first and last scenes.

In the first scene we hear that a servant owes his master ten thousand talents. He cannot pay that gigantic sum. The creditor gives orders for harsh measures, after which the servant begs for postponement of the payment. Clearly both parties assume that the debt really can be paid. But neither the measures which the lord orders nor the postponement which the servant begs for can offer any comfort in the given situation: the debt is simply far too great. The tension leads to a denouement in which the lord has mercy on his servant and forgives him the whole amount.

In a number of respects the second scene runs parallel to the first. In the first scene the lord appears as the creditor, whereas in the second scene the servant plays this role. The situation of the fellow-servant resembles that of the servant in the first scene. The parallel comes out most clearly in v.29, which corresponds almost literally to v.26:

26 Thereupon the servant prostrated himself before him and asked: 'Have patience with me, and I will pay you everything.'

29 Thereupon his fellow servant prostrated himself before him and besought him: 'Have patience with me, and I will pay you.'

But now the situation is by no means as hopeless as it was before. The servant has to ask only one hundred denarii from his colleague, while he himself must find ten thousand talents (probably sixty million denarii; a denarius is the daily wage for an agricultural worker, see Matthew 20.1). But although the servant has just been released from his impossible obligation, he demands that his fellow servant shall indeed pay back the amount that he owes.

Just as the second scene has all kinds of connections with the first, so too there are all kinds of connections between the third scene and the two preceding ones. This comes out best in v.33, 'Should not you have had compassion on your fellow servant, as I had compassion on you?' The first part of this sentence refers to the second scene, the second part to the first scene. Furthermore v.34 ('his lord was so angry') shows a change from v.27 ('the lord had pity on this servant'). Now the servant gets a taste of his own medicine; he is affected by the same measures that he had wanted to impose on his colleague for payment: v.34 ('until he had paid back all his debt') corresponds with v.30 ('until he had paid back his debt').

It is interesting that in a certain respect the third scene also gives a distorted picture of what we have been told earlier. Here I am referring to the words of the lord in v.32, 'You wicked servant! I forgave you all that debt when you begged me to.' This does not fit with the servant's request in v.26. He had by no means spoken about forgiveness of the debt, but had begged for payment to be postponed. This inconsistency is by no means insignificant. It shows what the narrator is up to. The narrative emphasizes the writing off of financial debts, and in v.35 that element is related to the obligation of Jesus' disciples to forgive one another from the bottom of their hearts.

In v.35 not all the content of the parable is used. The conclusion above all takes up the harsh punishment which the lord imposes on the hard-hearted behaviour of his servant. Just as the lord takes strict measures, so too will the heavenly Father, if anyone does not forgive his brother. An important element of the parable is left out here: the servant should have had compassion on his colleague, because his lord showed him so much compassion. So too must Jesus' followers forgive one another because God has forgiven each one of them.

Mark 12.18–27: Jesus in conversation with the Sadducees

18 Sadducees also came to him. They deny that there is a resurrection. They asked him the following question:

19 'Master, Moses prescribed for us: If a man's brother dies and leaves a wife with no children, his brother must marry this wife, and father descendants for his brother. 20 Now there were seven brothers. The first took a wife, and he died without offspring. 21 And the second married her; he too died with no offspring. And the third likewise. 22 The seven had no offspring. Last of all the woman also died. 23 When they rise at the resurrection, whose wife will she be? For all seven had her as wife.'

24 Jesus said to them,

'Are you not on the wrong track, because you know neither the scriptures nor the power of God? 25 For when they rise from the dead, they neither marry nor are given in marriage, but are like angels in heaven. 26 And as for the dead being raised, have you not read in the book of Moses, in the passage about the bush, how God said to him, "I am the God of Abraham, and the God of Isaac, and the God of Jacob"? 27 He is not God of the dead, but of the living. So you are clearly on the wrong track.'

Construction

This passage consists of two sub-divisions. In the first the Sadducees put a question to Jesus; in the second Jesus gives an answer to this question. The question is quite a long one, and so is the answer. A structural analysis brings out that the Sadducees take three successive steps (a–b–c). These steps return in Jesus' answer, but in precisely the opposite order (c'–b'–a'). The structure of the text is given schematically in Table 3:[5]

Introduction	v.18ab			
I	vv.18c–23		Question from the Sadducees to Jesus	
	1	v.18c	Introduction to the direct speech ('They asked him the following question')	
	2	vv.19–23	Direct speech	
		a	v.19	Quotation of texts from the Torah (Deuteronomy 25.5–6; Genesis 38.8), introduced with 'Moses prescribed for us.'
		b	vv.20–22	Case
		c	v.23	Question
II	vv.24–27		Jesus' answer to the Sadducees	
	1	v.24a	Introduction to the direct speech ('Jesus said to them')	
	2	vv. 24b–27	Direct speech	
		c'	v.24b	Counter-question
		b'	v.25	Correction of the case presented
		a'	vv.26–27	Replacement of the texts quoted with another text from the Torah (Exodus 3.6), introduced with 'God said to him [= Moses]'

Table 3: Construction of Mark 12.18–27

Argument

The form and content of a text cannot be dissociated. In the case of Mark 12.18–27 that is very clear. The structure already shows how the content of the discussion goes.

First the Sadducees are introduced to the reader: they are people who claim that there is no resurrection. That one point forms the subject of their dispute with Jesus. At this moment the narrator does not think that any other views that they hold (see Acts 23.8) are important.

The Sadducees occupy the entire first round of the debate. Right at the beginning they allow Moses to speak. Here we find direct speech within the direct speech. The precepts of Moses are to be found in Deuteronomy 25.5–6 (see also Genesis 38.8) and relate to levirate marriage. This institution meant that a childless widow had to remarry a brother of her dead husband. The first child born from the new alliance was regarded as a descendant of the dead man. In this way some ongoing existence of the dead man here on earth was secured. To these regulations the Sadducees attach a bizarre case from practice: in succession a woman marries seven brothers, all of whom die childless. After that they jump to the question whose wife the woman will be at the resurrection. The tenor of their question is that belief in the resurrection is completely ridiculous.

In the second round Jesus speaks. This sub-division contains an inclusion: Jesus begins with a counter-question ('are you not on the wrong track?'), which he himself answers at the end of the passage ('so you are clearly on the wrong track').

Then he corrects some elements from the Sadducees' argument. By making the resurrection look ridiculous they indicate that they have a limited idea of the power of God. They assume that even God must yield to the power of death. Their story about the woman with the seven husbands, along with the question about the resurrection attached to it, also needs correction. The question implies that life after death is a copy of life as we now know it. Jesus makes a correction here: the resurrection implies an existence that is quite different from life now. Then there will no longer be any question of marriage and giving in marriage; the dead will lead an asexual existence: they will be like the angels in heaven.

The last step is that Jesus replaces the text of scripture quoted by the Sadducees (Deuteronomy 25.5–6) with another text (Exodus 3.6). Like his opponents, Jesus too draws on a book of

Moses. He does this deliberately, since the authority of the books of Moses is also fully recognized by the Sadducees. They did not attach the same importance to later parts of scripture, and in their eyes oral traditions had no authority at all. Jesus too allows another speaker his say (again direct speech within the direct speech!). The speaker whom Jesus brings on the scene is God himself. The quotation that Jesus uses in the dispute must thus be aimed higher than the quotation that his opponents came up with, since that related to a precept of Moses.

According to Exodus 3.6, God made himself known to Moses as the God of Abraham, the God of Isaac and the God of Jacob. Jesus regards this statement as a proof of belief in life after death. He introduces the quotation with the assertion that Exodus 3.6 relates to the question whether the dead are raised, and immediately after the quotation he says that God is not a God of the dead but of the living. Can all this be read in Exodus 3.6? The Sadducees will have seriously doubted that. What Jesus comes out with must in their eyes have looked very much like a circular argument. But Jesus says that they are on a false track. He presupposes that his own argument is thoroughly convincing.

How this argument works can be clarified in two ways. The first explanation is that Jesus takes up later traditions – not recognized by the Sadducees – in which Exodus 3.6 is regarded as a proof text for the resurrection. The second explanation remains closer to Mark's text: the quotation and the following statement that God is a God of the living are both premises in an argument the conclusion of which is not mentioned. The first premise is that God is the God of Abraham, Isaac and Jacob. The second premise is that he is a God of the living. The unspoken conclusion is that in that case the patriarchs are still alive many centuries after their deaths.[6]

Luke 16.19–31: Do not make the earth hell!

Text

In Luke 16.19–31 there is the story about Lazarus and the rich man which is now world-famous. Here is the text.

I 19 There was a rich man, who was clothed in purple and fine linen and who feasted sumptuously every day. 20 At his gate lay a certain Lazarus; he was poor and full of sores. 21 He longed to be fed with what fell from the rich man's table, but no, the dogs came and licked his sores.

II 22 Then the poor man died; the angels carried him to Abraham's bosom. The rich man also died, and was buried. 23 In Hades, being in torment, he lifted up his eyes, and saw Abraham far off and Lazarus in his bosom, and he called out,

> 24 'Father Abraham, have mercy upon me; send Lazarus in order that he may dip the end of his fingers in water and cool my tongue; for I am in anguish in this flame.'

25 But Abraham said,

> 'Child, remember that you in your lifetime received good things, and Lazarus always evil things; but now he is comforted here, and you are in anguish. 26 And besides all this, between us and you a great gulf has been fixed; even if someone wanted to pass from here to you, he would not be able; nor may anyone cross from there to us.'

27 But the rich man said:

> 'Then I beg you, father, to send him to my father's house, 28 for I have five brothers. Let him go and warn them, so that they do not also come into this place of torment.'

29 But Abraham said,

> 'They have Moses and the prophets; let them hear them.'

30 But he said,

> 'No, father Abraham, but if some one goes to them from the dead, they will repent.'

31 But Abraham said to him,

> 'If they do not hear Moses and the prophets, neither will they be convinced if someone should rise from the dead.'

Structural analysis

The narrative of Lazarus and the rich man consists of two sub-divisons.[7] The break comes between v.21 and v.22. The first sub-division comprises vv.19–21, the second vv.22–31. This division rests on the following arguments: (a) vv.19–21 take place in and around the rich man's house during the lifetime of Lazarus and the

rich man, whereas vv.22–31 take place in the underworld, after
their deaths; (b) in v.22 a new character is introduced, namely
Abraham.

The first part of the narrative depicts how the rich man is
clothed in purple and the finest linen and feasts sumptuously every
day. There is a blatant contrast between his situation and the fate
of the beggar by his house. This man is covered in sores and longs
to assuage his hunger with what falls to the ground from the rich
man's table. He is outside the gate, surrounded by the dogs of the
street; the rich man is inside the house. There is no mention of any
communication between them.

At the beginning of the second part a reversal takes place: both
die. Now Lazarus is mentioned first and only then the rich man.
The second part takes place in the underworld: there the rich man
is racked with pain and the poor man is in Abraham's bosom. If in
the first part they were still near to each other, now there is emphasis on the spatial distance between them ('from afar'), but
despite this distance they can see and hear each other. The second
part consists primarily of a conversation between the rich man and
Abraham. The rich man does not address Lazarus directly, but
talks with Abraham about Lazarus. The two conversation partners
speak alternately, the rich man in vv.24, 27–28, 30 and Abraham in
vv.25–26, 29, 31. Abraham is constantly addressed by the rich man
as 'father Abraham' or as 'father'. That he is a child of Abraham is
confirmed by Abraham in v.25.

Some exegetes think that the conversation relates above all to the
reversal of relationships between the position of the rich man and
the poor man after their deaths.[8] They see the narrative as an
illustration of statements elsewhere in Luke (1.53; 6.20–26;
14.12–14, 24). That earthly relationships have been reversed after
death indeed plays a role in the text. This is evident from the statement with a chiastic order in v.25:

A 'Child, remember that you in your lifetime received good things,
B and Lazarus always evil things;
B' now he is comforted here,
A' and you are in anguish.'

This verse takes up the chiastic form of narration in vv.19–22, where the situation of the rich man (A) and the poor man (B) during their lifetimes are compared with the new situation of the poor man (B') and the rich man (A') after their deaths.

But the reversal of the situation is not the most important narrative motive. After all, this does not recur after v.25. The unity of the narrative is governed by the moves from one place to another (whether these are made or not):

vv. 19–21: the rich man is in his house and does not come into contact with the beggar on the street, while Lazarus is outside and makes no attempt to go in;

v.22: both leave the earth and find themselves in the underworld;

vv.24–26: Lazarus cannot cross from the place where he is to the place where the rich man is, nor is it possible to go in the opposite direction;

vv.27–31: Lazarus can act as link between the underworld and the rich man's father's house, but this move is rejected by Abraham as meaningless.

Lazarus' movements form the subject of the conversation between the rich man and Abraham. Three times (vv.24, 27–28, 30) the rich man makes a request which relates to this. His first request (v.24) has two parts: 'Have mercy upon me and send Lazarus.' The purpose of sending Lazarus is worked out in a final sentence ('in order that...'); the reason why Abraham must have compassion is expressed in a causal sentence ('for...'). The questioner expresses his own situation in this round of conversation. He asks Abraham to send Lazarus to him to cool his tongue with a couple of drops of water, since he is in anguish. Just as Lazarus was earlier tormented by hunger and longed for what fell to the ground from the rich man's table, so now the rich man suffers tormenting thirst and burns with longing for the cooling water which is evidently available to Lazarus. This request for material help is rejected by Abraham for two reasons. The first reason is given in v.25 and the second in v.26. In v.25 Abraham refers to the reversal of situations after death. In v.26 he adds why it is impossible to move from one division to another in the realm of the dead: there is a great gulf between the two divisions.

After this answer the rich man no longer goes on with his own situation. He clearly sees that he is irrevocably lost and now turns his attention to his five brothers in their father's house. Whereas formerly he paid no attention to the beggar at his house, now he is anxious about the future fate of his family. His second request shows a clear parallelism with the first. Again he asks Abraham to entrust Lazarus with a task. This time Abraham is to send him to earth so that (again a final sentence) the rich man's five brothers are prevented from ending up in the same situation as himself. Now he is asking for immaterial help. This request is rejected with a reference to Moses and the prophets.

The rich man is not convinced by this answer (cf. 'no...' in v.30); he repeats his request, but extends it with the argument that someone who has risen from the dead carries more powers of conviction than Moses and the prophets. Abraham does not accept this argument. The five brothers must make do with what they have at their disposal: the writings of Moses and the prophets provide a sure compass. The narrative has an open ending: we are not told whether or not the five brothers convert. It is left to the reader to draw an appropriate conclusion from this narrative.

A gate and a great gulf

The conclusion is not that poor people on earth must hold on because they can expect a glorious future after death. Nor that the poor and the rich simply live in worlds which are hermetically sealed off from each other. No, the story drives us in a completely different direction. To make that clear, let me refer to a sharp contrast between the two sub-divisions of the narrative: gate <—> great gulf. During their lifetimes the poor beggar and the rich gourmet had no contact with each other, but this would have been quite possible, since Lazarus lay at the gate of the rich man's house. A gate indicates the possibility of communication. After their death they both find themselves in the realm of the dead. Even now they again have no direct contact with each other. Lazarus lives in a different division of Hades from the rich man. Things have changed, and it is now completely impossible for the one to go to the place where the other is. A great gulf gapes between the two divisions.

Thus the situation in the second part of the narrative is completely different from that in the first. This difference is particularly instructive. In the first half it is still possible to overcome the social division between poor and rich: the rich can still seek contact with the poor on earth. In the second part that is no longer possible. There can be no question of crossing the boundary between the rich and the poor after their deaths.

Readers turn the story upside down when they immediately assume that the opposition between poor and rich already has a definitive character on earth. Really they are already replacing the gate with a great gulf, still on earth. In so doing they make the earth a Hades, a realm of the dead, in which relations are already frozen, while on earth the possibility of crossing frontiers is still completely there. The narrative is opposed to this thought. The gloomy rules from the realm of the dead are not applicable on earth during our lifetime. Now we still live in a world in which the gates can be opened.

John 18.1–12: Jesus is arrested

Text

A   18.1 After these words, Jesus went with his disciples across the Kidron valley. There was a garden there, which he and his disciples entered. 2 Judas, who betrayed him, also knew the place; for Jesus often met there with his disciples. 3 Judas went there, with the cohort and some legal officers from the chief priests and the Pharisees, equipped with lanterns, torches and weapons.

B   x   4 Jesus, who knew all that was to befall him, went out and said to them,
         'Whom do you seek?'
     5 They answered him,
         'Jesus of Nazareth.'

He said to them,
   'I am he.'
y   Judas, who betrayed him, was also standing with them. 6 When
he said to them, 'I am he,' they drew back and fell to the ground.
x'   7 Again he asked them,
   'Whom do you seek?'
They said,
   'Jesus of Nazareth.'
8 Jesus answered,
   'I told you that I am he; so, if you seek me, let these men go.'
9 This was to fulfil the word which he had spoken, 'Of those
whom you gave me I lost not one.'

A'   10 Simon Peter had a sword, drew it, struck the high priest's
slave and cut off his right ear. The slave's name was Malchus. 11
Jesus said to Peter:
   'Put your sword into its sheath. Shall I not drink the cup
   which the Father has given me?'
12 Thereupon the cohort, the captain and the legal officers of the
Jews seized Jesus and bound him.

Structural analysis

John 18.1–12 forms the beginning of the passion narrative. This
passage has a unity of time and place. The narrative takes place at
dead of night. With good reason Judas and his companions have
provided themselves with lanterns and torches. In terms of time,
18.1–12 follows on from 13.30 ('it was night'). The scene of the
action is a garden on the other side of the brook Kidron. The narrator mentions that Jesus had often met there with his disciples.
This information explains why Judas is so infallibly in a position to
find this place. The text does not say that Judas also enters the
garden. He is outside the hedge. Anyway, Jesus has to leave the
garden (18.4, 'he went out') to make contact with the squad which
is to arrest him. After Jesus has allowed himself to be arrested, a
new location is mentioned in 18.15, the palace of the high priest.

The text speaks of two parties. On the one hand stand Jesus and
his disciples; over against them stand Judas and his consorts. These
two parties are introduced in 18.1–3 (A). This sub-division is

closely connected with 18.10–12 (A'), where one person from each of the two groups is mentioned by name: Simon Peter and Malchus. There are yet other connections between A and A'. The opposing party have weapons which they do not *need* to use, since Jesus hands himself over to them voluntarily; Peter is provided with a sword which he *may* not use, for in his attempt to prevent Jesus' arrest he forms an obstacle to Jesus, who is going to fulfil his Father's will. The cohort and the legal officers from 18.3 are again mentioned in 18.12 where they seize Jesus. That happens only after the person being arrested assures them that he willingly surrenders himself to all that awaits him.

The heart of the passage is formed by 18.4–9 (B). This subdivision B again shows a triptych (x –y – x'). The beginning (x) and the conclusion (x') both contain a short dialogue between Jesus and the opposing party; each time Jesus here has the first and the last word:

question from Jesus:	'Whom do you seek?'
answer from the opposing party:	'Jesus of Nazareth'
Jesus' reaction:	'I am he'

This repeated dialogue is interrupted by narrative text (y): 'Judas, who betrayed him, was also standing with them. When he said to them, "I am he," they drew back and fell to the ground.' Here the narrator creates a pause in which Jesus' reaction is repeated once again. The result of this is that 'I am he' is said three times in total. The emphasis thus falls on this part of the dialogue. Moreover these words are here framed by the verbs 'stand' and 'fall': the whole of the team involved in the arrest (the cohort alone consists of 760 infantrymen and 240 auxiliaries!) cannot remain on their feet when they hear these words and fall to the ground. This indicates that Jesus' reaction means more than just a confirmation of the answer from the opposing party. Of course, if the question was only about Jesus as the person sought, then he could simply have been identified by Judas. We find 'I am he' (in Greek *egō eimi*) in the Septuagint, the earliest Greek translation of the Old Testament, repeatedly in the framework of a theophany

(Deuteronomy 32.39; Isaiah 41.4; 43.10; 46.4; 48.12; 52.6). In this way God makes himself known to mortals who often react in deep reverence. Jesus now speaks the same words. They indicate that he is most deeply bound up with the Father, whose will he carries out. He will drink to the dregs the cup that the Father has given him. His arrest is not the work of the heavily armed squad that he sees in front of him. No, Jesus allows himself to be taken voluntarily. He rejects Peter's armed opposition. The appropriate response is not opposition but surrender.

There is yet another implication of the fact that Jesus makes the opposing party say so explicitly that they are seeking him. Taking this up, in 18.8 he pleads that his disciples may go free. The narrator links this with the report that here Jesus is fulfilling a saying uttered earlier. It is not so clear precisely where this statement is to be found. There are two possibilities. We can think of 10.28, where Jesus says of his sheep, 'They shall never be lost; no one shall pluck them from my hand.' We can also refer to 17.12, 'While I was with them, I kept them in your name, which you have given me; I have guarded them, and none of them is lost.'

The strength and weakness of structural analysis

Together with surveying the demarcation, the study of the structure of a text is one of the fixed ingredients of any serious exegesis. These are the first and necessary steps. They must always be taken before we put further questions to the text. If we omit these steps we attach ourselves to loose elements at too early a stage and then give them a meaning or a function which has not been sufficiently tested by their place in the whole.

The text itself is a firm point of reference in any structural analysis. We concentrate on phenomena which in principle are visible to any reader. For beginners, this is an attractive area in which to practise, and in which results can be achieved quickly. Some discipline is required in engaging in the search for lines and patterns consistently from a synchronic perspective and not loading the text with what we have read in commentaries about the history of its development.

Critical questions also have to be put to this undertaking. Don't we run the risk of getting entangled in our own reading strategies or letting ourselves be guided by the compulsion of schematism, constantly reading the same pattern (for example a concentric structure) into totally different texts? This danger is by no means imaginary. In order to reduce the risk, we must allow ourselves to be guided by structures which have been deliberately introduced by the author; however, that device too brings us back to the text, for where else but in the text can we find traces of the author's intention? And what author is aware of all the patterns that can be found in his or her text?

3

Narrative analysis

Narrative texts form the object of scholarly study within narratology, a discipline which in the meantime has also won itself a place in biblical exegesis. The first experiments had been with the Old Testament and its many brilliant narratives.[1] By now the necessary pioneering work has also been done in the sphere of the New Testament, where we find narratives with a certain elegance only in the four Gospels and the Acts of the Apostles. These books speak in a narrative fashion about Jesus and his first followers. At the moment a narrative study is available for each of the Gospels.[2]

This chapter begins with some concepts from the investigation of narrative texts as a means of communication. Afterwards I shall use John 10.4 to 11.54 to demonstrate the possibilities and limits of a narrative analysis.[3] Starting from a translation of the Greek text, I shall discuss the demarcation and composition, the course of action, the main characters, the setting (space and time) and some textual perspectives. Where necessary I shall intersperse my analysis with notes on theory.

Narrative communication

Narratives do not circulate only on paper. From time immemorial they have been handed down by word of mouth, and today they also reach us by the TV screen, the cinema or the theatre. In all these cases we can speak of a process of communication in which three factors play a role: a sender (a) transmits the narrative (b) to a receiver (c). Whenever a narrative reaches us through a text we can replace 'sender' by 'author' and 'receiver' by 'reader'. That gives us the following model: author ⟶ narrative ⟶ reader. The author and the reader stand outside the narrative; they are human beings of flesh and blood. They do not communicate with one another directly, but through the narrative text.

Precisely how the textual communication takes place, how an author works on the reader through a text, has been intensively studied. The diagram developed by S.Chatman has been very influential:[4]

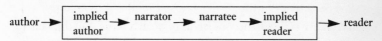

The starting point is that the author, the maker of the narrative, actually does not matter any more once the narrative is on paper. The readers are not confronted with a writer of flesh and blood. They look at a text in which a kind of representation is worked out of what the author wants to achieve with the narrative. The guiding factors by which they are governed in their reading are together termed the implied author. This means the principle that underlies the total organization of the text, the overall view of the narrative, the elements which produce unity and coherence.

Readers of flesh and blood come in many shapes and sizes. Because it is extremely uncertain whether readers who really exist all react to a text in the same way, it is not appealing to take this type of reader as a point of reference. The narratologist prefers to look at the image of the reader worked out by the author in the text, the implied reader. In writing a text, authors create a notion of their expected reader which is represented in the text. Signals relating to this are contained in the text itself: the reader must be familiar with the language in which the text is set down; the vocabulary used indicates that the recipient must also have a particular vocabulary; some customs and institutions are not explained because they are thought to be known, whereas other things *are* explained; foreign terms may be explained or not; it is expected that the reader agrees with the positive or negative evaluations that are to be found in the text. These examples demonstrate that the implied reader does not coincide with the actual reader. There is a good chance that the implied reader has knowledge that the reader of flesh and blood lacks; conversely, however, the reader who really exists can be acquainted with things that the implied reader does not need to know.

In what has been said above, the emphasis lies on the receptive role of the reader, but a narrative also contains more activating elements. The connection between a series of episodes is not always equally clear; when there are no indications of time and no causal particles, the readers themselves must provide temporal and causal links. The activity of the reader is also mobilized by questions that are not followed by answers. Such questions make an appeal to the readers. A good narrative leaves room for the imagination. Frequently there are gaps in the information given; there are a number of white spaces which the reader must try to fill in. Open-ended narratives are a special phenomenon. Such a form of narration activates the readers to think of an appropriate ending themselves on the basis of the possibilities which presented themselves earlier in the narrative.

Narrative theory also speaks of the narrator or the narrative voice. Another notion corresponds to this, namely that of the hearer, referred to as the narratee. The narrator does not coincide with the person or group which has written the story, nor with the implied author. So too the 'narratee' is not the same as the actual reader or the implied reader. In Luke we come upon a narratee within the text who is referred to as Theophilus (Luke 1.3). In John we find a narratee who is indicated with the second person plural (e.g. in 20.31: 'In order that *you* may believe that Jesus is the Christ, the Son of God, and that through believing *you* may have life in his name').

The narrator is the intermediary to whom the implied author delegates the presentation of the narrative; this is the voice that can be heard when we listen to the text as narration. The possibility of hearing the narrative voice is greatest when the narrator indicates himself as an 'I' or a 'we'. In the Gospels that is the case, among other instances, in Luke 1.3 ('*I* have decided to write an orderly account of all things from the beginning'), in John 1.14 ('the word came to tabernacle among *us* and *we* have seen his glory') and in

John 21.24 ('*we* know that his testimony is trustworthy').[5] The narrator can also appear as a character in the narrative: one example of this is the we-passages in Acts 16.10–17; 20.5–15; 21.1–18; 27.1–28.16; in the Fourth Gospel the narrator identifies strongly with the Beloved Disciple, if he is not in fact the same person. Usually, however, the narrator remains in the background in the Gospels. He tells of others without explicitly putting himself in the picture.

At particular points in the narrative the narrative voice addresses the reader directly. When this happens the term used is 'commentary sentences'. One example of this is John 12.6, in which Judas is characterized as a thief. Commentary sentences contain supplementary information, give a further explanation of the story being narrated or indicate what its meaning is. The information thus offered is not accessible to the characters in the narrative and reaches only the reader, with the effect that the reader soon knows more than the characters.

The narrative voice is regularly delegated to a character. We then speak of character text. The words of the character are not on the same level as those of the narrator; the character text is always embedded in the narrator's text. Here there is nevertheless a difference in degree between direct and indirect speech. In passages in direct speech the character usually gets the opportunity to speak on his or her own account, although of course we must remember that the words spoken directly by a character have also been chosen by the narrator. In the case of indirect speech the character does not get the opportunity to express his or her thoughts and feelings directly; these are indeed the thoughts and feelings of the character, but they are presented by the narrator.

After all this we can give a general definition of a narrative. A narrative consists of happenings presented in a particular way which are presented to a reader by means of a particular medium (in our case the text). The communicative aspects of the narrative belong to the heart of the definition. The narrative is a construction by the narrator, a world-in-words, which is presented to the readers for their judgment. It stands at some distance from the world known to us, but on the other hand the distance is again not so great that what is narrated becomes totally unimaginable, since the narrative would lose its communicative function were it completely unrecognizable. By reading a narrative we enter into a world which is to some degree fictional, a fantastic universe, which can give us a new perspective on the reality that surrounds us.

Translation of John 10.40–11.54

The translation which now follows is as literal as possible. In the margin I indicate how the text can be divided up (X – I – II – III – IV – X'). Moreover in the layout the difference between narrator's text (e.g. 10.40), commentary sentences (e.g. 11.2) and character text (e.g. 10.41b), is made clear.

X   40 He went away again to the other side of the Jordan, to the place where John at first baptized, and there he remained. 41 Many came to him and said,

> 'John did no sign, but everything that John said about this man was true.'

42 And many began to believe in him there.

I   11. 1 Now a certain man was ill, Lazarus of Bethany, the village of Mary and her sister Martha.

> 2 Mary was the woman who anointed the Lord with ointment and wiped his feet with her hair; the sick Lazarus was her brother.

3 The sisters sent to him, saying,

> 'Lord, behold, he whom you love is ill.'

4 When Jesus heard this he said,

> 'This illness will not end in death; it is for the glory of God, for the Son of God must be glorified through it.'

5 Jesus loved Martha and her sister and Lazarus.

6 When he had heard that Lazarus was ill, he stayed two days longer in the place where he was.

7 Then after that he said to his disciples,

> 'Let us go into Judaea again.'

8 The disciples said to him,

> 'Rabbi, just now the Jews were seeking to stone you, and are you going there again?'

9 Jesus answered,

> 'Are there not twelve hours in the day? If anyone walks in the day, he does not stumble, because he sees the light of this world. 10 But if anyone walks in the night, he stumbles, because the light is not in him.'

11 He said this, and after that he said to them,

> 'Lazarus our friend has fallen asleep, but I am going there to awaken him out of sleep.'

12 The disciples said to him,

> 'Lord, if he is asleep, he will recover.'

13 Now Jesus had spoken of his death, but they thought that he meant taking rest in sleep.

14 Then Jesus told them plainly,

> 'Lazarus is dead; 15 and for your sake I am glad that I was not there, so that you may believe. Come, let us go to him.'

16 Thomas (that means the Twin) said to his fellow disciples,

> 'Let us also go, that we may die with him.'

II   17 Now when Jesus came, he found that Lazarus had already been in the tomb four days.

18 Bethany is near Jerusalem, about fifteen stadia off.

19 Many of the Jews had come to Martha and Mary to commiserate with them for the loss of their brother. 20 When Martha heard that Jesus was coming, she went to meet him, but Mary remained in the house. 21 Martha said to Jesus,

> 'Lord, if you had been here, my brother would not have died. 22 And even now I know that whatever you ask from God, God will give you.'

23 Jesus said to her,

> 'Your brother will rise again.'

24 Martha said to him,

> 'I know that he will rise again in the resurrection at the last day.'

25 Jesus said to her,

> 'I am the resurrection and the life; he who believes in me shall live, even if he is dead, 26 and whoever lives and believes in me shall never die. Do you believe that?'

27 She said to him,

> 'Yes, Lord, I firmly believe that you are the messiah, the son of God, he who is to come into the world.'

28 When she had said this, she went and called her sister Mary, and whispered to her,

> 'The master is here, he is calling for you.'

29 When she heard that, she rose quickly and went to him.

> 30 Now Jesus had not yet come to the village, but was still in the place where Martha had met him.

31 The Jews who were with her in the house, commiserating with her, saw Mary rise quickly and go out, and they followed her, supposing that she was going to the tomb to wail there. 32 When Mary came to the place where Jesus was, as soon as she saw him, she fell at his feet, saying to him,

> 'Lord, if you had been here, my brother would not have died.'

33 When Jesus saw her wailing, and the Jews who came with her also wailing, he was moved with indignation and troubled, 34 and said,

> 'Where have you laid him?'

They said to him,

> 'Lord, come and see.'

36 Jesus began to weep. 16 The Jews said,

> 'See how he loved him!'

37 But some of them said,

> 'Could not he who opened the eyes of the blind man have kept this man from dying?'

III   38 Then Jesus, again moved with indignation, came to the tomb. It was a cave, and a stone lay against it.

39 Jesus said,

> 'Take away the stone.'

Martha, the sister of the dead man, said to him,

> 'Lord, by this time there is already an odour, for he has been dead four days.'

40 Jesus said to her,

> 'Did I not tell you that if you would believe you would see the glory of God?'

41 They took away the stone. Jesus lifted up his eyes and said,

> 'Father, I thank you that you have heard me. 42 I knew that you hear me always, but I have said this on account of the people standing by, that they may believe that you sent me.'

43 After these words, he cried with a loud voice,
> 'Lazarus, come out.'

44 The dead man came out, his hands and feet bound with bandages, and his face wrapped with a cloth. Jesus said to them,
> 'Unbind him, and let him go.'

45 Many of the Jews, therefore, who had come with Mary and had seen what he did, began to believe in him. 46 But some of them went to the Pharisees and told them what Jesus had done.

IV   47 So the chief priests and the Pharisees held an assembly, and said,

> 'What are we to do? For this man performs many signs. 48 If we let him go on like this, everyone will come to believe in him, and then the Romans will come and take away from us both our holy place and our people.'

49 One of them, Caiaphas, who was high priest that year, said to them,

> 'You know nothing. 50 You do not understand that it is in your interest that one man should die for the people, and that the whole people should not perish.'

51 He did not say this of his own accord, but being high priest that year he prophesied that Jesus should die for the nation, 52 and not for the nation only, but to gather into one the scattered children of God.

53 So from that day on they were resolved to put him to death.

X'   54 Jesus therefore no longer went about openly among the Jews, but went from there to the region near the wilderness, to a town called Ephraim; and there he remained with his disciples.

Demarcation and composition

The narrative begins with a short sketch of Jesus' stay on the other side of the Jordan (10.40–42). There he receives the report of Lazarus's sickness and there he speaks two days later with his disciples about his plan to go to the place of the disaster, to Bethany in Judaea (11.1–16). The narrative does not end with the raising of Lazarus but gets a sequel in 11.47–53, where the Jewish leaders resolve to kill Jesus. The one who has been condemned to death thereupon retreats to a safe place (11.54). His reaction is the same as in 10.42. The repetition of 'he went away' and 'he remained' emphasizes that the whole narration is enclosed by 10.40–42 (X) and 11.54 (X').

The narrative is presented chronologically. Table 4 contains the four sequences which can be distinguished within this whole, together with some substructures.

X	10.40–42	Jesus stays on the other side of the Jordan
Sequence I	11.1–16	Lazarus' sickness and death
	11.1–6	Report on Lazarus' sickness
	11.7–16	Conversation between Jesus and his disciples on his plan to go to Judaea (first round: 11.7–10) and raise Lazarus from the sleep of death (second round: 11.11–16).
Sequence II	11.17–37	Jesus' encounter with Martha and with Mary and the Jews
	11.17–19	Introduction
	11.20–27	Encounter with Martha
	11.28–37	Encounter with Mary and the Jews
Sequence III	11.38–46	Lazarus is raised to life
Sequence IV	11.47–53	The high priests and the Pharisees resolve to kill Jesus on the advice of Caiaphas
X'	11.54	Jesus and his disciples stay in Ephraim, close to the wilderness

Table 4: The composition of John 10.40–11.54

The first sequence has a unity of place: Jesus is still on the other side of the Jordan. Within 11.1–16 the first six verses are about the report to Jesus about the sickness of his friend: the key words here are 'sickness' and 'be sick'. Two days later Jesus talks at length with his disciples (11.7–16). In this section 'the disciples' and 'go to Judaea' function as key words. The conversation consists of two rounds (11.7–10 and 11.11–16), both of which begin with 'after that'.

The second sequence takes place in Bethany and at a place on the edge of the village where Jesus is staying. There is much coming and going between the two locations. First Jesus has an encounter with Martha, and after that with her sister. There is a dispute as to whether the sequence ends with 11.37. 11.32 could also be an appropriate conclusion. But I would argue for seeing 11.28–37 as a single whole, since this section contains so many words that are connected with mourning and gives an impressive picture of the state of mind of the characters.[6]

The third sequence begins in 11.38 with the departure to the tomb, which is close to Bethany. At the beginning and end of the sequence Jesus addresses a command to the bystanders (11.39,44). Like the second sequence, the third also ends with a twofold reaction from the Jews present (see 11.36–37 and 11.45–46). Within the total narration, III forms the pendant to I: in III what Jesus had announced in I takes place.

The fourth sequence takes place in Jerusalem. It is the only sub-division of the story in which Jesus is not present on stage. But he is the only point on the agenda at the gathering held in Jerusalem. The narrator makes Jesus draw a conclusion in 11.54 from the resolution of the high priests and Pharisees ('therefore') without mentioning how Jesus has heard of their decision.

The course of the action

The story has two cores. The first is that Jesus brings his dead friend to life; the second is that Jesus' enemies want to kill him.

The first core is developed as follows. At the beginning it is said very emphatically that Lazarus is sick. Two days later it proves that Lazarus has died. His death is connected with Jesus' absence. That is stated not only by Martha, Mary and the Jews (11.21, 32, 37) but also by Jesus himself (11.15). No one doubts that Jesus could have healed his friend. From the beginning Jesus indicates that sickness and death do not have the last word. He asserts that Lazarus' sickness will not end with death (11.4) and that he is going to wake him from his sleep (11.11). The tension is heightened by the reports that Lazarus has already been in the tomb four days (11.17) and that the process of decomposition must already have begun (11.39). Despite the seriousness of the situation, Jesus does not go into action immediately. After receiving the report of Lazarus' sickness he lets two days go by before he makes arrangements to travel. When he arrives in Bethany, he tells Martha of the need to believe that in his own person he is the resurrection and the life. Standing before the open tomb, he thanks God that things have turned out well, even before the dead man has left his last resting place. In only a few words, the narrative sketches out how Lazarus indeed emerges living from the tomb at Jesus' call.

The second core consists of the efforts of the opposition to kill Jesus. His stay on the other side of the Jordan was already the direct consequence of the fact that the Jews in Jerusalem had wanted to stone him (10.31, 39). The disciples remind Jesus of this incident (11.8). Nevertheless he travels to Bethany, which is close to Jerusalem. Among the Jews who have come to Martha and Mary to commiserate with them are some minions of Jesus' deadly enemies. After Lazarus' resurrection they bring a report to the Pharisees, who begin to take counsel with the chief priests over counter-measures. Caiaphas sees only one solution: Jesus must die for the people. The story ends with Jesus retreating back to a safe place. When his hour is to come is not determined by the high priest.

The real aim of the narrative is expressed by Jesus himself. Lazarus' sickness must lead to the glorification of God and of his son (11.4). Jesus rejoices that the manifestation of this will bring the disciples to believe (11.14). These statements are combined in 11.40 as follows: 'Have I not told you that you shall see the glory of God if only you believe?' Jesus' action has the status of a sign (cf. 12.18). That is even recognized by his enemies (11.47). The signs make Jesus' glory manifest (2.11); they show that Jesus comes from God and that God is with him (3.2); they serve to awaken faith that Jesus is the messiah, the son of God (20.30–31). All this can also be found in our narrative. Jesus wants to lead his disciples and the people at the tomb to faith (11.15, 42). He does indeed achieve this effect with many people (11.45). Later, too, we hear that many Jews began to believe in Jesus because of what had happened (12.11, 17–19). The fear of the leaders that everyone is going to believe in him (11.48), does not come out of thin air.

Characters

Making character portraits

Character portraits are constructions which are gradually built up during the process of reading. They are not there ready-made in the text. When we try to form a picture of a character, we must allow ourselves to be guided by facts from the texts. These have been listed very well by R.Alter.[7] According to him, characters expose themselves by what they say and do (and also by what they do not say and do), by their relations with other actors, by the way in which the character is depicted by other actors and by illumination given by the narrator in commentary sentences.

In making a character portrait we must note the positioning of the character within the narrative as a whole. In what sub-divisions do we find the character? The characteristics attributed to the character when first presented give this character a certain degree of predictability. Readers must regularly supplement their portrait on the basis of new information. Perhaps it will prove that later in the narrative a character will assume different characteristics from before. A book may also contain different portraits of one and the same character.[8]

I shall now go on to draw a portrait of the main characters. I shall consider in succession the disciples, Mary and Martha, and Jesus.[9]

The disciples

The disciples appear as a group and stand in a close relation to Jesus. He is their rabbi, they go off with him and are ready to share his fate. Jesus in his turn associates closely with his followers. He makes use of the inclusive 'we' (11.7: 'Let us go back to Judaea'; 11.11, 'our friend'; 11.15, 'Let us go to him'). At the same time there is a certain difference between Jesus and the disciples. He wants to go to Judaea and the disciples do not; he knows that Lazarus is dead, they do not, and only with some difficulty does this truth sink in. What they do know is that Judaea is a dangerous area. They remember all too well what happened there shortly beforehand. Even if they cease their opposition to Jesus' travel plans, they still regard the journey to Judaea as a journey to death.

After 11.7–16 the disciples are mentioned again in 11.54. In the intermediate part their presence is presupposed, but nowhere mentioned explicitly. And that although Jesus rejoiced that the coming events would lead the disciples to believe (11.15)! The explanation for this remarkable phenomenon could be that in that long passage Mary and Martha take on the role of the disciples. Let's look at this more closely.

Mary and Martha

Mary and Martha are mentioned in John for the first time in 11.1, as is Lazarus. Although all three are new characters, only Lazarus is treated as an unknown figure who needs further introduction. The narrator presents him as someone who comes from Bethany, the village of Mary and her sister Martha. The two sisters are regarded as well-known figures. In view of 12.9–11,17–18, where we hear of the great fame which Lazarus enjoys after his resurrection from the dead, we would have expected rather that Lazarus was a well-known figure and that it was his two sisters who had to be introduced to the reader through him.

In 11.1 Mary comes first. It is said of Martha that she is Mary's sister. In 11.5 the order is completely reversed: 'Martha, her sister and Lazarus'. In 11.1 Martha is thus Mary's sister, and in 11.5 Mary is Martha's sister. This is a signal addressed to the readers. They must compare these two characters to see which of them they can best reflect.

The two sisters appear together in 11.3–5. That they send Jesus a report implies that they know that Jesus is on the other side of the Jordan, where he has sought refuge after the unsuccessful attempt on his life in Jerusalem. They let Jesus know that the one whom he loves is sick, and they assume that Jesus can offer help in this emergency. Later they repeat this, each individually, in 11.21, 32: 'Lord, if you had been here, my brother would not have died.' The same perspective is expressed by some Jews (11.37): 'Could not he... have kept Lazarus from dying?'

Martha

From 11.17 on, Mary and Martha no longer play the same role. As soon as Martha hears that Jesus is on the way, she goes to meet him, while Mary stays at home. In her conversation with Jesus, Martha shows a thorough knowledge of religious doctrine. To her rebuke that her brother would not have died had Jesus been in Bethany at the critical moment, she adds in the same breath: 'And even now I know that whatever you ask from God, God will give you.' First she associates Lazarus' death with the absence of Jesus, and then she declares that everything is again open now that he is present. Martha thus confirms that life and death are closely connected with the presence and absence of Jesus. It is also striking that she does not indicate *what* Jesus must ask God: she leaves that entirely to him. She does so because of her belief in the role of Jesus as mediator: she sees him as someone who has access to God.

Jesus' answer is put in the future tense ('your brother will rise again'). He does not say when that will happen. Martha repeats Jesus' words and fills them out with a temporal definition ('my brother will rise at the resurrection on the last day'), as if she wants to make the precise meaning of resurrection clear to Jesus. She associates the resurrection of her brother with a moment in the distant future.

However, Jesus has a quite different idea of the resurrection. He corrects Martha's view by saying that he himself is the resurrection and the life. The victory over death is not bound up with the end time but with his person (cf. 14.6). Jesus has the ability to give authentic life now, already, but he does this only to people who are totally in tune with him. Hence too his question to Martha, 'Do you believe this?'

Her reaction is: 'Yes, Lord, I believe that you are the messiah, the son of God, he who is to come into the world.' This threefold creed is a detailed statement of who Jesus is. Martha does not say that he has just arrived from the region on the other side of the Jordan. No, she speaks of a quite different journey: Jesus comes from God and is now in the world. The correctness of her confession is confirmed in 11.41 where Jesus addresses God as his Father and points to himself as the one who has been sent by God.

We find the predicates used by Martha once again in 20.31. There the narrator says that he wants to lead his readers to the belief that Jesus is the messiah, the son of God. Thus the readers of the Fourth Gospel can model themselves on Martha. She sets an example that is worth following.[10]

Nevertheless, it may be asked whether Martha's reaction is quite so unequivocally positive.[11] There are some reasons for doubting that. In the Greek text of 11.27 the perfect form *pepisteuka* is used (cf. 6.69: *pepisteukamen*). This form indicates an action begun in the past, the result of which still continues. Thus Martha is saying that she has always cherished the categories which she uses and that she continues to do so (hence the translation 'I firmly believe'). She does not explicitly confirm that her vision of life and death has been radically changed by the previous statement by Jesus, but she uses predicates which have already been applied earlier by others to Jesus (1.41; 4.29; 7.41; 9.22: 'messiah'; 1.34, 49: 'son of God': 6.14: 'the one who is to come into the world'). So she is really using standard notions, precisely as she did when she stated her belief in the resurrection.

That Martha has not developed any new perspective on Jesus is also evident from what follows. When talking to Mary she calls Jesus 'the master' (11.28);[12] this designation is comparable with the 'rabbi' used by the disciples (11.8). It is even more important that she certainly does not play the role of the perfect believer when she tries to thwart the execution of Jesus' command to take the stone away from Lazarus' tomb. There is a clear opposition between what she thinks she is going to see (a body in a state of dissolution) and what according to Jesus she is going to see if only she believes (the glory of God). By introducing his words with 'did I not tell you', Jesus refers back to his earlier conversation with Martha. Evidently at that time she was so caught up in her own schemes that she did not allow Jesus' statement that he is the resurrection and the life to get completely through to her.

These elements together produce the following portrait. Martha plays an independent role and is very enterprising. Her role is comparable with that of the disciples: she addresses Jesus as 'Lord', she calls him 'the master', and for him she is a worthy conversation-partner, as much so as the disciples (11.7–16). Martha has a wealth of knowledge of faith. The narrator makes her express the traditional Jewish belief in the eschatological resurrection, in order then to weaken it with Jesus' saying that life is already accessible now to those who believe in him. The intention is for Martha to abandon her old framework and show herself receptive to the new perspective offered by Jesus. She is described as a dynamic character who is undergoing an intensive process of learning. Her learning curve is instructive for readers: they too are expected to have their categories supplemented by what Jesus has to say.

Mary

In 11.1 and 11.5 the searchlight is directed on Mary and Martha alternately. But Mary already immediately has a marked advantage over her sister, since in 11.2 in a commentary sentence the narrator characterizes her as the woman who anointed the Lord and dried his feet with her hair. This information is extremely surprising, for although Jesus' anointing has yet to take place (12.1–8), it is here already spoken of as if it were an event from the past. The narrator assumes that Mary's action is already known to the reader from other sources. Here we can think of oral traditions, but reference can also be made to Mark 14.3–9 and Matthew 26.6–13 (in Bethany Jesus' head(!) is anointed by an anonymous woman) or Luke 7.36–50 (about the anointing of Jesus' feet by a woman with a bad reputation). The special feature of John 11.2 (and 12.3) is that here the anointing is attributed to Mary of Bethany. Already before she has gone into action in the story she is portrayed as someone with a deep respect for Jesus.

While Martha goes to Jesus, Mary remains at home mourning, surrounded by Jews who have come to commiserate with the two sisters (11.19), but who later are associated only with Mary (11.31,45). She leaves the house only when she hears from Martha that Jesus is calling her. So she does not get moving of her own accord, like her enterprising sister; in comparison with her, she is more receptive by nature. When she sees Jesus, she throws herself at his feet, a gesture with which she shows her deep respect for his person (cf. 11.2). Even before a word has been exchanged between them, Mary pays Jesus the respect that is due to him; Martha expressed her faith verbally and did so only at the end of an intense conversation about doctrine. From her position at Jesus' feet Mary repeats the words with which Martha began in 11.21: 'Lord, had you been here, my brother would not have died.' We do not hear Martha's further words from Mary's mouth. There are no speculations about Jesus as mediator or about the eschatological resurrection. Instead of this there is intense sorrow at the loss of her brother. Her bond with Jesus does not take her tears away, but the opposite is equally true: her confrontation with death has not swept away her trust in Jesus.

Up to this moment in the story the emphasis lay on the supremacy of Jesus. According to 11.15 he himself was delighted that he was not in Bethany at the critical moment, for the death of Lazarus is part of a wider scenario which is focussed on the glory of God and the faith of the disciples. Now that Jesus sees how deeply immersed Mary and the Jews are in mourning, he himself is in the grip of powerful emotions: he is moved with indignation and troubled (11.35,38), and bursts into tears (11.35).[13] This last is explained clearly in the text. According to the Jews, Jesus' tears show how much he loved Lazarus. The bystanders cannot see that Jesus is moved with indignation and troubled, since he does not express these emotions. However, the narrator does know how Jesus is feeling and he conveys his knowledge to the readers. How are they to interpret Jesus' irritation? I do not think that we can accept that Jesus is offended at Mary's sorrow, since her mourning leaves her faith intact. Is he then offended at the remark by some Jews that he could have avoided this death? Or is he annoyed at the fact that he has been expected for so long and has not gone into action earlier? It seems to me best to understand Jesus' powerful emotions in the light of what follows immediately afterwards: he asks where Lazarus lies buried (11.34) and goes to the tomb (11.38). He is annoyed at the power of death which is still as tangible as ever and now resolutely goes into action. Evidently the lamentations of Mary and the Jews have acted as a catalyst; the story now gains momentum.

In the scene at the tomb (11.38–46), Mary is mentioned only in 11.45, where the Jews who come to believe on seeing Jesus' sign are associated with her. There is no reaction from Mary herself. It is striking that she has no part in the doubt expressed by Mary, who is here referred to as 'the dead man's sister', as if Lazarus had only one sister.

Mary's reaction is expressed only in 12.1–11. During a feast in honour of Jesus in Bethany, Mary anoints Jesus' feet with a large quantity of oil of nard and then dries his feet with her hair. The anointing of someone's feet after the meal has already begun is not an everyday activity, but is not completely unusual.[14] The strange thing is that Mary dries Jesus' feet immediately after anointing them. Commentators here are fond of referring to Luke 7.38, 44, but in that passage the order is different: the woman dries Jesus' feet after first having wet them with her tears, and only after that does she anoint them with balsam. An additional detail which is puzzling is that Mary uses her hair and not a cloth. What she means by all this is not stated explicitly in the text. It is important for us that we also find the sequence which Mary observes in 13.5: during a meal Jesus washes his disciples' feet and dries them with the apron around his waist.[15] Her role thus resembles that of Jesus. In both cases we come across a sign of respect, an indication of love.

In 12.1–11 Mary's action is connected in different ways with Jesus' imminent death. The respect shown by her to Jesus contrasts markedly with the negative reaction of Judas Iscariot, who here is characterized by the narrator as the one who is to hand Jesus over. The role assigned to Judas should really have been fulfilled by Mary and the others present, since the chief priests and the Pharisees had given orders that the one who knew where Jesus was staying should provide information about this (11.57). The most explicit reference to the end of Jesus' life is made by Jesus himself (12.8). He makes a connection with the day of his burial. This gives the anointing by Mary the character of a burial ritual. This fits the picture that we had gained of her earlier extremely well. In John 11 she is described as someone who was in deep mourning because of the death of her brother. Here she expresses her affection and respect for Jesus, who is soon to die, and this is emphasized once again in 12.11 (the chief priests resolve *also* to kill Lazarus; the formulation is almost identical with the death sentence on Jesus in 11.53).

Summing up, we can now say that Mary too has the features of a disciple. She expresses her faith in Jesus in what she does. Her respect implies the recognition of his glory that – and this is a paradoxical fact – will become visible in the end of his life, which is to be expected very soon. Mary is a different character from her sister. The positive lines in the portrait of Mary are complementary to the strong characteristics in Martha. Each represents a particular way of being a disciple. Some readers of the book will be able to identify more with Mary, the others more with Martha.

Jesus

Jesus is given various titles. The narrator, the disciples and Martha and Mary call him 'Lord' (11.2, 3, 12, 21, 27, 32, 39); the speakers in 11.34, who are not identified more closely, also address him in this way. Moreover he is the rabbi (11.8) and the master (11.28) for his disciples. We find a great concentration of titles in Martha's creed: Jesus is the messiah, the son of God, the one who is to come into the world. These indications also occur often in the rest of the book. In this sub-narrative they are given a new dimension by the statement which Jesus himself makes about his identity: I am the resurrection and the life.

In the narrative Jesus is the main figure, not so much because he is on the stage almost continuously (sometimes he is absent for a short period: 11.19, 28, 47–53), but above all because in one way or another the other characters' roles are determined by his movements and undertakings. Although he is fully involved in the event that is being related, he is not confined in it. No, he determines what is going to happen and each time chooses precisely the right moment. An example of this is that after the report of Lazarus' sickness he remains where he is for some days and only after that proposes to travel to Bethany, regardless of the fact that this is a dangerous destination. According to Martha and Mary he keeps them waiting a long time; according to the disciples he is showing too much haste.

Jesus is also the one who foresees events (11.11) and can already interpret them beforehand (11.4). His knowledge does not depend on the actual course of time. In his prayer before the raising of Lazarus he speaks in the past tense, as if the dead man is already standing before him alive ('I thank you that *you have heard me.* I *knew* that you hear me always'). What he has to do is determined by the Father; human characters have no influence on this.

This image of the omniscient Jesus, who is superior to the power of death, stands in tension with the way in which he is depicted at his encounter with Mary and the Jews (11.28–37). He bursts into tears and has to be told by the bystanders where Lazarus lies buried. For him, the death of a beloved person is clearly not the happy event of which he was still speaking in 11.15. Jesus too is a dynamic character, who in the course of the narrative takes on different appearances.

Do the two faces of the main figure indicate a deep division in his person? This is in fact the last thing that the narrator wants us to believe. For him the power and powerlessness of Jesus, his superior distance and his compassion, lie very close together. Jesus has not overcome the darkness of death without himself being touched by it. Or in terms of 11.51–52, by dying for God's children he saves them from destruction and brings a new community into being.

Space and time

Indications of place

The events of a narrative stand in a particular setting: they take place somewhere (space) and at a particular moment (time). In analysing the space we begin by mapping out the different indications of place. Then we look for an answer to a number of questions. How are the characters arranged in space? Do they move from A to B? What significance do the indications of place assume in the narrative? Are there spatial oppositions, and is there a boundary between one space and the other?

In John 10.40–11.54 we come across various indications of place.
A first grouping provides the following result:

1. In 10.40–11.16 Jesus is in a place on the other side of the Jordan,
   which is described as the place where John had once baptized. On
   the basis of 1.28 the reader knows that Bethany is meant, on the
   other side of the Jordan.
2. The village of Bethany in Judaea, close to Jerusalem, is different
   from this. The house of Mary and Martha is in this village and there
   is a burial place in the immediate vicinity. Jesus' encounter with
   Martha and Mary and the Jews takes place outside the boundaries
   of the village (11.30).
3. In 11.46 some Jews go to the Pharisees. Given their connection with
   the high priests and with Caiaphas we may assume that 11.47–53
   takes place in Jerusalem.
4. In 11.54 Jesus and his disciples withdraw to the town of Ephraim,
   in the region close to the wilderness.

This list is not complete. The text also mentions a sphere outside
and above the world, where God dwells. Jesus has been sent to the
world by him and lifts up his eyes whenever he addresses God in
his prayers (11.41–42). The narrator, who surveys all other
locations and in this sense is 'omnipresent', is completely dependent on his main character for information about God, for only
Jesus has seen God and has perceived from God what he must do
and say on earth. Jesus makes 'the world above' present here below
for those who believe in him.

In the narrative an intensive traffic develops between the
locations mentioned. Mary and Martha seek contact with Jesus in
the region beyond the Jordan and leave their house to meet him
outside the village. With a crowd around him, Jesus goes to the
tomb, which is shut off from the outside world by a stone. The
report that Lazarus has been raised is passed on by some of the
bystanders to the authorities in Jerusalem, whereupon Jesus moves
to a region where he is safe.

Jesus has two motives for his journey to Bethany: he is driven by
his love for Martha, Mary and Lazarus (11.3, 5, 35) and by his
concern to make the glory of God shine out in the dark domain of

death. Moreover, directly or indirectly, he influences the movements of all the other characters. The space in the narrative is completely dominated by him.

What is the colouring of the different locations in the narrative? The tomb is the place of death and decay. The stone marks the sharp division between the dead and the living. The house of the two sisters is a place of mourning and comfort. Like the tomb, Jerusalem too, indeed the whole of Judaea, stands under the sign of death. Shortly beforehand the Jews wanted to stone Jesus in Jerusalem, and now the death sentence is pronounced on him there, to avoid the Romans destroying the city. Over against these places stamped by death stand the regions where Jesus is staying at the beginning and the end of the narrative. Both on the other side of the Jordan and in the region close to the wilderness he is protected from attacks on his life and is surrounded exclusively by supporters (10.42: people who are beginning to believe in him; 11.54: his disciples).

The places mentioned are thus dominated by the sharp contrast between death and life. However, black is not set statically over against white, for the frontier between death and life shifts with the movements which Jesus makes. Life and resurrection become reality where he encounters faith: the other side of this is that those who reject him enter the kingdom of death. This deep truth is expressed by Jesus himself at the edge of Bethany. At this place belief in the life that Jesus makes present and sorrow at the death of Lazarus meet. In connection with this we see how Jesus gives orders for the stone at the entrance of the tomb to be taken away and thus for the world of death to be unbolted. After that command has been carried out, the giver of life stands face to face with death and decay. Just as Jesus got Mary going by calling her, so too he calls Lazarus to come out. By hearing Jesus' call, Lazarus crosses the frontier between death and life. This scene shows that there are good reasons to believe Jesus' statement in 11.25 that he is the resurrection and the life. Everyone who hears this statement has a share in life, for ever.

Passage of time

In the study of the setting of a narrative, temporal aspects are also important. Here the point of departure is formed by indications of time which together give a picture of the course of time within the story that is related.

The narrative from John 10.40–11.54 takes place between the feast of the dedication of the temple, which is celebrated in the winter (10.22), and the feast of passover in the spring (11.55). The duration of Jesus' stay beyond the Jordan is not defined more closely; nor do we hear how long he hides in Ephraim (according to 12.1 he is back in Bethany around a week before Passover).

Although the events of 11.1–53 (or rather the conversations, for the majority of the text consists of direct speech) follow one another chronologically, it is impossible to indicate precisely how much time elapses here. All that is clear is that 11.17–46 takes place on one day, namely the fourth day after Lazarus has been laid in his tomb (11.17,39). The impression is given that the authorities deliberate on counter-measures that same day. An indication of that is the concluding note in 11.53 which begins with 'from that day onwards'. Proportionally, the most attention is thus paid to the fourth day.

At first sight the course of time in 11.1–16 causes no problems, since this passage contains a precise indication in 11.6: two days after receiving the report of Lazarus' sickness, Jesus tells his disciples that the man has died. After this conversation the narrator continues with the information that Jesus arrived in the neighbourhood of Bethany. Whether he set off immediately after the conversation and how long the journey took is not said (this is an ellipse, an omission), so that readers curiously ask themselves how the 'two days' of 11.6 relate to the 'four days' of 11.17. I see two possible ways of resolving this question. The first is that Lazarus died on the day on which Jesus received the report about his sickness: the two days of 11.6 are then included in the four days of 11.17. The second possibility is that Lazarus died only shortly before the conversation between Jesus and his disciples, thus two days after Jesus was notified of his sickness. In this case the four days of 11.17 follow the two days of 11.6 and therefore in total six days pass between the receiving of the report and the arrival in Bethany. We cannot straighten out this complication. It is abundantly clear at this point that the narrator is not interested in the precise moment of Lazarus' death but is exclusively focussed on Jesus' reaction to the sickness (11.4) and death (11.11, 14–15) of his friend. We cannot infer from his words how these events are to be fitted into the normal course of time: the only important thing is that it is still day and that the night has not yet come (11.9–10). With these metaphorical words Jesus indicates to his disciples that he can confidently go to Bethany, because the hour of his death has not yet come.[16]

In 11.49, the narrator names Caiaphas as the 'high priest of that year' in order to put particular emphasis on the year of Jesus' death; within the many years during which Caiaphas held office (AD 18 to 36) he focusses on the one year which was of such crucial importance within the total activity of Jesus. By the category of time 'from this day' the narrator betrays that chronologically he is far removed from the event narrated. He is looking back on the events that he narrates from a later standpoint.

Retrospects and anticipations

In a narrative, the course of time which is sketched out is regularly interrupted by references to the past (retrospects) and the future (anticipations).[17] In studying this phenomenon we begin from the primary story. In our case this story consists of the activity of Jesus, lasting around two years, as that is described in John.

Retrospects can be divided into three sub-categories. An internal retrospect recalls happenings which were mentioned earlier in John; it is a reference back to an earlier moment within the primary story (for example 10.40; John had *once* baptized there). An external retrospect relates to a moment in time which lies completely outside the primary story (1.17: the law is given by Moses). A mixed retrospect is a reference back to an event which begins outside the primary story and ends within it (9.33: no one has ever heard of a person who has opened the eyes of someone who was born blind).

We can make the same distinctions in the case of anticipations. An internal anticipation relates to a future moment in time which falls completely within the primary story (11.51: Jesus is to die for his people), an external anticipation points forward to a moment which lies completely outside the primary story (11.48: the Romans will assault Jerusalem), and a mixed anticipation points forward to an event which begins within the primary story but still goes on outside it (14.13: I must go away but I shall return).

The internal retrospects and anticipations contribute to the cohesion of the book. The retrospects lead the reader to read the part of the narrative that is now being related in the light of what has gone before, whereas the anticipations already give an impression of the further course of the story that is being related.

The mixed and external retrospects relate the ministry of Jesus to moments from the preceding history of Israel. The mixed and internal anticipations in turn connect the narrative about Jesus with the period between his resurrection and the end of time. The readers of John are situated in this long period. Here we can make a distinction between the original readers and the later readers. For the original readers, who must be situated towards the end of the first century, some events which are presented in the book as future already lie in the past (the capture of Jerusalem in the year 70); other events indicated as future take place in their own time (the hostility between the Pharisees and Jesus' followers). Later readers are at a still greater distance from what is related in the book. However, for them, too, not everything from the book is past time. In their case, too, the statements about the eschaton or the end time relate to something that is still to come.

Armed with these distinctions we can now go in search of retrospects and anticipations in 10.40–11.54. We find such references above all in commentary sentences by the narrator and in the conversations which the characters have with one another. I have collected these together in Table 5, in such a way that within each series there is an increasingly great distance from 'the present' (the course of time described in our narrative).

Retrospects	
11.7–16	Jesus says that Lazarus has died in the meantime; the death has taken place shortly before he speaks of it.
11.21, 32	Martha and Mary recall on the fourth day after Lazarus' burial that Jesus was absent when their brother was sick.
11.37	The Jews go further back into the past and refer to the healing of the man born blind (9.1–7).
11.8	The disciples speak of recent attempts on Jesus' life (8.59; 10.31) and earlier visits to Judaea (3.22; 7.1–3).
11.27, 42	Martha calls Jesus the son of God who has come into the world; Jesus calls himself the one who has been sent by the Father. Both references are to Jesus' origin in the unfathomable depths of God.

Anticipations	
11.11, 14	Jesus announces – first in ambiguous words, then outspokenly – that he is going to arouse (raise) Lazarus.
11.8,16	The disciples expect that not only Jesus but also they themselves will be liquidated by the Jewish leaders.
11.48	The chief priests and the Pharisees speak of the death of Jesus and of their own downfall at the hands of the Romans.
11.51–53	The narrator discusses the positive significance of the death of Jesus for his readers and looks back on this crucial event from his own time.
11.24	Martha speaks about the resurrection at the last day.

Table 5: Retrospects and anticipations in John 10.40–11.54

Both series end up in an event which really cannot be fitted into the events that we can survey. That Jesus has been sent by God and was already inwardly bound up with him 'in the beginning' (1.1) is expressed with the help of an indication of time and situated in the past, but this does not mean that it is an event of the same order as the other events from the past. *Mutatis mutandis* the same thing is true of the resurrection on the last day. This day certainly lies within the perspective of the readers, but it is not a day like the other days which still lie before them. For want of a better word, in the first case we can speak of a prehistoric or suprahistorical past which supports and provides the foundation for the whole of further history, whereas in the second case we can speak of the eschatological future in which the whole of history finds its consummation.

In John, both this ultimate past and this extreme future are bound up with Jesus, the son sent by the Father, who floods believers with the life that comes from God. In Jesus' voice the Word that was from the beginning with God resounds. He anticipates the eschaton by saying that an hour *is coming* when all those who lie in the grave will hear his voice and will emerge (5.28–29), but really this voice is now resounding already, as he says this, and therefore he can just as well assert that the decisive hour has already dawned: 'An hour *is coming*, indeed it *is* already *here* when the dead shall hear the voice of the son of God and those who listen to it shall live' (5.25). Everyone who believes in him now already has a share in life, for ever (11.25–26). His voice also reaches the readers who take up the book in which these words are written.

Perspective

So far I have regularly made a distinction between narrator text and character text and I have drawn attention to commentary sentences, which occupy a separate position within the narrator text. These distinctions put us in a position to hear different voices in the text, which do not always emphasize the same thing or do not always express the same standpoint. So we see that in the narrative divergent interpretations clash and struggle with one another for pre-eminence. Yet in this maelstrom the reader is almost irresistibly driven in a particular direction. It is worth looking at this phenomenon rather more closely.

Recently Ellen van Wolde and José Sanders have presented a

linguistic model for the analysis of the textual perspective of narrative biblical texts.[18] Starting from the usual distinction between narrator text and character text these two scholars have developed a refined conceptual apparatus which I reproduce in Table 6.

NARRATOR TEXT			CHARACTER TEXT (embedded in the narrator text)			
1 direct narrator text		2 indirect narrator text	3 indirect character text		4 direct character text	
1a commentary sentence	1b direct narrative sentence	2 indirect narrative sentence	3a indirect rendering of the words of the character (indirect speech)	3b indirect rendering of the perception of the character	4a direct rendering of the words of the character (direct speech)	4b direct rendering of the perception of the character
influence of the narrator					influence of the character	

Table 6: Forms of perspective

Text types 1 to 4 inclusive are based on linguistic markings in narrative texts: the verb forms (present, past, future), the person forms (first, second and third person) and the referential force of indications of place and time ('here', 'there', 'then', 'now'); moreover we have to note time and again who is responsible for which utterance. At these points changes regularly take place in a narrative text which indicate a change of perspective.

The model developed by van Wolde and Sanders shows that the different voices or perspectives are often intertwined. When the narrator is speaking, sometimes something of the perspective of a character is echoed, and conversely the narrator is not completely out of range when a character is speaking. The bottom part of Table 6 indicates that here we have a sliding scale. As the influence of the narrator decreases, that of the character increases, and as the characters have less chance to indicate something by themselves, the perspective of the narrator comes more clearly into the picture.

I shall discuss the technical terms in the table briefly and illustrate them with some examples from John 10.40–11.54. Narrator text is easy to recognize: here the narrator himself is speaking. Really it is a particular type of direct speech, since we could preface the narrator text with an explanation in the style of: 'I tell you this…' It is characteristic of the narrator text in our passage that the narrator speaks in the past tense and in the third person, and that through his choice of 'then' (11.14) and 'there' (10.40, 42) instead of 'here' and 'now' (11.21–22, 32: character text!) he shows that he is presenting the events related as it were from outside. He himself does not appear in the story and adopts a standpoint from which he surveys the whole.

That the narrator text is a layered whole is evident from the distinction between direct and indirect narrator text. Direct narrator text is bound up with the perspective of the narrator: he presents the actions or events without picking anything up from the perspective of the character. One example is 11.1: 'A man was sick' (it does not say 'Lazarus felt sick'). Commentary sentences are a subgroup within the direct narrator text. They differ from direct narrative sentences in that the narrator communicates directly with the readers and gives them more information about the event being related, which at that moment has come to a standstill. We encounter this type of sentence in 11.2, 5, 13, 18, 30, 38b, 51–52. Commentary sentences also give an impression of the profile of the readers. In 11.18 and 11.38b it is presupposed that the readers do not know the precise location of Bethany and are not familiar with a rock tomb. Here, however, I must add that the sentences mentioned are at the same time also extremely functional within the narrative: 11.18 is a preparation for 11.46, whereas 11.38b is necessary for a good understanding of Jesus' command in 11.39.

In indirect narrator text the reader already sees something of the perspective of the character come through in the presentation of the actions or events. The narrator gives an account of the feelings of the character, but it is the narrator who is accountable for the description of this feeling (11.33: Jesus was moved with indignation and troubled).

The difference between an indirect and a direct mode of

presentation is also to be found in the character text. The best-known phenomenon is that the words of the character can stand in direct or indirect speech (both recognizable by verbs like 'say', 'ask', 'tell' and the like). There is an abundance of direct speech in our passage: twenty-eight times in all. In almost half of these cases Jesus is the speaker (thirteen times); after him Martha scores the highest (five times); the disciples plus Thomas speak three times and other speakers (like Mary and Caiaphas) only once. In this type of character text the reader hears directly what a character says; the use of the present tense, of the first and second person, and of words like 'here' and 'now', is characteristic of this category. With indirect speech the character's own perspective is less visible, since then his or her words are given by the narrator (11.46: some told the Pharisees what Jesus had done).

An innovative element in the Van Wolde/Sanders model is that they note not only words of a character reported directly or indirectly but also perceptions, thoughts, feelings and experiences (recognizable from verbs like 'hear', 'see', 'think', 'believe' also fits into this series). In this 'mental' character text, too, there is a distinction between direct and indirect presentation. In our passage we find only examples of an indirect presentation in which the narrator expresses the perception (11.20: Martha heard that Jesus was coming; 11.31: the Jews saw Mary get up quickly and go outside... they thought that she was going to the tomb to wail; 11.33: Jesus saw her wailing and the Jews wailing with her; 11.45: the Jews had seen what he had done).

When we apply the theory to our narrative in detail, we discover that the precise distinctions from the scheme do not always work. A sentence can sometimes contain two forms of perspective. Thus 11.13 is a commentary sentence (direct narrator text); however, the sentence also contains indications of the consciousness of Jesus and the disciples which are given indirectly: Jesus had spoken about Lazarus' death, whereas the disciples thought that he meant the rest of sleep. In 11.3 the report of the two sisters is given directly, but they do not mention Lazarus by name, nor do they speak of their brother (as each of them does in 11.21, 32, 'my brother'), but present him from Jesus' perspective ('the one whom you love'). In

11.40 we come upon indirect speech within the direct speech ('did I not tell you that you should see the glory of God?').

The same event can be mentioned in different types of text. The sickness of Lazarus is a fine example of this. This is mentioned in a sentence that is direct narrative (11.1), in a commentary sentence (11.2), in a direct piece of character text (11.3) and in a perception described indirectly (11.6).

The spontaneous impression that the narrator is clearly focussing on Jesus is clearly supported by an analysis of the perspective. Jesus is present in almost every sub-division (except in 11.47–53, but there he is the subject of the conversation); he speaks particularly frequently, and primarily about himself. In total he comes into conversation with six different partners (the disciples, Martha, Mary, the bystanders, God, Lazarus). The other characters mostly address their words to Jesus (11.3, 8, 12, 21–22, 24, 27, 32, 34, 39), and if this is not the case, as a rule they speak about him (11.16, 28, 36–37, 47–48, 49–50). A special characteristic of the text is that it is so strongly permeated with direct character text. The number of direct narrative sentences is quite small, given the length of the narrative. This means that really very little happens in it. The main event is that in their conversations together, starting from the sickness and the death of Lazarus, the characters develop a particular perspective on Jesus in his relation to God. We find contrasting perspectives during the conversation between Jesus and his disciples and his conversation with Martha. The disciples remain imprisoned in their sombre perspective on death, although their master is already speaking about waking up (rising). Martha in turn encloses herself in the hopeful prospect of the end-time resurrection, but it does not penetrate to her that resurrection is already attainable now by Jesus.

The narrator associates himself very strongly with his main figure. He shares the perspective presented by Jesus. Jesus for his part speaks from the perspective of God. We can express this relationship as follows: the narrator stands to Jesus as Jesus stands to God. Just as Jesus is inwardly bound up with God, so the narrator is intimately bound up with Jesus. With his narrative the narrator tries to communicate his own perspective to the readers. The opposite to the narrator's perspective is expressed by Jesus' enemies, the high priests and the Pharisees, figures with whom the readers had better not associate themselves. It is striking that the narrator hardly lets them speak their own language, although he reports their words directly. With some irony the narrator makes Jesus' enemies express the perspective that he himself holds without their being aware of it: Jesus' signs lead people to faith (11.47–48) and he dies for his people (11.49, repeated in the commentary sentence which follows).

The most important results listed

The narrative analysis of John 10.40–11.54 has kept us occupied for a long time. We have studied the different aspects of the narrative one by one. What are the most notable results of this exercise?

A core decision was that 10.40–11.54 must be understood as a consecutive whole in which two motifs are woven together: the raising of Lazarus and the threat to liquidate Jesus. From the beginning Jesus announces that the sickness of his friend will result in the manifestation of God's glory. After Lazarus has died, Jesus travels to Judaea, in the certain expectation that the events which will take place there will have a positive influence on the further maturing of the faith of his disciples. However, whether this effect intended by Jesus is indeed achieved remains open, since after 11.16 the disciples quietly disappear from the scene (they are mentioned again only in 11.54). The place which is opened up is occupied by the two sisters of the dead man. In his conversation with Martha Jesus makes it clear, taking up her belief in the resurrection of the dead at the end of time, that he himself is the resurrection and the life. Mary is able to combine her sorrow at the loss of her brother with an undeterred trust in Jesus; she expresses her faith more by what she does than by what she says. The two women do not need to be played off against each other: each functions as an illuminating model for the later readers of the narrative.

By consistently applying concepts from narratology it was easy to see that the narrative in part escapes these categories. That was the case above all when we turned our attention to the setting (space and time) and the perspectives. The text contains many details which relate to concrete locations and situate the narrative within the brief time-span of only a few days. However, the concrete details regularly come under pressure, since matters are presented within that 'framework' which cannot be captured in the usual experience of space and time. It gradually emerges from the narrative that the journeys undertaken by Jesus stand in the light of his 'journey' from God to the world and back again. The usual course of time is also disturbed. The eschatological resurrection is associated with the current presence of Jesus, who gives authentic and full life now already to those who believe in him. His special status derives from the fact that his origin from the beginning lies hidden in the unfathomable depth of God. Whatever happens is consequently determined by him. Even the plans of Jesus' enemies are completely dominated by what he does and says. We also saw that the different perspectives which in theory can be so precisely distinguished from one another sometimes overlap in the text. The narrator leaves a good deal of room for the perspectives of Jesus. In the narrative other voices also resound, which bring out a perspective that differs from the view represented by Jesus. But even the enemies of Jesus speak his language, and the misunderstandings formulated by the disciples and Martha put Jesus in the position of being able to sharpen further what he has to say.

Justified and unjustified criticism

Narrative analysis picks up the fact that many biblical texts, including the Gospels, have a narrative character. Narrative analysis is a markedly literary approach and thus offers a refreshing counterbalance to the (obsolete) view that biblical narratives must be read solely as a historical account or can be reduced to cold, theological statements. A narrative, the slogan goes, is a world-in-words which can give a new perspective on the world in which the readers find themselves.

The range of instruments used is taken from modern narratologists like M.Bal, S.Chatman and G.Genette. They have not developed their refined conceptual apparatus for narrative texts from the Bible. But it has been transferred over to the Bible. This move raises critical questions. Can texts from antiquity be studied meaningfully with the help of categories which have been developed on the basis of texts from a completely different culture? Are the concepts applied by exegetes in the spirit of those who developed them? Do not exegetes, intent as they are on the analysis of concrete texts, make all too selective use of the jargon of literary criticism? These questions are legitimate. There must be no question of a purely mechanical application. In that case texts from the Bible or the Gospels would be pressed into an alien strait-jacket. The application of narratalogical concepts in exegesis must go hand in hand with the necessary supplementations and with a distinctive contribution to further formulations of theory.

Narrative analysis puts much emphasis on the implicit reader, who is guided in a model way by the perspectives of the narrator or implicit author. I would point out that the implicit reader is a hermeneutic construction. Exegetes must be careful to avoid using this term in such a way that it is only a surrogate of themselves. By using it, researchers shelter behind the hedge of the text. Little attention is paid to readers who really exist and to their questions and their perspectives. The readers of flesh and blood must identify with the implicit reader and they must 'believe' in the narrative and the ideas presented in it, but does this imply that they have to take over all the views and values (or non-values) from the text uncritically? Stories should also be read with a certain degree of suspicion. They contain options which are extremely problematical for real readers from later times. Here is an example. In many narratives in the Bible a splendid role is reserved for men, thus giving the impression that masculine and human are identical. Or they describe the position of women in society one-sidedly from a male perspective, without illuminating the thoughts, feelings and experiences of the women who appear in the story. Here narrative analysis cannot be content with a description of what there is in the text without adding a note of criticism.

Undeserved criticism is also directed towards narrative analysis. The range of instruments used is said to be too complex, given the relative simplicity of the biblical texts; the investigation is said to produce little that is new; the investigator is said to deny the right of other approaches to exist; and narrative analysis is said to give ammunition to the reprehensible idea that the Gospels belong purely to the realm of fiction.[19] This criticism blocks the further development of a branch on the exegetical trunk which is still young. The presupposition is that narrative analysis claims a monopoly. That is not the case. The narrative approach is no more – but also no less – than one new route on the exegetical street plan.

4

Meaning in context

Words in their context

What the meaning of a word is, why a speaker or a writer chooses this particular term and not others, are questions with which anyone concerned with texts and language is confronted. Such questions can also be studied systematically. That happens in semantics, a sub-division of linguistics which is concerned with investigating the expression of meaning through language. Some facets of this are discussed in this chapter. Its aim is to provide a first introduction to factors that determine the way in which words and expressions take on meaning in written linguistic utterances.

Semantics can be engaged in from two different perspectives. In exegesis the diachronic perspective has dominated the field for a long time. The characteristic of this branch is that it attempts to map out the changes in the meaning of a particular word that have taken place in the course of time. The term is put on a trajectory which can be traced historically. *Doxa* is a well-known example: in Attic Greek the term denoted an opinion, knowledge which had not yet been thought through, whereas in the Hellenistic Greek of the Septuagint and the New Testament, under the influence of the Hebrew *kabod* it is loaded with another meaning: glory, splendour.

Semantics can also be practised from a synchronic perspective. A powerful stimulus toward this was given by the Swiss linguist F.de Saussure, and this is becoming increasingly influential in exegesis.[1] Synchrony here means that a word is dependent for its meaning on a more comprehensive network within which it is included. It takes on its meaning through its connection with other elements. Here we can distinguish two dimensions: a word is defined on the one hand by its place and function within a concrete text, and on the other by its position within the language to which it belongs.

The first dimension can be illuminated as follows. In writing a sentence I cannot put the words together in an arbitrary fashion: 'sentence together fashion arbitrary' is nonsense. There is a syntactical connection between words which follow one another in linear fashion. The sequence of sentences also obeys particular rules. A sentence takes on its sharpness and colour from the sentences that stand around it. On a yet higher level the words, clauses and sentences take on their meaning by functioning in a text. A technical term for this phenomenon is that they are positioned on a syntagmatic axis. The sub-divisions of a text being put together stand in a particular order and show a certain connection. The ordering or structure of a text is of great importance for the meaning of the words and sentences from which the text is constructed.

Therefore no writer likes to see his or her words being taken out of context. However, if that does happen, they do not become completely meaningless. As well as in texts, words also function within another network: they belong to a particular language. Their meaning is also defined by that. A language is no more a collection of loose elements than a text is. The word 'bier' does not mean the same in English and German. In both cases the signifier (the linguistic sign) is the same, but the content is completely different. This is because the meaning of 'bier' in English is governed by the relationship between this word and terms relating to death and funerals, whereas in German it is governed by terms denoting drinking and having a good time. So words point to other words from the same language; they function within a particular linguistic paradigm or, to use a technical term, they are situated on a paradigmatic axis.

A word has more or less fixed meanings as a result of its relations with other words in the same language. More or less, for language is constantly developing. The general, fixed meanings are not dependent on the use of a word in a particular text. These general meanings can be looked up in a dictionary or a lexicon. Such a book gives a description of the rich repertory of language at different moments in its history (usually the plan is completely diachronic). In a scholarly study of the Gospels we make use of Greek lexicons, since these works were originally written in Greek. It is preferable to consult a lexicon which covers the whole corpus of ancient texts written in Greek.[2] In addition there are lexicons which are specially concerned with the Greek of the New Testament and early Christian literature.[3]

The meanings found in lexicons cannot be applied directly to the use of a word in a particular text. Here the literary context plays a large part. The meaning of the term used is coloured by the surrounding linguistic phenomena; the term takes on a particular connotation as a result of its use. The connotation does not obliterate the general meaning. By its usage in a text, certain general meanings of a word are excluded (not meanings A and B, but A or B); furthermore the meaning selected is specified and nuanced in a particular direction. Finally the word can be enriched through its usage with aspects which are not mentioned in the dictionary.

So a text is a realization of the language paradigm. In a semantic analysis of a text we must constantly relate the register of the text to the rich repertory of the language. Why does the word A stand here? Why hasn't the equivalent B or the synonym C been chosen? Within the language, A belongs to a particular word-group to which B and C also belong. A has been selected from that semantic field. We must also note the connections which A has with X, Y and Z within the text. So word A is at the crossing of two lines. That also applies to the other linguistic phenomena contained in the text. We constantly see how the syntagmatic and the paradigmatic axes cross each other.

As well as lexicons we use other aids in a semantic analysis. A concordance is a valuable tool. This is a list of all the words from a particular literary corpus in alphabetical order, indicating the places where they are used. A concordance of the Bible contains all the words in this corpus, beginning with Genesis and ending with the book of Revelation; at the same time part of the sentence is printed in which the term concerned is used.[4] Such lists have also been produced with the aid of computer programmes which have been specially developed for Bible study.[5] Used together with a lexicon, a concordance offers excellent possibilities for relating the syntagmatic axis to the paradigmatic axis.

So far I have been emphasizing the fact that linguistic elements have meaning because they refer to one another: they function within the network of language and within the network of oral or written linguistic expression. But that does not yet complete the picture. There are yet other factors which are of influence in the process of giving meaning. Linguistic communication presupposes that there are users of language who give a particular picture of the reality around them by means of language and text. So we cannot be content within the assertion that words have a general, fixed meaning through their place within the linguistic system which is further coloured in a concrete linguistic expression. Words also stand in a relationship to real objects, persons, places, processes and events in reality outside language. This relationship is indicated by the term 'denotation'. It is important that the denotation is not dependent on the use of a word in a particular context. Thus the noun 'lake' refers to a stretch of inland water of a certain extent. Detached from a concrete situation, the term 'lake' has a general meaning: it refers to a particular class, without it being clear precisely which lake is meant. If 'lake' is used in a concrete linguistic expression, the word comes to refer to a specific extralinguistic reality. The sentence 'Jesus was again walking by the lake' (Mark 2.13) refers to Lake Gennesaret, which has already been mentioned in 1.16. In this case the writer is referring to a particular stretch of water in an area known to his readers. That a speaker or author is using a word to refer to a specific phenomenon in extralinguistic reality is indicated by the term 'reference'.

The lexical meaning and denotation are closely connected, but they do not coincide completely. The same is true of the pair 'denotation' and 'reference'. In turn the denotative aspects are closely connected with the connotative aspects, but again without the one level completely coinciding with the other. The different levels permeate each other, and sometimes there are partial overlappings. 'Meaning' is thus a layered concept. In other words, in a text a variety of layers of meaning lie on top of one another. We are confronted with a complex interplay and we have to be careful not to make one aspect all too independent from another. This applies particularly to the relationship between the 'world' which is unfolded in a narrative text and extralinguistic reality. The referential aspects are so closely woven together with other layers of meaning that we cannot regard them as a blueprint for extra-linguistic reality. In the case of texts from a distant past – like the Gospels – it is extremely difficult to discover the referential meaning. These texts refer to a world which in many respects is different from the context of the present-day reader. For a good understanding of the text, a far-reaching knowledge of the histori-cal and socio-political context of the time is needed. Without that we are all too easily inclined to project present-day institutions, views and customs back on the past.

After these theoretical reflections, here are some examples, which are characterized by an increasing degree of difficulty. First I shall show that the meaning of the word 'neighbour' shifts to a surprising degree in a relatively short textual unit (Luke 10.25–37). Then I shall present two word-studies which have been made with the help of concordances: what is the meaning of 'one of these little ones' in Matthew and 'son of God' in Mark? The series will be concluded with 'king of the Jews' in John 18–19. The special feature of this last example is that an attempt is made to understand the title applied to Jesus against the background of the political situation in Palestine under Pilate's administration.

'Neighbour' in Luke 10.25–37

The parable of the Good Samaritan is one of the best-known texts in the Gospels. It is less well known that the parable is part of an extended conversation between a lawyer and Jesus. It is even the case that the parable comes properly into its own only when it is read within this connection. The total text reads as follows:

I   25 A lawyer came to him to put him to the test, saying,
        'Teacher, what must I do to inherit eternal life?'
     26 He said to him,
        'What is written in the law? How do you read it?'

27 He answered,
> 'You shall love the Lord your God with all your heart, and
> with all your soul, and with all your strength, and with all
> your mind; and your neighbour as yourself.'

28 He said to him,
> 'You have answered right; do this, and you will live.'

II   29 But in order to justify himself, he said to Jesus,
> 'Yes, but who is my neighbour?'

30 Jesus replied,
> 'A man was travelling from Jerusalem to Jericho, and he fell
> into the hands of robbers. They stripped him and beat him,
> and departed, leaving him half dead. 31 Now by chance a
> priest was going down that road; he saw him and passed by
> on the other side. 32 So likewise a Levite, when he came to
> the place and saw him, passed by on the other side. 33 Then
> a Samaritan, as he journeyed, came to where he was; and
> when he saw him he had compassion, 34 and went to him and
> bound up his wounds, pouring on oil and wine. Then he set
> him on his own beast and brought him to an inn, and took
> care of him. 35 And the next day he took out two denarii and
> gave them to the innkeeper, saying, "Take care of him; and
> whatever more you spend, I will repay you when I come
> back." 36 Which of these three, do you think, was a neigh-
> bour to the man who fell among the robbers?'

37 He said,
> 'The one who showed mercy on him.'

Jesus said to him,
> 'Go and do likewise.'

When we write out the text like this, we immediately see that the
whole passage takes the form of a conversation. The lawyer and
Jesus each speak four times. This is a particular kind of conversation, namely a didactic conversation. The opening question is
what someone has to do to have a share in eternal life. The answer
is that such a person needs to observe the Torah, which can be
summed up briefly by Deuteronomy 6.5 (love of God) and
Leviticus 19.18 (love of neighbour). The rest of the discussion
is about the second rule. The central question here is who the
neighbour is.

In my presentation of the text I have distinguished two parts. The first comprises vv.25–28, the second vv.29–37. This division can be justified as follows. Both parts begin with a question from the lawyer. Each time the narrator indicates the purpose of the man's question (v.25: he wants to put Jesus to the test; v.29: he wants to justify himself). Twice (vv.27 and 37) the lawyer gives the right answer to Jesus' question. Both parts end with a call to the lawyer to put that good answer into practice.

I have presented this text because here we can see well how the meaning of the key word ('the neighbour') is defined by the context. This term occurs three times (vv.27, 29, 36). It is introduced in v.27, where it is found in a quotation from Leviticus 19.18. For readers who think that love of neighbour is a typical characteristic of Christianity, this is a complete surprise. The commandment to love one's neighbour is already stated in the Old Testament. In the Jewish tradition, along with Deuteronomy 6.5 it is regarded as the heart of the whole Torah. The lawyer is familiar with this and indeed gives the expected answer. But that is not the whole story. Jesus did not ask him just *what* the law said but also *how* he read it. The discussion is focussed on this. In the second round of the conversation the lawyer comes up with a new question, 'Yes, but who is my neighbour?' This term from Leviticus 19.18 is evidently open to more than one explanation. Jesus tells the parable of the good Samaritan in order to clarify his standpoint on this question.

Before we go into Jesus' view of the neighbour, let's pause over the meaning of 'neighbour' in Leviticus 19. At the end of the day, that is the text which is under discussion here. In this part of Leviticus there is alternate mention of 'your neighbour', 'your brother' and your 'fellow countryman'. The text thus gives the impression that neighbour simply means another member of one's people or one's faith. However, this limited view of neighbour is already attacked in Leviticus 19 itself. According to v.32 of the same chapter one must also love the stranger as oneself and regard him or her as if he or she were an Israelite by birth. This observation is important for two reasons. First, on the basis of Leviticus 19 we can opt for either a more limited or a broader interpretation of the word 'neighbour'; perhaps that is why the lawyer is asking who his neighbour is. Secondly, we could think that Jesus tells the parable in order to release the term 'neighbour' from its limited meaning, but that cannot be his purpose, since in Leviticus that term already takes on a broader scope.

With his parable Jesus gives an interpretation of 'neighbour' which cannot be derived from Leviticus. What Jesus thinks comes to light when he turns the lawyer's question into a new question:

10.29 The lawyer asks, 'Who is my neighbour?'

10.36 Jesus ends his parable with the question, 'Who was a neighbour to the man who fell among the robbers?'

In v.29 the neighbour is the *object* of love. In other words, the lawyer is asking to whom he must direct his love. In v.36 the neighbour is the *subject* of loving. It is not the half-dead man who is the neighbour, but the one who gives him help. Thus as a result of the parable the term 'neighbour' has taken on a new and unexpected content. It has become an extremely dynamic concept: you are not someone's neighbour, but you must strive to become someone's neighbour; the neighbour is not the one who receives love but the one who gives it. In the light of the parable that programme of action takes on a quite specific colouring: becoming someone's neighbour means that with great compassion you leap to the support of someone who is in need. You do not make this choice because the sufferer is your neighbour but because at that moment you have to fulfil the role of neighbour. You yourself are the neighbour!

This didactic conversation does not stop at theoretical reflections. The lawyer himself already began with the question what he was to do. His question is given a twofold answer: he must make the core texts of the Torah the guideline for his life (v.28), but he must also regard the surprising content which Jesus gives to the term 'neighbour' as a new point of action (v.37).

'One of these little ones' in Matthew

In Matthew a group of people appear who are referred to as 'the little ones'. According to the lexicon 'little' (in Greek *mikros*) relates to the extent of one's body, age, reputation or influence. The term can be used both literally and figuratively. In Matthew it is used in the latter sense. There it is about adults with particular characteristics, but the thought is not of their age or the length of their bodies. First I shall set out the texts:

10.42 Whoever gives to *one of these little ones* even a cup of cold water because he is a disciple, truly, I say to you, he shall not lose his reward.

18.6 Whoever causes the downfall of *one of these little ones* who believe in me, it would be better for him to have a great millstone fastened around his neck and to be drowned in the depth of the sea.

18.10 See that you do not despise *one of these little ones*; for I tell you that in heaven their angels always behold the face of my Father who is in heaven.

18.14 So it is not the will of my Father who is in heaven that *one of these little ones* should be lost.

Time and again we come across the same combination of words: the number 'one', the demonstrative pronoun 'these', and an adjective noun which is used as a noun ('little ones').

In the case of an oral linguistic expression a demonstrative pronoun does not cause us particular problems. The communicative situation makes it sufficiently clear to whom the pronoun refers. Moreover the speaker can accompany his or her words with an evocative gesture of the hand. In a written linguistic expression the referential force of a demonstrative pronoun is preserved, but in this case to whom the pronoun refers must be inferred primarily from the literary context.

Who are meant by 'these little ones' in Matthew? They belong among the followers of Jesus. That can be read explicitly in 10.42 ('because he is a disciple') and in 18.7 ('who believe in me'). On the basis of this information we might think that 'the little ones' is a synonym for 'the disciples'. Another possibility is that 'the little ones' is a term for particular disciples, for a sub-group within the wider circle of the disciples. And perhaps the sub-group is not always the same. To become clearer, let's look closely at the texts one by one.

In 10.42 the little ones are characterized as disciples. Here it is evident from the context that the twelve apostles are meant (10.1–5; 11.1). Apostle is derived from the Greek and means a person who is sent. The twelve are sent out by Jesus to drive out unclean spirits, to heal all sickness and disease and to announce the nearness of the kingdom of heaven. They may not take money, a bag, a spare set of clothing, sandals or a staff on their travels. For eating, drinking and lodging they are completely dependent on the help of the people they meet on the way. Jesus has a particular sympathy for these little ones, and even God identifies with them: 'He who receives you receives me, and he who receives me receives him who sent me' (10.40).

18.6, 10,14 are also about followers of Jesus. This can be inferred from the periphrasis in v.6, 'one of these little ones who believe in me'. But there is no reason here to think of the twelve apostles (as in 10.42) or to regard the little ones as a designation for all disciples. Of course all disciples are called to become like children (18.3), but verses 5–14 show that only a limited group obeys the call and is hindered in responding by people from their own group who do not make the same choice. I think that I can support this from the negative activities mentioned in the text. The little ones encounter much hostility: there are those who are trying to bring them down and who look on them in a condescending way. The result of this is that the little ones are beginning to distance themselves from the community and risk going astray. The contempt which they suffer from their fellow-believers stands in sharp contrast to the high respect which God has for them. No matter what it costs, the Father in heaven will see that they are not lost. His special care for the little ones must be a stimulus to the community to restore its wandering members to their rightful place.

This description is also based on the parable of the stray sheep in vv.12–13. This parable relates to the situation of the little ones. That is evident both from the sentences which frame it (vv.10, 14) and from the emphasis that the parable itself puts on the fate of one sheep from a large flock (v.12: 'one of them', surely there is good reason why the number comes first!). This one sheep is not lost, as in Luke 15.3–7, but has gone astray. So the little ones are the victims of internal tensions in the community. That is particularly tragic because they are the ones who have set such store on Jesus' ethical ideal.

Up to now we have been discussing four texts which speak of 'one of these little ones'. 25.40,45 also belong in this series. There we find the same combination of words, the only difference being that in this case the superlative is used, 'one of the least of these'.

25.40 Truly I say to you, as you did it to *one of the least of these* my brethren, you did it to me.

25.45 Truly I say to you, as you did it not to *one of the least of these*, you did it not to me.

Here we have a mention of the least. They are even smaller than the little ones. But what makes them so small? Only one answer can be given to this question from the context: the fact that they have to suffer so much. They are hungry and thirsty, they are naked or strangers, they are sick or in prison. Followers of Jesus can easily end up in such a situation (cf.10.42), but the text gives no indication that we must think only of them. These words can just as well be about sufferers who do not belong to the community. It is again clear that Jesus identifies completely with the least: what you do for them, you do for him. Moreover he regards them as his brothers and sisters. These terms indicate how much Jesus feels bound up with them.

The conclusion of this analysis is that the little ones (the least) is a dynamic term and that its meaning changes. In 10.42 and 18.1–14 'the little ones' refers to sub-groups from the community of faith; in 25.40,45 'the least' has a broader significance: this term refers to all those in need, whoever and wherever they are.

'Son of God' in Mark

In Mark, Jesus is called 'son of God' eight times. The complete list looks like this:

1.1 The beginning of the good news of Jesus the messiah, *the son of God*.

1.11 'You are *my* beloved *son*, with you I am well pleased.'

3.11 And whenever the unclean spirits beheld him, they fell down before him and cried out, 'You are the *son of God*!'

5.7 [he] cried out with a loud voice, 'What have you to do with me, Jesus, *son of the most high God*? I adjure you by God, do not torment me.'

9.7 And a cloud overshadowed them, and a voice came out of the cloud, 'This is *my* beloved *son*, listen to him.'

13.32 'But of that day or that hour no one knows, not even the angels in heaven, nor *the son*, but only the Father.'

14.61 Again the high priest asked him, 'Are you the messiah, the *son of the Blessed*?'

15.39 When the centurion... saw that he thus breathed his last, he said, 'Truly this man was *the son of God*.'

'Son of God' does not occur in all these passages. In 14.61 God is called the Blessed; in 13.32 there is only mention of the son, and in 1.11 and 9.7 we have 'my son', but here God himself is speaking.

We shall now try to discover what son of God means in Mark. This investigation is worthwhile, at least if we read the texts closely and do not burden them with what we think we already know about this designation.

First we shall ask *by whom* this title is used. In 1.1 the narrator himself is speaking. In all the other cases he puts the title into the mouth of a character: God (1.11; 9.7), a demon or an unclean spirit (3.11; 5.7), the high priest (14.61) and a Roman centurion (15.39). Jesus himself speaks of the son only in 13.32, but he does not add whether he means himself by it. However, the title can hardly refer to anyone other than Jesus. It is striking that 'the son of God' is used above all by non-human speakers (God, a demon, an unclean spirit) who possess supernatural knowledge. Only in the passion narrative do human characters refer to Jesus as the son of God. That is done in a hostile manner by the high priest (14.61), and soon after Jesus' death the centurion gives him this title (15.39). The title cannot have a hostile tone in the mouth of the centurion, since he begins his remark with 'indeed' or 'truly'.

After this first survey we shall try to see *the meaning* of 'son of God' in Mark. For this we must go through all the passages once more and each time look at the surrounding verses. In this investigation we must keep open the possibility that 'son of God' does not have precisely the same meaning everywhere. Perhaps we will come across different aspects of meaning or small semantic shifts. We must also remember that as readers we hear everything that is said in the book about Jesus: not only the report of the narrator in 1.1 but also the statements by the different characters. Thus the readers find themselves in a privileged position; soon they know more than the characters who populate the book.

The first passage from the list (1.1) is at the same time the first sentence of the whole book. Often such a first sentence contains a key to the whole. That is also the case here, certainly if we regard 1.1 as the title of Mark's book. The first sentence runs as follows: 'The beginning of the good news of Jesus the messiah, the son of God.' It is not certain that 'son of God' was in the original text. Perhaps it is a later addition. We have only manuscripts from later centuries, and they are not unanimous here. The title appears in a number of important manuscripts, but not in others (which are equally authoritative). I give preference to the first group and thus assume that in the first verse of Mark Jesus is designated in two ways: he is the messiah and he is the son of God. The original readers, probably Christians from Rome around 70, will not have found this strange. They were probably already familiar with these designations before they had a sight of Mark's book. By using well-known designations in the title of the book the narrator arouses the expectation that he has something new to say about these terms. In this first verse he contents himself with the report that the beginning of the good news lies with Jesus himself: Jesus himself is the bringer of the good news. But the sentence can also be understood differently: 'beginning of the good news about Jesus'. In that case Jesus is the content of the message.

Almost immediately afterwards Jesus himself hears that he is God's son (1.11). No less than God tells him this, and none other than Jesus hears this news (apart, of course, from the readers). God addresses him in the second person: 'You are my beloved son, with you I am well pleased.' This statement contains allusions to some texts from the Old Testament (Psalm 2.7; Isaiah 42.1). So the meaning of 'son of God' must be derived primarily from scripture. There this term sometimes refers to non-human beings who are located in heaven and make up part of the heavenly court (Psalm 82.6). In Job 1.6 the Satan, too, is part of this company. The term also refers to the people of Israel. God has called this people to life and chosen it as his covenant partner. Indeed God is called Israel's Father and the Israelites are God's sons and daughters (Exodus 4.22; Deuteronomy 1.31; 32.5–6, 18–20; Jeremiah 31.9,20; Hosea 11.1; Psalm 80.16). The term is also applied to David and Solomon, to their successors (II Samuel 7.14; I Chronicles 17.13; 22.10), and to the king who as God's anointed resides on Zion and to whom the pagan assailants must submit (Psalm 2.7, 11). Against this background it is clear that 'son of God' denotes the intimate relationship of Israel or of representatives of the people with God. In Mark 1.11 God declares that Jesus is in the same position.

As well as God, the demons are familiar with the identity of Jesus. Whenever they are confronted with him, they cry out, 'You are the holy one of God' or 'you are the son of God' (1.24; 3.11; 5.7). It is striking that Jesus muzzles them and forbids them to disseminate their knowledge. The people who encounter Jesus do not in fact really know who they have before them. They ask themselves who he is and try to answer this question, but their knowledge is extremely defective. Even the disciples grope in the dark for a long time over this. The readers see all that the characters have to say about Jesus: he blasphemes God (2.7), he is mentally ill (3.21), he is in the power of an unclean spirit (3.30), he is the reincarnation of John the Baptist (6.14), he is Elijah or he is a prophet like other prophets (6.15; 8.28). Because from the beginning the readers have been enlightened by the narrator, they can see that these are false ideas or half truths which they had better not accept.

Halfway through the book it begins to dawn on the disciples. After Jesus has fiercely rebuked them for being blind and deaf, the great statement is made. Peter, the spokesman of the disciples, declares, 'You are the messiah' (8.29). Jesus forbids the disciples to tell anyone about him, since their concept of messiah is still extremely imprecise. They cannot reconcile the idea that Jesus is the messiah with the prospect that he will have to suffer and die.

The disciples remain burdened with this fault to the end. Whenever Jesus speaks of his suffering and death they are not in a position to fathom the meaning of his words.

In 9.7 the voice of God resounds again. He repeats his report from 1.11 but now this is directed to Jesus' companions: '*This is* my beloved son.' Now something new is added, 'Listen to him.' Given the context, this can only mean that the disciples must take Jesus' teaching about his suffering and death to heart.

These lines reach their climax in the passion narrative. Then the moment has come when Jesus' identity can be expressed bluntly, for in this phase of the narrative there is no danger that the reader will dissociate being son of God from a shameful death. When asked by the high priest whether he is the messiah, the son of the Blessed, Jesus replies, 'Yes, I am.' Now he himself breaks the command to silence that he had imposed on others. Immediately after his death the curtain in the temple is torn in two. The curtain removes God from sight. The fact that the curtain is now torn means that the aura of mystery which has always surrounded Jesus is now definitively removed and that now his inner relationship to God comes into public view.

The exclamation of the centurion under the cross, 'Truly, this man was the son of God,' is confirmation of this. For Mark it was important that a high-ranking Roman made this statement: for the Christians in Rome it must have been an important stimulus. But above all Mark wants to see the truth about Jesus spoken at the moment of his death. Only in this way does it become really clear that the title 'son of God' relates to someone who has entered his glory through suffering and death. The readers must not be deterred by suffering and death from the way on which Jesus has gone before them. By the way in which they deal with their own situation they can show that they are giving the right answer to the question of Jesus' identity.

'King of the Jews' in John 18–19

Jesus' kingship is an important motif in John's passion narrative. This motif is expressed in the words king, kingship, king of the

Jews. They are concentrated in the passage in which Jesus is being judged by Pilate:

18.33 'Are you the *king of the Jews*?'
18.36 'My *kingship* is not of this world. If my *kingship* were of this world, my servants would fight, that I might not be handed over to the Jews; but my *kingship* is not of this world.'
18.37 Pilate said to him, 'So you are a *king*?' 'Yes,' said Jesus, 'I am *king*.'
18.39 'Shall I release *the king of the Jews*?'
19.3 'Hail, *king of the Jews*!'
19.12 'Every one who makes himself *king* sets himself against Caesar.'
19.14 'Here is your *king*.'
19.15 Pilate asked them, 'Shall I crucify *your king*?' The chief priests replied, 'We have no *king* but Caesar.'
19.19 Pilate also wrote a title and put it on the cross; it read, 'Jesus of Nazareth, *king of the Jews*.'
19.21 'Do not write "*King of the Jews*", but, "This man said, I am *the king of the Jews*."'

That Jesus is king is understood by the narrator in quite a different way from the way in which Pilate understands it. In the narrative the two perspectives are intertwined. We shall begin with the narrator's view; after that we shall try to look through Pilate's eyes.

The first line: the narrator's view

The narrator has a paradoxical message: that Jesus is king comes to light precisely through his suffering and death. In a private conversation Pilate asks Jesus whether he is king. Jesus does not immediately take up this term, but speaks of his kingship. He asserts that he is making a different world present in this world, a world which is completely pervaded by the truth. Jesus himself is the truth in his own person, and his kingdom is formed by people who listen to his voice. Within the narrator's perspective Pilate is gradually convinced of Jesus' special position, so much so that he tries to convince the Jews (the chief priests are meant) that Jesus is their king. Without themselves being aware of it the soldiers also contribute to the manifestation of Jesus' royal dignity. They put a crown on his head and a purple cloak over his shoulders. Really this is no less than the investiture of Jesus. Immediately after this Jesus is displayed in this outfit to his Jewish subjects. Pilate publicly proclaims him king. In the view of the narrator the governor is definitively persuaded: he bows under the power with which Jesus is clothed by God himself. Pilate's positive attitude contrasts strongly with that of the Jews: they throw away their messianic expectations and claim that they have no other king than the Roman emperor. Pilate writes on the board above the cross in three languages, 'Jesus of Nazareth, king of the Jews'. In this way he makes the whole world share in the insight that he has gained.

The second line: Pilate's perspective

The narrative takes on quite a different significance when we relate it to the political situation in Palestine at the time and assume that Pilate has an agenda of his own which diverges from that of the narrator.[6] The text then speaks of a harsh confrontation between the Roman occupation forces and the Jewish striving for national autonomy. The Roman state is represented in the narrative by Pilate. For him, maintaining political peace has top priority. As a calculating governor he seizes on the Jesus case with both hands in order to bring down the Jews and their struggle for freedom.

To identify this second line of meaning, let's go through the narrative again. We note that Pilate is the first to use the title 'king of the Jews'. The Jews did not use these words when they formulated their accusation against Jesus (they called him a criminal). For Pilate, 'king of the Jews' has purely political connotations. It is unthinkable to him that anyone other than the emperor could claim this title. Because he is so mesmerized by the political connotations, what Jesus has to say about his kingship completely escapes him. He has no access to the truth.

After his conversation with Jesus, Pilate asks the Jews whether he must release their king to them. He wants to test them with his question. If they say yes to it, they confirm that they have a king of their own and want to detach themselves from Rome; if they say no to it, then they drop their striving for autonomy, for what people allows its own king to be executed? The Jews are able skilfully to avoid this dilemma. They make use of the fact that in his offer Pilate spoke only of the king of the Jews, without naming a candidate. So in the Greek text their answer runs: *mē touton alla ton Barabban* ('No, not him, but Barabbas!'). The Greek text allows the following paraphrase: no, not this king of the Jews, but someone else whom we put in the same category, namely Barabbas. They are not opting for a king like Jesus, who will not let his servants fight for him, but for a bandit, who is not afraid of plunder and killing. The Jews thus maintain their longing for a king of their own, and they give a content to that concept which is extremely threatening to the Romans.

Pilate then brings Jesus out with a crown of thorns on his head and a purple cloak on his shoulders. The governor presents him as a joke king and so shows once again how thoroughly he detests the Jews' striving for a king of their own. Indeed he proclaims Jesus their king, and he can do so confidently, for he already knows in advance that the Jews are not set on this ridiculous king. When the Jews proclaim that they have no other king than Caesar, Pilate has achieved his purpose. He was never concerned with anything other than the loyalty of the Jews to Rome. Whether or not Jesus is guilty is of no further interest to him. He hands him over to be crucified, and moreover that gives him the opportunity to write in three languages that the Jews' ideal of a king of their own has been written off.

Thus Pilate cleverly manipulates the process in such a way that it ends up with a confirmation of the loyalty of the Jews to the Roman empire. Throughout this game Jesus is no more than a pawn on a political chess board. He is not the only victim: with him the Jewish national ideals are also nailed to the cross.

The two lines together

The two lines that I have drawn are rather different. The first line is dominated by the perspective of the narrator. His voice is so dominant that even the words and actions of Pilate become ambiguous. Without being aware of it, and contrary to his own purposes, the prefect makes his contribution to the disclosure of a deeper reality which remains hidden from the man himself, namely that the real victor is none other than Jesus. By manifesting himself as the true king, Jesus dethrones any kinship that is rooted in this world. The second line relates to a political trial of strength between Pilate and the Jews. Here the prefect is given a perspective of his own, which is fundamentally different from that of the narrator. Pilate is the advocate of a kingdom that is 'of this world'. Within this line he wins: cunning as he is, he knows precisely how to achieve what he wants.

Because the two lines run contrary to each other at many points, the interweaving of them leads to paradoxes and contrasts. Here are some examples. Jesus' glory takes shape in his deepest humiliation; the outcast is the one who really dominates the situation; his cross becomes a throne; the true king gives his life for his own, while his opponent is a bandit who sows death and destruction. The paradoxical convergence of the two lines shows how God makes himself present on earth in Jesus. Jesus is God's word which has been made flesh and has put up its tent among us (1.14). The purpose of his descent from heaven is for him to give his flesh for the life of the world (6.51). His incarnation culminates in his suffering and death, which are thus transformed from a tragic nadir to a revealing climax. In Jesus, suffering and death lose their meaninglessness and cynicism because they become bound up with God. The cynicism of the established power is unmasked by a kingship which is of a totally different order and which is invulnerable precisely in its vulnerability. A complete Roman cohort falls to the ground when Jesus utters the words 'I am (he)' (18.6). Pilate's cunning is developed at length in order to bring out better its ultimate ineffectiveness.

The intertwining of the two lines preserves us from a one-sidedly spiritual interpretation of Jesus' kingdom. That his kingdom is not of this world does not mean that it leaves the world with its concrete power structures untouched; no, precisely because it is qualitatively so totally different, it reveals how rotten these structures are. Sometimes this is not sufficiently shown in exegetical studies. The Johannine narrative of the trial of Jesus is

said to have an apologetic purpose; according to John, Jesus'
kingship is said to be capable of peaceful co-existence with the
prevailing state system; the author is said to be defending himself
against the allegation that followers of Jesus pose a threat to the
political order in the Roman empire; at this point they should be
distinguished clearly from Jewish rebels. Given the link between
the two semantic lines, that this is the purpose of the narrator
seems extremely doubtful. The manifestation of God's dwelling
among us in Jesus (line 1) implies that he exposes any apparatus of
state which divinizes itself (line 2). His kingdom does not have its
origin in this world and makes no use of the means of power which
score so highly in this world, but precisely by emphasizing this the
text provides the reader with arguments for a critical attitude to the
current political system. Followers of Jesus must put God above
the emperor. They find an ally, perhaps unexpectedly, in Jewish
freedom movements which put God's sovereignty higher than the
sovereignty of the state.

The window of synchrony

With this brief introduction to semantics, the synchronic palette is
complete and the first part of this book is coming to an end. In
succession I have looked at the demarcation, the structure, the
narrative organization and the meaning of a text. Together they
form a four-leaved clover. All along the line we have been con-
centrating on texts from the Gospels in their final form. The
literary aspects have always been in the foreground. The four
separate steps supplement one another, and form a cumulative
whole. The questions about meaning which have been discussed in
this fourth chapter were already emerging when in Chapter 2
I investigated the structure of a text or when in Chapter 3
I sketched a character portrait of Martha or Jesus. The examination
of structures and patterns in Chapter 2 and the sketch in Chapter
3 of narrative communication came through in the way in which
the semantic aspects of a text have been illuminated in the present
chapter.

   The window of synchrony gives a varied view of Jesus, the main figure in the Gospels. Every textual unit, however small, puts its own emphases on the way in which he is portrayed. Together the Gospels contain a series of portraits of Jesus which sometimes strongly resemble one another and sometimes clearly differ from one another. As well as being attracted (or irritated) by the portraits of Jesus, the reader can be struck by the diversity of reactions which Jesus provokes among the other characters, and by the different points of view presented by the narrators. The diversity as such is not regarded as a problem within the synchronic approach. As long as what is narrated remains imaginable, conflicting elements in a narrative can be taken together, and together they produce significant effects.

Synchrony must be given priority. A refined analysis of the literary aspects of a text is a necessary basis for any further step. In the next part of this book we enter the domain of diachrony. In this framework literary-*historical* questions arise which are deliberately ignored in a synchronic analysis: how have the texts gradually assumed their present form? Which theory gives the best explanation of the many agreements and differences between the Gospels? Here the diversity is regarded as a problem. To resolve that, the textual fabric which is so central in a synchronic approach is separated into earlier and later levels. Of course this operation gives a completely different view of Jesus.

Part II The window of diachrony

5

Diachronic methods

Survey

This chapter contains a survey of different methods with a diachronic profile. I shall present them in the order of their origin: (a) textual criticism; (b) historical criticism; (c) literary criticism; (d) form criticism; (e) redaction criticism.

Textual criticism has the oldest credentials. In antiquity readers already had to grapple with the problem that the original made by the author (the so-called *autographon*) had been lost or was no longer known. They still had copies, *antigrapha*. On the basis of these they tried to establish how the text had originally run. This type of investigation has been considerably refined over past centuries. Modern textual criticism is a specialist profession with a highly scientific content.

The other diachronic approaches have only been developed since the seventeenth and eighteenth centuries. Redaction criticism is concerned with the text in its final form, whereas literary criticism and form criticism are concerned with the literary stages preceding the text that we now have. Together they provide a picture of the history of the development of the text. Historical criticism is different from this again. This branch of the investigation is not concerned with the history of the origin *of* the text but with the history *behind* the text. Starting from the text and the stages in its development, the researcher tries to gain access to the historical facts and events which are depicted in the text or to which the text points.

The particular perspectives of the different diachronic methods and the connection between them is clarified in Table 7.

historical criticism	the historical facts and events
	↓
literary criticism and form criticism	the preliminary stages of the text: (a) oral traditions (b) written traditions
	↓
redaction criticism	the text in its final form
	↓
textual criticism	the different versions in which the text circulated after its origin

Table 7: Diachronic methods

The history of the development of the text is indicated here with arrows pointing downwards. However, we must realize that the investigation of it goes in precisely the opposite direction. The starting point lies with textual criticism, the mother of all exegesis: on the basis of manuscripts and old translations we try to arrive at a trustworthy reconstruction of the text as this was set down in writing by the author or redactor. Then this text is in turn regarded as the final result of a long development which – in a number of cases – finds its origins in particular historical facts or events.

Historical criticism remained in use when literary criticism and form criticism developed. So too form criticism has not been outdated by the rise of redaction criticism. There is a cumulative process. The different approaches have not just developed *after* one another but also continue *alongside* one another. Certainly a new method often made a correction to an already existing method. Moreover it is true of all diachronic methods that they are further refined in their use. By being applied to different texts and gradually being accompanied by other approaches, they are purged of impure elements or uncritical presuppositions. All this is part of the normal development of scholarship. Sitting on the shoulders of the giants of the past, dwarves can look further and see more than the giants themselves![1]

Textual criticism

What is textual criticism?

Text-critical investigation is necessary when we only have copies of the original, so-called *antigrapha*. Through the *antigrapha* the textual critic tries to offer a reliable version of the copy made by the final redactor, the so-called *autographon*. I have adopted the following general definition from J.H.Greenlee: 'textual criticism is the study of copies of any written work of which the autograph (the original) is unknown, with the purpose of ascertaining the original text.'[2]

Textual criticism is applied to all texts from the past where the original has not been preserved or is unknown, and where we are dependent on manuscripts. Textual criticism is also indispensable in the study of the Gospels. No original has been preserved of a single book of the New Testament. In our translations of the Bible and also in scholarly editions of the text a text is printed which is the result of textual criticism.

Applied to the New Testament, the definition runs as follows. Textual criticism strives to arrive at the earliest text of the New Testament that we can still get to on the basis of available manuscripts, old translations and quotations from the New Testament in the church fathers, observing a number of basic rules. In most cases we can safely assume that this earliest form is also the original one.

Some elements in this definition need elucidation. The original text of the New Testament books was written in Greek. The manuscripts mentioned in the definition are also written in Greek. In total, at the moment we have around 5500 manuscripts.[3] This number has grown rapidly in the twentieth century. In 1908 C.R.Gregory arrived at about 4000 items.[4] Of no work from antiquity are so many copies known. The high figure also explains why there are so many textual variants.

There are also ancient translations of the New Testament into Syriac, Coptic and Latin. They are of great importance, since they are far older than many Greek manuscripts (the majority of which do not go back before the fourth century). Yet they have a different status from the Greek manuscripts, since only indirect conclusions about the formulation of the Greek original can be drawn from a translation.

In their writings the church fathers quote sentences from the New Testament. These quotations are also important for textual critics. They give indications of the original formulation of the text. Here too caution is needed, since the quotation need not be a literal rendering of the original.

The most-used critical edition of the text is the *Novum Testamentum Graece*, edited by Barbara and Kurt Aland and other scholars. The most up-to-date edition is the twenty-seventh, from 1993.[5] This edition of the text stands in a long tradition. The first edition was made in 1898 by Eberhard Nestle. From the thirteenth edition (1927) the edition contained a text-critical apparatus, compiled by Erwin Nestle. From 1952 until his death in 1994 Kurt Aland made an inestimable contribution. Therefore the book is often referred to as Nestle-Aland for short.

The twenty-seventh edition of Nestle-Aland contains a continuous Greek text of the whole of the New Testament. This text is the result of a critical reconstruction on the basis of many manuscripts, old translations and quotations in church fathers. It is an eclectic edition. That means that the text as printed in Nestle-Aland cannot be found precisely in this formulation in a single separate manuscript. A well-founded choice has been made from the different witnesses to the text. The experienced user can make a critical judgment of the choices made, since as well as the reconstructed text, Nestle-Aland offers a very extensive critical apparatus in which by means of an ingenious system many divergent readings are given, each time with a mention of the sources in which these readings are to be found. Since the appearance of the twenty-sixth edition (1979), the text printed in Nestle-Aland has been identical with the text in another important edition of the text: *The Greek New Testament*.[6] This book offers far less information about divergent readings. It is intended above all for Bible translators. The text offered by both editions enjoys wide international and interconfessional recognition. Without exaggeration we can say that we now have an extremely trustworthy reconstruction of the original text of the New Testament. Therefore the compilers speak of the new standard text. But despite all that has been achieved at this level, we must not lose our critical sense. This standard text too must constantly be studied, with a view to periodical improvement.

Examples

Here are four examples to illustrate the work of textual criticism. At the same time they give me the opportunity to mention some basic rules which were mentioned in the definition.

There are two versions of Matthew 5.22a. Most manuscripts render this sentence as follows: 'But I say to you that everyone who is angry with his brother without cause shall be liable to judgment.' Over against this stand some manuscripts in which the words 'without cause' (in Greek *eikēi*) are absent. Which is the more original? The answer does not depend on pure numbers. A very old rule is that manuscripts must not be counted but weighed. Thus it is not the quantity but the quality that is decisive. In this case the minority has it right. This group includes an old papyrus and two authoritative manuscripts, the Codex Sinaiticus and the Codex Vaticanus.[7] Both lack the Greek word translated 'without cause'. So here Jesus' statement is much more radical: what he says applies regardless of the question whether or not someone is angry with his brother with good cause. It is obvious that this strict statement is original. We can easily imagine how attempts were soon made to tone down Jesus' harsh statement in some way. In other words, the version in which 'without cause' does not appear is the most recalcitrant. A rule of textual criticism is that such a difficult reading is probably the most original. Another rule is that what is presumed to be the original reading must provide a reason for the origin of the variants. Both rules clearly apply here.[8]

In Mark 1.2–3 we find a combination of two Old Testament quotations. In v.2 Malachi 3.1 is quoted, and in v. 3 there is a quotation from Isaiah 40.3. The two quotations are introduced at the beginning of v.2. Here we find two different readings: 'as it is written in the prophet Isaiah' and 'as it is written in the prophets'. The latter is correct, since here we have quotations from two prophetic books. But this correct formulation is doubtless a correction of the statement that the words quoted are all to be found in Isaiah. A copyist changed 'in the prophet Isaiah' into 'in the prophets'. We cannot imagine the opposite happening. An extra argument is that 'in the prophet Isaiah' is backed up by earlier manuscripts than the alternative reading.

An interesting example is to be found in Mark 9.49. There are three formulations of this verse:

(a) 'For everyone will be salted with fire.' This formulation has the support of a small number of witnesses of good quality.

(b) 'For every sacrifice will be salted with salt.' Mark 9.49 then contains a quotation from Leviticus 2.13. We find this formulation in the Codex Bezae.[9]

(c) 'For everyone shall be salted with fire, and every sacrifice shall be salted with salt'. This reading is supported by the majority of witnesses.

Here too the weight of the manuscripts again plays a role in the assessment. A text-critical judgment usually begins at that level. This requires a long and thorough training. Only when the scholar has considered a large number of cases can he or she form an independent judgment on the value of the different manuscripts. In this case other considerations also play a role. Statement (a) is particularly obscure. The development presumably was as follows. At an early stage a copyist already noted in the margin that in his judgment 'for everyone shall be salted with fire' must be understood against the background of Leviticus 2.13. This gloss was then taken up into the text to replace the enigmatic sentence which stood there before. Another development is that this gloss was added to the enigmatic statement: that produced variant (c).

A more difficult problem is how the conclusion of Luke 3.22 originally ran. We have the choice of two alternatives. The first possibility is that here God is saying to Jesus, 'You are my beloved son, in you I am well pleased.' We find precisely the same thing in Mark 1.11. In Luke 3.22 some witnesses read something completely different: 'You are my son, today I have begotten you.' In this case Luke 3.22 contains a quotation from Psalm 2.7. It is not simple to arrive at a well-founded choice. The first variant mentioned ('You are my beloved son, in you I am well pleased') is perhaps not original, since it is possible that at this point Luke 3.22 was subsequently adapted to the formulation in Mark. In that case we have a harmonization under the influence of a parallel text from another Gospel. Most scholars are very mistrustful of this phenomenon. But in the case of the second variant ('You are my son, today I have begotten you') we can use a similar argument. Luke 3.22 can have been adjusted to Psalm 2.7 at a later stage. Here too we could speak of influence from a parallel, in this case from the Old Testament. This phenomenon is treated with the same suspicion as an adaptation to a parallel from another Gospel. All in all my preference is for the second variant. The first then came about through an adaptation to the parallel in Mark. I think it less likely that at a later stage an already existing parallel with Mark was given up by an adaptation to Psalm 2.7.

These examples are only a selection from a quite endless series. They show something of the way in which textual criticism works. That is sufficient within the framework of this book.[10] I have presented textual criticism briefly to emphasize that it is not always one hundred per cent certain how the text originally ran. We must constantly keep this in view, whatever method we apply.

Historical criticism

'True, but did not really happen.' This statement about the Bible which is often heard stands in a long tradition. Already towards the end of the seventeenth century the idea arose that not every *story* from the Bible is also *history*. The background to this idea is that only something that can be documented historically is true. Only facts are true; the rest is fiction.

Historical criticism has become so dominant over recent centuries that many exegetes today sum up all diachronic methods under one heading and refer to this as 'the historical–critical method'. That is a gross exaggeration. Historical criticism is only one particular method alongside other diachronic approaches.

Once historical criticism had put down its roots in the ground of biblical exegesis, the historicity of texts from the Gospels was also soon put in doubt. The Jesus whom we meet there – said critical investigators – need not be the true Jesus. Also under the influence of the natural sciences with what was then their predominantly causal-deterministic model of explanation, miracle stories above all suffered. Could Jesus really walk on water? And calm a storm?

The old historical criticism had a rationalistic slant. People sought a natural explanation for the events that were related, so that they fitted into a course of events which could be tested scientifically. Furthermore historical criticism initially had an anti-dogmatic colouring. The investigators fought against the doctrines developed by dogmatics and cultivated by the churches. There was criticism of the ahistorical formulation of the truths of faith: they were being presented as a coherent system of unchangeable and timeless statements. A third characteristic of historiography in the eighteenth and nineteenth century was its one-sided fixation on bare facts and loose data. Some researchers claimed that they could give a neutral description of the past as it really was from a 'stand-point without a standpoint'. They had no inkling of their own historicity and failed to notice sufficiently that their own prejudices and interests influenced the picture of the past that they developed. This positivistic idea was abandoned towards the beginning of the twentieth century.

Despite these shortcomings, the old historical criticism has provided a wealth of worthwhile knowledge about the world in which Jesus lived: geographical and topographical facts, information about the socio-economic conditions and about religious customs. Through such realities we have begun to anchor the Gospels more firmly in their historical context. An awareness has been aroused that the situation in the first century was aeons away from the world in which we live. This includes the fact that at that time different thought-models were used from those of today. A complete reformulation is needed to make the thought world of that time accessible to people of modern times.

Another gain is that historical criticism proved a stimulus to the rise of literary criticism. The historical question who Jesus really was functioned as a catalyst for the investigation of the character and antiquity of the writings in which he is mentioned and of the relationship between them. That brings me to literary criticism.

Literary criticism

Given the purpose of this chapter, here I shall limit myself to the diachronic content of literary criticism.[11] But even then this method is still characterized by a certain diversity. I shall touch on three problems which can be solved in a meaningful way by literary criticism.

1. Literary criticism is applied to the quest for a scholarly solution to questions about the author. Is Moses really the author of the Torah, as an age-old tradition would have us believe? Is Matthew written by one of the twelve apostles, a former toll collector? Does Mark go back to a companion of Peter, and Luke to a companion of Paul on his travels? Was the Fourth Gospel written by 'the disciple whom Jesus loved', and does this character coincide with the apostle John? Were the New Testament letters which bear the name of Paul (thirteen in total) really all written by him? These questions relate to authenticity or inauthenticity. The answer given to them is of some importance, for establishing the author has direct consequences for the time in which the writing concerned was composed. Here literary criticism does good service. With the help of this method the language, style and theological motifs of the texts are examined. It also investigates whether their content can be fitted into what we know of the life of the supposed author. Literary criticism has contributed to new insights at this level. That the Torah came from one author, called Moses, is now regarded as a statement of faith and not as a historical assertion. In their present form the Gospels were set down on paper only towards the last quarter of the first century. Of the letters handed down in the name of Paul, seven were certainly written by him (Romans, I–II Corinthians, Galatians, Philippians, I Thessalonians and Philemon); it is uncertain whether some letters (Colossians and II Thessalonians) come from Paul himself; the authenticity of other letters is seriously doubted or denied (Ephesians, I–II Timothy and Titus).

2. Usually literary criticism coincides with source criticism. Starting from the text as we now have it, the exegete tries to reconstruct older traditions which originally had an independent existence, apart from their present literary setting. Thus this is a search for the sources of the text. That is a meaningful enterprise if there are good reasons to assume that in terms of both form and content the text is not an *original* unity but a composite whole consisting of sub-units of different origin. The starting point is thus that the text has particular characteristics which indicate that the author or redactor has used already existing material and has put this in a new meaningful context. What indications are these? Scholars base themselves on a variety of literary phenomena: the text contains unnecessary repetitions and stylistic unevennesses; words occur in the text which the author does not use elsewhere or which occur only rarely in his book (this phenomenon is all the more striking when we meet this terminology in abundance in other passages which do not come from the same author); the text contains statements which do not match one another in content or which completely contradict one another; the flow of the argument is interrupted in what seems to be an arbitrary way. These phenomena make it difficult to read the text coherently, but they find an appropriate explanation when they are regarded as indications of a complex history of development. Reconstructing this is a highly hypothetical business, above all because here the exegete tries to go back to the sources which were already circulating in the pre-literary stage of oral tradition and thus were not yet fixed in writing.

3. Literary criticism also relates to the investigation of the literary relationship between two or more texts which show many agreements but which at the same time clearly differ from one another. We find examples of this in plenty in the Synoptic Gospels. *That* there must be a literary relationship in such a case is highly probable when there are a number of agreements in the vocabulary of text A and text B. The answer to the question precisely *what* the literary relationship is also depends on the differences between the texts. Sometimes we do best to opt for a direct literary relationship (text B is dependent on text A, or in other words, the author of B has used A). Sometimes we must opt for an

indirect relationship (text A and text B are independent of each other, but both go back to text C).

The heyday of classical literary criticism fell in the second half of the nineteenth century and the beginning of the twentieth. Hypotheses formulated then can sometimes still be used now. One example of this is the two-source theory, which I shall now present.

The two-source theory

Harmonization

If we put the Gospels of Matthew, Mark and Luke side by side, we discover not only a number of agreements but also notable differences. Sometimes the differences are even so great that the reader gets the impression that the texts contradict one another.

An example will clarify this general problem. In Mark 10.46–52 there is a healing story that we also find in Matthew 20.29–34 and Luke 18.35–43. According to Mark a blind beggar, called Bartimaeus, was sitting by the wayside when Jesus went away from Jericho (10.46). Luke also speaks of a blind man, but he does not give his name and makes the story take place when Jesus comes near to Jericho (18.35; only in 19.1 is it said that Jesus came to Jericho and went through the city). In Matthew this story takes place, as in Mark, when Jesus is leaving Jericho, but now there are two blind men by the wayside and neither of them is named (20.29–30).

What are we to do about these differences? Must we ourselves bring order here by putting the three versions together to form one continuous whole, without contradictions? This way of working is called harmonization. The result of this operation might look like this: Jesus healed a blind man on entering Jericho (Luke), and after that he healed another blind man on leaving the city (Mark); Matthew has combined these two incidents, so in his Gospel two blind men are cured of their affliction. In this new story the differences have largely been smoothed over. If we were to do that all along the line we would get a Gospel harmony, a continuous description of Jesus' life composed of Matthew, Mark and Luke.

Although the Gospel according to John takes its own course in many ways, we can also include this writing in such a new creation. Then the harmony is composed of all four Gospels. An ancient example of this is the *Diatessaron*, which was created by Tatian around AD 170 (the Greek *dia tessarōn* means 'through four [Gospels]').

Many children's Bibles and biblical histories are made on the same pattern. The underlying thought is that the Gospels, from which the elements for such a retelling were taken, cannot contain any historical inaccuracies, because they are inspired by the Holy Spirit.

The Synoptic problem

In exegesis scholars do not work with a Gospel harmony, but with a synopsis (= survey). This is a book in which corresponding passages from the Gospels are printed side by side in columns, so that they can easily be compared with one another.[12] Above all the first three Gospels suit themselves to this well. Hence we also refer to Matthew, Mark and Luke as the Synoptic Gospels, or the Synoptics for short. A synopsis is an indispensable means of making a serious study of the parallel passages from more than one Gospel. This tool indicates what passages can be regarded as parallels to one another, and it puts us in a position to make a detailed comparison of the formulation in one version with the wording in the other version(s).

With the help of a synopsis we can form a good picture of the Synoptic problem. This term denotes the phenomenon that the first three Gospels resemble one another strongly and at the same time differ markedly from one another. There are a number of agreements in the material, its order and its formulation.

Material

Matthew, Mark and Luke offer seven different possibilities in the agreement and difference between their material. This number seven gives the maximum number of possibilities for three writings between which there is a literary relationship. Following W.Hendriks, I shall speak here of Synoptic classes.[13]

class 1   a passage occurs in Matthew, Mark and Luke
class 2   a passage occurs in Matthew and Mark
class 3   a passage occurs in Matthew and Luke
class 4   a passage occurs in Mark and Luke
class 5   a passage occurs only in Matthew
class 6   a passage occurs only in Mark
class 7   a passage occurs only in Luke

Class 1 contains the material that occurs three times. The material that occurs twice belongs to classes 2, 3 and 4. The material occurring once (usually called special material) falls into classes 5, 6, and 7; in each of the Synoptic Gospels a particular part of the material belongs to this last category.

Thumbing through a synopsis, we find these classes easily enough. A number of texts are printed in all three columns; other texts occur in two columns (Matthew//Mark; Matthew//Luke; Mark//Luke); in the case of material which occurs only once, of course only one column is used, while the other two columns contain no text.

Hendriks indicates both in absolute figures and in percentages how the total wordage of Matthew, Mark and Luke is divided between the different Synoptic classes.[14] Here I shall quote only his percentages (Table 8):

material	Matthew	Mark	Luke	class
material occurring three times	31.53%	53.23%	30.12%	1
material occurring twice	14.86%	26.58%	–	2
	20.52%	–	18.30%	3
	–	9.33%	4.86%	4
material occurring once	33.09%	–	–	5
	–	10.86%	–	6
	–	–	46.72%	7

Table 8: Wordage of Matthew, Mark and Luke in percentages and divided between the Synoptic classes

This table demonstrates that Mark has relatively little special material (class 6). The rest of the material in Mark has a parallel in Matthew and/or in Luke (classes 1, 2 and 4). Matthew has far more material of his own (class 5). The rest of the material in Matthew has a parallel either in Mark (classes 1 and 2) or in Luke (class 3). Luke contains the most special material: almost half of this Gospel belongs in that category (class 7). The rest of the Lukan material has a parallel either in Mark (classes 1 and 4) or in Matthew (class 3).

Order

A further point which deserves our attention is the order of the material. At this level, too, there are marked agreements between the three Synoptics. These Gospels have the same basic framework. If we put Matthew 1–2 and Luke 1–2 in brackets, all three run from the ministry of John the Baptist to the resurrection of Jesus from the dead. In the period marked out in this way Jesus is first active for a long time in Galilee; after that he travels to Jerusalem, where he is arrested within a week and crucified on the orders of Pilate. This common pattern stands out even more when we note that John has quite a different order. Here Jesus travels to Jerusalem four times (2.13; 5.1; 7.10; 12.12). Large parts of the book take place in this city (2.13–3.21; 5.1–47; 7.10–10.39; 12.12–20.29). In total the passover is mentioned three times in John. The first mention comes at the beginning of Jesus' ministry, the last at the end of the book; in 6.2 passover is mentioned once more. Because each time around a year passes between two passovers, the total duration of Jesus' ministry in John amounts to around two years.

The order of the material in the Synoptic Gospels can be studied in even more detail. If we line up the passages from the Synoptic classes 1, 2 and 4, we see that the order of the material in Mark usually corresponds to the order of the same pieces in Matthew or in Luke, and often to the order in both Matthew and Luke. In some cases Matthew or Luke does not follow the order in Mark, but in these cases time and again only one of the two does not take over the order, while the other does. As a rule they do not combine in going against Mark's order.

Something similar is also true of the material in class 3, the twofold material which Matthew and Luke have in common. In Matthew and Luke this material is used in different ways. In Matthew it is primarily concentrated in Jesus' five long discourses (the Sermon on the Mount, the Mission Discourse, the Parable Discourse, the Community Discourse and the Eschatological Discourse), while the pericopes in Luke which belong to this category stand side by side in two great blocks (Luke 6.20–8.3 and 9.51–18.14). Because of this difference, it is not evident that the order of the separate pericopes more or less agrees in each case. However, broadly speaking that is so.

Formulation

The parallel texts from the Synoptic Gospels also correspond at a number of points in the vocabulary used. This is true above all of the material from classes 1, 2 and 4. These classes comprise material from Mark which also occurs in Matthew and/or Luke. In class 3 (the material common to Matthew and Luke) the number of words which are literally the same is somewhat lower, but here too they amount to more than fifty per cent of the total vocabulary.

If we are comparing parallel texts, the best way is to mark the different words with a particular colour. E.Charpentier has given some useful advice here.[15] As in the division of the material, we can distinguish seven possibilities. Each of these possibilities gets its own colour. Here Charpentier begins from three primary colours: red, blue and yellow. He assigns a primary colour to each of the Synoptics: red to Matthew, blue to Mark and yellow to Luke. The other colours needed are formed by mixing two or three primary colours together. Schematically, it all looks like this:

A word that in a particular text is peculiar to Matthew	red
A word that in a particular text is peculiar to Mark	blue
A word that in a particular text is peculiar to Luke	yellow
The same word in Matthew, Mark and Luke	brown

The same word in Matthew and Mark	purple
The same word in Matthew and Luke	orange
The same word in Mark and Luke	green

A solution to the Synoptic problem

We saw above that the Synoptics on the one hand resemble one another closely and on the other differ from one another markedly. The question now is how we are to explain this phenomenon. How can the Synoptic problem best be solved?

One conclusion imposes itself irresistibly. Given the great degree of agreement in the choice of the material, the ordering of the material and its formulation, there must be some sort of literary relationship between these writings. The question is not *whether* they are related in literary terms, but *how* the relationship between them can best be described. Furthermore, it is plausible to presuppose that the first three Gospels go back to earlier material in the tradition (sayings of Jesus and stories about him), which circulated in the earliest Christian communities partly in oral and partly in written from.

In past centuries the validity of almost every conceivable solution to the Synoptic problem has been investigated. Already in the nineteenth century the two-source theory was proposed above all by C.H.Weisse and H.J.Holtzmann. I shall first present this theory in a scheme (Table 9) and then give the necessary explanation.

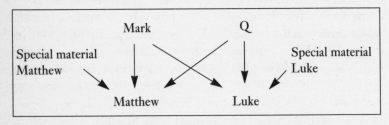

Table 9: A schematic diagram of the two-source theory

The two-source hypothesis consists of the following elements:
1. Mark is the earliest Gospel.
2. Matthew and Luke have – independently of each other – made

use of Mark in the composition of their Gospels. They have drawn part of their material from Mark; they have also often kept the order in which the material appears in Mark; finally, they have to some degree also conformed to the way in which this material is formulated in Mark. Mark has thus functioned as a source for the two other evangelists. This part of the hypothesis explains the striking agreements in the Synoptic classes 1, 2 and 4.[16]

3. In writing their Gospels, Matthew and Luke have made use of a second source in addition to Mark. They have taken over a good deal of narrative material from Mark. In addition they have many passages in common which are lacking in Mark. These primarily consist of logia (= sayings) of Jesus. According to the two-source theory they have taken this material from a second source, the Logia source (denoted with the letter Q, the initial letter of the German *Quelle* = source).[17] Probably Q was a document written in Greek which was itself in turn a collection of yet older material from the tradition. This part of the two-source theory offers an explanation for the high degree of agreement within class 3. Unlike Mark, Q is a lost source. It is very likely that an old collection of sayings of Jesus existed. Already at an early stage followers of Jesus began to put together similar material from the tradition. There is no doubt that here they had a certain preference for sayings of Jesus. The plausibility of the idea that sayings of Jesus were a popular 'collectors' item' is further increased by the discovery in 1945 of the Gospel of Thomas, which consists of 114 logia. That Q underlies Matthew and Luke is more hypothetical than the statement that Matthew and Luke based themselves on Mark. After all, this last source is still at our disposal. So we can accurately compare the Gospels of Matthew and Luke with this alleged source. In the case of Q such a comparison is far more complicated.

The two-source theory gives an appropriate explanation for the agreements in classes 1, 2, 3 and 4. The material from classes 5, 6 and 7 remains unexplained. That the two-source theory gives no explanation for class 6 (the special material in Mark) is no problem, since there is not much of this material (around 30 verses in all). The difficulty lies above all in classes 5 and 7. This is the material which occurs either only in Matthew or only in Luke. In the case of Matthew, within the total wordage the material amounts to around one third of his book, and in Luke to almost half! Theoretically we could elaborate on the idea that Matthew and Luke used written sources. Doesn't class 5 indicate that in addition to Mark and Q Matthew also used another source of his own which has left no traces in Luke? And doesn't class 7 leave room for postulating a separate source for Luke? If we answer these questions in the affirmative, the total number of written sources of the Synoptic Gospels goes up to four instead of two. One particular variant of this idea was defended by B.H.Streeter.[18] Matthew's special material is said to go back to a source M, and Luke's to a source L. However, most scholars do not accept this proposal because the material from classes 5 and 7 is very diverse. If this material had come from written sources, the special material of Matthew and of Luke should have displayed a more homogeneous character. The alternative to written sources is that here Matthew and Luke adopted material from the broad stream of oral tradition, each in his own way.

Although the two-source theory leaves a number of questions unanswered, this theory does give a reasonable explanation of many details in the Synoptic Gospels. Moreover the application of this theory has proved particularly fruitful in practice. Later developments in exegesis (like redaction criticism) have increased the plausibility of the two-source theory rather than raising questions about it.

Form criticism and redaction criticism

In the investigation of the Gospels, form criticism and redaction criticism attach a great deal of importance to the history of the development of these books. Here form criticism emphasizes the preliminary stages of the text, and above all the small literary units from which the Gospels are constructed. Redaction criticism focusses on the final stage of this development. This method is above all directed towards uncovering the theological motives which are determinative for a Gospel as a whole.

Form criticism emerged after the First World War. Those who

did pioneering work in this area include K.-L.Schmidt, M.Dibelius and R.Bultmann.[19] They built on the work of the Old Testament scholar H.Gunkel and the classicist E.Norden. In form criticism the Gospels are regarded as anthologies or collections of small literary units (for example logia, parables, healing stories, exorcisms) which can be isolated from one another on the basis of literary unevennesses and inconsistencies. These small units are older than the writings in which they are now to be found. Originally they often led an independent existence, detached from the context in which we now find them. A number of them go back to Jesus; others came into being in the earliest Christian communities. These units were handed down orally, and in the course of that process of tradition they were developed further and constantly reinterpreted. Probably small collections of similar material were already made at a very early period (Q is one example of this). The Gospels in their present form are thus the result of a long development. Form criticism tries to reconstruct the original form of the units of which the Gospels are constructed and to sketch a picture of the history which they have undergone before being set down in the Gospels.

Form criticism distinguishes a large number of literary forms. A literary form has certain fixed characteristics (style, structure), which are also determined by the cultural and social situation in which it came into being. The existence of divergent literary forms is thus explained by the great difference in situations in which linguistic expressions are produced. In this context form criticism uses the technical term *Sitz im Leben*. This technical term denotes historical and sociological situations with which the origin and ongoing existence of a literary form are connected. Here we do not have a single historical event but a typical situation or form of action within the community. Thus the *Sitz im Leben* in the community is extremely important. Alongside this, scholars talk of the *Sitz im Leben Jesu*, but initially (under the influence of R.Bultmann) form criticism had great reservations about this.

Redaction criticism was developed in Germany from around 1950 onwards by H.Conzelmann, W.Marxsen and G.Bornkamm.[20] In its application to the Gospels, this method is focussed on the reconstruction of the distinctive emphases which the author/redactor gave to the tradition(s) that had been handed down. Here the exegete begins from the assumption that the intention of the author comes to light above all where in his own way he gives shape and meaning to the material of the tradition, and that the way in which the redactor has interpreted the material is also determined by his situation and by the particular situation of his original reading public. The purpose of the analysis is thus to outline and explain the distinctive share of the redactor as well as possible. To achieve this, it is necessary to put all the linguistic phenomena of a text – lexemes, combinations of words, and also the style and technique of composition – under the microscope. Time and again it has to be ascertained whether the relevant phenomena indicate the hand of the redactor; if that is not the case, we may assume that the element under investigation points to the use of already existing material from the tradition or of traditional ideas.

Redaction criticism can be regarded as a supplement and a correction to certain instances of one-sidedness in form criticism. Form criticism one-sidedly puts the emphasis on the process of the oral tradition of small literary units before they are fixed in writing. Not much attention is paid to the end-products, the Gospels themselves. For redaction criticism the Gospels are more than merely a collection of loose pericopes. This method also, and above all, is concerned with the final form and meaning of these writings, with the characteristic structure of the final text and with the function of the different sub-units within that whole.

Whereas within form criticism the evangelists are regarded as the ones who collect and hand down the material of the tradition, and their contribution to the process of tradition remains limited to the insertion of topographical and temporal notions into the material of the tradition, in redaction criticism they are seen as redactors with a theological perspective of their own. They show a degree of freedom towards the meaning of the material which has formed in the course of the tradition. The evangelists have interpreted the data of the tradition that has been handed down each in his own way. Thus we can speak of the theology of Matthew, Mark, Luke and John. The distinctive theological perspective of the evangelists can be reconstructed on the basis of an investigation of their choices from the material in the tradition, the changes, omissions and additions that they make compared to their sources, their choice of words, their technique of composition and the ordering of their material.

Form criticism (above all Bultmann) concentrates almost exclusively on the creativity of the earliest Christian communities and the *Sitz im Leben* in the community of the different literary units. Redaction criticism is also interested in the *Sitz im Leben* of the evangelists. This method pays a good deal of attention to the historical context in which the author wrote his book.

Two guides to reading

I shall now present two guides to reading. They relate to literary criticism and to form criticism and redaction criticism and are meant to build a bridge between theory and practice. These guides consist of questions relating to particular passages. They will help those who use them to become more systematic in the diachronic study of Synoptic texts.

Guide I: Passages from Mark with a parallel in Matthew and Luke

The first guide can be used in texts from Mark which have a parallel in Matthew and Luke (Mark//Matthew and //Luke).[21]

1. Mark's version
- Look at the way in which the pericope in Mark is connected with what comes before and after. There is a good chance that these connections have been made by the redactor of the Gospel of Mark. That is certainly the case when elsewhere in Mark we find similar connections between separate pericopes.
- Does the passage contain elements which indicate the hand of the redactor apart from the opening and closing sentences? Note here vocabulary that is typical of Mark. Make use of a concordance.
- Indicate which parts of the text are presumably taken from tradition. One indication of this is words which do not occur elsewhere in Mark or which are used only seldom by him.

- Now try to establish the extent of the material from the tradition used by Mark. What literary form does the material display? How far can the fixed characteristics of this literary form still be found in the text of Mark?
- What can be said about the original *Sitz im Leben* of the material from the tradition?
- Now study the elements which more or less certainly indicate the hand of the redactor. The purpose of this is for you to gain insight into the meaning and function of the text at the level of redaction. With what aspects of meaning has the redactor enriched the tradition? On which meanings has he put extra emphasis? Try also to indicate what function the redactional elements may have fulfilled within the communication between the author and his original readers. This involves your trying to make a connection between the final redaction and the so-called *Sitz im Leben* of the evangelist.

2. Synoptic survey
- Put the text of Mark and the parallel texts from Matthew and Luke in three columns side by side (or make a copy from a synopsis).
- Now list which words from Mark can also be found in the two other versions. Underline these elements with a brown crayon.
- Now note the agreements between Mark and Matthew (underline these elements in purple) and the agreements between Mark and Luke (green).
- Now come the differences: (a) changes (a linguistic element in Mark is rendered differently in Matthew or Luke); (b) omissions (an element in Mark is missing from either Matthew or Luke); (c) insertions or additions (Mark or Luke contain an element which is missing in Mark). In noting the differences use a separate colour for each evangelist (red for Matthew, blue for Mark, yellow for Luke). First compare Mark with Matthew, and then Mark with Luke.

3. Matthew's version
- The agreements suggest that Matthew has indeed used Mark's version. Indicate in your own words how far Matthew's text agrees with Mark's version.

- Then we concentrate on the differences. Indicate in your own words at what point the text of Matthew differs from that of Mark.

- We may not automatically assume that the differences are all to be attributed to Matthew. This evangelist could also have used material from the tradition that has not been included in Mark. Therefore we must investigate whether the differences noted go back to tradition or redaction. We need to examine them closely one by one, and in doing so we will use a synopsis and a concordance. If Matthew is also fond of using a particular word elsewhere, then there is a good chance that in our passage it also comes from him. That chance is particularly great when elsewhere in Matthew there are (the same) divergences from the vocabulary in Mark or Q.

- In this survey, at the same time we are trying to form an idea of what meaning the words that we are surveying have for Matthew. In noting this, we are collecting elements which may be useful in determining Matthew's own theological perspective.

- The literary context forms a separate focal point. Investigate whether the pericope in Matthew stands in the same context as it does in Mark. If this is not the case, then the phenomenon gives a good deal of support to determining Matthew's intention. The surrounding context does shed clear light on the meaning and function that the passage under investigation will have had for Matthew.

- After this analysis there is an attempt at a synthesis. Add the redactional elements together so that they make a more or less conclusive whole. What can you now say about the meaning and the function of the relevant passage in Matthew?

4. Luke's version

In analysing the differences between Mark and Luke we can again use the questions raised under 3 (of course each time 'Matthew' must be replaced with 'Luke').

Guide II: Parallel texts from Matthew and Luke (without a counterpart in Mark)

The second guide relates to material from Q (Matthew//Luke). In this case the following questions may be useful:

1. Comparison
- Compare the context of the text in Matthew with the context of the version in Luke. Are there relevant differences? If so, what light do these differences shed on the meaning and function of the text in Matthew? And on the meaning and function of the Lukan text?
- Put the versions of Matthew and Luke in two columns side by side (or make a copy from a synopsis).
- Now list which words the two texts have in common. Underline these words with a crayon (orange).
- Make a list in which you indicate in your own words how far the two texts contain the same statements.
- Now come the differences: (a) changes (a linguistic element from Matthew is given differently in Luke or vice versa); (b) omissions (an element in Matthew is absent from Luke or vice versa); (c) insertions or additions (Matthew contains an element which is absent from Luke or vice versa). In marking the differences use a separate colour for each evangelist (red for Matthew, yellow for Luke).

2. Matthew's version
- Does Matthew's text contain terms that indicate the hand of the redactor of this Gospel? With the aid of a synopsis and a concordance investigate how the words from Matthew's text which diverge from the formulation in Luke are used elsewhere in Matthew. These observations together give an idea of the way in which Matthew has understood the Q tradition used here.

3. Luke's version
- Does Luke's version contain terms that indicate the hand of the redactor of the Third Gospel? With the aid of a synopsis and a concordance investigate how the words from Luke's text which diverge from the formulation in Matthew are used elsewhere in Luke. These observations together give an idea of the way in which Luke has understood the Q tradition used here.

4. The formulation and tenor of the Q text

- We can probably no longer discover precisely how the Q version ran. However, we can assume that the elements common to Matthew and Luke (coloured orange) go back to Q. The original Q formulation may have been preserved either by Matthew or by Luke. For this, look at the non-redactional elements in both passages: they probably come from Q. Try to combine the non-redactional elements of the two versions. What can you now say about the formulation of Q on the basis of these observations?

- Can you indicate what the literary form of the Q text is? How far can the typical characteristics of this literary form still be found in the text of Matthew? And how far in the text of Luke?

- Can you indicate what was probably the original meaning and *Sitz im Leben* of the Q text?

These guides form the background to the analysis of the Synoptic texts in Chapters 6 and 7.

6

Texts in triplicate

In this chapter there follow some examples of a form-critical and redaction-critical analysis of texts from the threefold tradition. In order not to complicate matters needlessly I have opted for quite short narratives:

- the baptism of Jesus (Mark 1.9–11; Matthew 3.13–17; Luke 3.21–22);
- the healing of Peter's mother-in-law (Mark 1.29–31; Matthew 8.14–15; Luke 4.38–39).

The baptism of Jesus

Survey

The narrative about the baptism of Jesus occurs in all the Synoptic Gospels. First I shall present a translation of the three versions in which I shall mark the literal agreement typographically. Words which we find in all three authors are printed in bold; agreements between Mark and Matthew are underlined; terms which Mark and Luke have in common are printed in italic.

Matthew 3.13–17	Mark 1.9–11	Luke 3.21–22
13 Then **Jesus** arrived from <u>Galilee</u> to <u>John</u> at <u>the Jordan</u>, to be **baptized** by him. 14 John would have prevented him, saying, 'I need to be baptized by you, and do you come to me?'	9 And *it happened* in those days that **Jesus** came from Nazareth in <u>Galilee</u> and was **baptized** in <u>the Jordan</u> by <u>John</u>.	21 Now *it happened* – when all the people were baptized and **Jesus** [also] had been **baptized** and was praying –

15 But Jesus answered him, 'Allow [me] now; for thus it is fitting for us to fulfil all righteousness.' Then he allowed him. 16 When Jesus had been baptized, <u>he arose immediately from the water</u>. And behold, <u>the heavens</u> were opened, and <u>he saw</u> the spirit of God descend like a dove, and alight on him. 17 And behold, a voice [came] from heaven, which said, 'This is my beloved son, with whom I am well pleased.'

10 <u>Immediately</u> when <u>he arose from the water, he saw the heavens</u> torn and the spirit descend on him like a dove. 11 And a voice *came* from heaven, '*You are* my beloved son; with *you* I am well pleased.'

that the heaven was opened, 22 and the holy spirit descended on him in bodily form, like a dove, and a voice *came* from heaven, '*You are* my beloved son; with *you* I am well pleased.'

The literal agreements indicate a literary relationship, but how must we imagine this? The two-source theory begins from the assumption that Mark is the earliest Gospel. That is also most probable in this concrete case. The best explanation of the fact that at particular points Matthew agrees with Mark, and that at other points Luke in turn agrees with Mark, is that Mark is the origin of the two other versions.

Mark's version

With a few small exceptions (which I shall touch on later), the vocabulary in Mark 1.9–11 is not typical of Mark in his role as redactor. Indeed we can safely assume that the narrative comes from the tradition. The text has the form of a vision followed by an interpretation (German exegetes speak here of a *Deute-Vision*, an interpretation vision).[1] Such a narrative has the following fixed characteristics:

(a) The text begins with the sketch of a situation (here: Jesus is being baptized).

(b) Then follows a vision. In this case it relates to a visionary experience of Jesus ('he saw'), which contains two inter-connected elements: he sees the heavens torn open and he sees the spirit descending upon him like a dove.

(c) This vision is interpreted by a voice from heaven, i.e. by God. The words of God consist of a combination of two quotations from scripture (Ps.2.7 and Isa.42.1). God calls Jesus his beloved son. This term denotes a relationship and indicates that God has a special bond with Jesus.

The narrative was already circulating in the earliest Christian communities, perhaps already in Palestine. Part of its core is that Jesus was baptized by John at the beginning of his activity. This fact is beyond doubt historical. It cannot have been invented by Jesus' disciples. They would never have arrived at the idea of making Jesus' career start with his baptism by John unless the facts compelled them to, since this event suggests that Jesus, the one who is being baptized, is inferior to John, the baptizer. Probably this thought was raised at a very early stage. The old story, which Mark has preserved almost word for word, already tries to correct this offensive idea. It propagates precisely the opposite: although Jesus was baptized by John (that is a fact), one may not conclude from this that John is superior to Jesus. No, in this case the person being baptized has a higher status than the person baptizing.

The special position of Jesus is expressed by the fact that here he is referred to as son of God, an honorific title which God himself has bestowed on him. So Jesus does not owe this title to John. He has received it only *after* his baptism, in a visionary experience which put him in contact with no less than God himself. The Christians who formed this story were steeped in the belief that Jesus is the son of God. It must have come into being when that picture of Jesus had been developed.

Mark has hardly changed anything in the story. Only two small details point in his direction. First, in 1.10 we have the word 'immediately' (in Greek *euthus*). That word is a great favourite of Mark's. He uses it regularly, and this gives his narrative of Jesus a somewhat rushed character. This fast tempo is striking in the first chapter (here we have 'immediately' in 1.10, 12, 18, 20, 21, 23, 28, 29, 30, 42, 43; in total Mark uses this word 41 times in his Gospel). A second redactional element is 'from Nazareth' in v.9. That is the place from which Jesus comes. Only he comes from this village in Galilee; the other candidates for baptism who gather around John come from Judaea and Jerusalem (1.5). The mention of Jesus' place of origin serves what follows in Mark's book. In it Jesus is often called 'the Nazarene' (1.24; 10.47; 14.67; 16.6). It is also important that for a long period his ministry is set in Galilee.

Mark has given the narrative about Jesus' baptism a place in the prologue of his book (1.2–13).[2] This leads to all kinds of relationships between that old piece of tradition and other parts of the prologue:

it happened (v.9: in Greek *egeneto*)	John appeared (v.4: similarly *egeneto*)
Jesus came (v.9)	comes after me... (v.7)
Jesus (v.9)	someone who is stronger than I (v.7)
in the Jordan by John (v.9)	by him [= John] in the river Jordan (v.5)
the spirit of God descends upon Jesus (v.10)	he shall baptize you in holy spirit (v.8)

The connections have solid semantic effects. The announcement by John of someone who is coming after him (originally perhaps someone who is treading in his footsteps, who is his disciple) is already fulfilled in v.9 when Jesus goes to John. The combination of v.7 with v.9 makes it clear that the 'someone who is stronger than I' means Jesus. That this view is correct is confirmed by God, the highest possible authority. The combination of v.8 with v.10 makes it clear that Jesus will baptize people with the spirit, with the divine power that he himself has received. He is the bearer of the spirit *par excellence*. That will emerge time and again from Jesus' words and actions which Mark has collected in his book.

That Jesus is the son of God is a Leitmotif in the Gospel according to Mark.[3] The voice from heaven resounds again in 9.7, and at the end of Mark this voice is echoed by the earth (15.39). The narrative of Jesus' baptism and the brief scene which describes the centurion under the cross (15.38–39) are very closely connected:

1.10 the heavens were torn open	15.38 the curtain of the temple was torn in two from top to bottom
1.10 Jesus saw that...	15.39 when the centurion saw that...
1.11 'You are my beloved son'	15.40 'Truly, this man was the son of God'.

How does Matthew present Mark's narrative?

In my commentary on Matthew's version I assume that he has used Mark's narrative. Matthew 3.13 is very like Mark 1.9: the same thing is true of Matthew 3.16–17 and Mark 1.10–11. The remaining verses (Matthew 3.14–15) have no counterpart in Mark. They belong to Matthew's own material, the so-called special material.

I begin with the material which Matthew and Mark have in common. The opening sentence (Matthew 3.13) corresponds word for word at a number of points with Mark 1.9: both evangelists mention the same characters (Jesus and John) and the same indications of place (Galilee and the Jordan; Matthew omits Nazareth) and they speak about 'being baptized'. A small but evocative difference is that coming *and* being baptized in Mark stand side by side in parataxis, whereas in Matthew it is said that Jesus goes to John in *order* to be baptized. Thus Jesus has a clear purpose in view when he goes to John. No one can stop him, not even John (see Matthew 3.14–15).

There are yet other differences. Matthew replaces 'in those days' with his favourite word 'then'. Moreover he speaks of 'arriving ' (in Greek *paraginomai*) and not of 'coming' (*erchomai*). Matthew uses the same verb in 3.1 where John appears on the scene. Thus John and Jesus are described in the same way. In Matthew all kinds of other examples can be found, with the effect that in many respects Jesus and John seem as like as two peas.[4] They stand for the same cause. However, this does not mean that Matthew does not put Jesus far higher than John the Baptist. In 3.14–15 he has presented this view by John himself!

Matthew's version also runs parallel to the text of Mark at the end. Most of the differences have merely a stylistic function. After the two inserted verses (3.14–15), Matthew again takes up the thread, and therefore at the beginning of v.16 he repeats some of the elements that we also already find in v.13: the proper name Jesus and the verb 'baptize'. 'The spirit' is changed into 'the spirit of God'; here Matthew makes Mark's purpose clear. The final point of the descent of the spirit is mentioned explicitly: the spirit alights on Jesus. It is striking that Matthew 3.16–17 twice contains the interpolation 'and behold'. The first evangelist uses this interpolation particularly frequently (62 times).[5] By it he indicates that things are coming up which deserve the special attention of the reader. In this case they are the descent of the spirit and the revealing words of God about Jesus' identity.

The most important difference is that the voice from heaven is not addressed to Jesus (as in Mark and Luke: 'You are...') but speaks of him in the third person ('This is...'). Because apart from Jesus no one is mentioned other than John, he has to be the one addressed here. That means that he receives confirmation from above of the correctness of his statements in 3.11 and 3.14, where John left doubt that he is inferior to Jesus.

Now we must pay special attention to the special material (3.14–15). The question is where this material comes from. Verse 15 contains various elements which are characteristic of the language and the style of Matthew. Jesus' command ('allow me') is carried out by John ('then he allowed him'). We often find this pattern in Matthew (e.g. 1.20 plus 1.24; 2.13–14; 2.20–21; 21.2 plus 21.6). Moreover there is no doubt that 'to fulfil all righteousness' indicates the hand of the redactor. 'Righteousness' is one of his favourite words, as is 'fulfil'.[6] According to v.15 Jesus and John stand for the same thing. That also indicates redaction, since Matthew is fond of emphasizing the parallelism between the ministry of the two of them (see e.g. 3.2 and 4.17).

He has good reason for doing so. Probably in his own time, long after Jesus' death, there were still people who were enthusiastic about John. This discussion forms the background to 3.14. That verse is about the relationship between Jesus and John, a question which also already played a role in Mark 1.9–11. Is not Jesus inferior to John, given that he has been baptized by John? In a very precise way Matthew knocks that idea on the head: he makes John himself say that he occupies a subordinate position. People who are enthusiastic about John are here told by their own idol that they are profoundly mistaken.

How does Luke present Mark's story?

We have read Matthew 3.13–17 against the background of Mark. In the way in which Matthew tells the story, we found elements of continuity and elements of discontinuity, a mixture of tradition and redaction. The tradition was handed on, but at the same time enriched with new emphases. We shall now be reading Luke's version in the same way. Here we assume that he too knew Mark's narrative and rewrote it creatively.

That Luke is dependent on Mark in literary terms is evident from the many elements that they have in common: 'it happened'/ Jesus is baptized/ the heavens are opened/ the spirit descends as a dove on Jesus/ a voice resounds from heaven/ the words which God speaks, are in Luke word for word the same as in Mark.[7]

But the narrative in Luke has quite a different tenor. Really we can no longer speak of a narrative about the baptism of Jesus, since this event has been completely forced into the background and is mentioned only in a subordinate clause. In the foreground stands what happens *after* the baptism of Jesus. That is clear when we note the grammatical construction of 3.21–22: 'it happened… that the heaven was opened and the holy spirit descended… and a voice came from heaven…'

These three events are presented quite differently from in Mark. There it is Jesus who sees the heavens torn open and the spirit descending; he is the one who also hears what the voice from heaven has to say. Thus this is a visionary and auditory experience on the part of Jesus. Luke transforms the personal experiences of Jesus into phenomena which everyone, and not only Jesus, could see and hear. Two details support that. In v.21 he mentions that the whole people is baptized. Thus it is presupposed that large masses of people are present and witness the special phenomena which now take place. Furthermore he adds that the spirit descends *in bodily form*. Thus the visibility of the spirit is empha-sized strongly.

We also find this more objectivizing presentation elsewhere in the two books written by Luke (Luke and Acts). Here are some examples.

- In Luke 24 the risen Jesus appears to the eleven and their companions (24.36–49). In their agitation and terror they think that they are confronted with a ghost (in Greek *pneuma*, the same word as in 3.22!). Jesus corrects this idea by saying: 'Look at my hands and my feet, it is I. Touch me and see; for a spirit does not have flesh and bones as you see that I have.' He then eats a piece of baked fish before their eyes.
- In the description of Jesus' ascension (Acts 1.9–11) Luke very strongly emphasizes the visibility of this event. Jesus is raised up before the eyes of his disciples. A cloud removes him from their sight. While his followers are still standing looking up to heaven, they are told by two men in white garments that they will see Jesus returning in the same way as they have seen him ascending to heaven.
- The Pentecost story in Acts 2.1–4 emphasizes that the descent of the spirit is coupled with phenomena that are audible and visible. There is a direct connection between this passage and Luke 3.21–22. Just as at the beginning of his ministry Jesus is endowed with the power of God's spirit, so too at the beginning of their world-wide mission his followers are filled with holy spirit.

Why has Luke opted for these vivid descriptions? Why so much emphasis on the visibility of things which we find difficult to accept as being visible to the naked eye? My answer to this question would be that within the group of Jesus' followers Luke already belongs to the second or third generation. He thinks it important to anchor his narratives in traditions which go back to the original eye-witnesses (Luke 1.2) who went out with Jesus from the beginning to the day of his ascension (Acts 1.21–22). This gives his narratives a solid foundation. Another factor is that in his time, many decades after Jesus' death, talk of Jesus was sometimes all too hazy, with the danger of making Jesus evaporate into a heavenly figure who was no longer really rooted in human history. Luke tries to correct this one-sided picture. From the beginning, from the baptism of John, to the day of the ascension – he emphasizes – Jesus' life has taken place in the sight of his disciples. The risen Christ may be totally different from the crucified Jesus; nevertheless he is one and the same figure: even if his glory has come, he still bears the marks of his death on the cross.

We are so used to the idea that Jesus was baptized by John that on a first and still somewhat superficial reading of Luke 3.21–22 it does not strike us that John is not mentioned here at all. The narrator reports only that all the people are baptized and that Jesus is baptized too. We are not told by whom. John does not appear at all, since shortly beforehand (in 3.20) Luke has mentioned that the Baptist has been imprisoned by Herod Antipas, a son of the feared Herod the Great. In Mark his arrest and imprisonment are mentioned only at a much later stage (Mark 6.17).

Here we come upon a form of narration which is characteristic of Luke. He is fond of rounding off one episode before going on to the next. After rounding off a long narrative about John (3.1–20) he switches over to Jesus (3.21–22). In the same way, in 1.56 he concludes the narrative about Mary's stay with Elizabeth before going over to the narrative of the birth of John. In 1.80 he makes that narrative in turn end in the report that in his youth John dwelt in solitary places until the day when he showed himself to Israel.

In 3.21–22 this form of narration has the additional effect of solving in a very original way the old problem of how the baptism of Jesus by John can be reconciled with Jesus' high status. John is literally written off![8]

Luke has changed a variety of other details. He has not only Jesus but all the people baptized. The people are already mentioned in 3.15. The report that *all* the people are baptized is somewhat exaggerated. Luke is fond of having whole like-minded groups appearing in the same way and plays down possible oppositions or internal conflicts.

It is also peculiar to Luke that Jesus prays after his baptism. Luke often depicts Jesus as someone who prays, above all at key moments in his life (see Luke 5.16; 6.12; 9.18, 28–29; 11.1; 22.41, 44, 45). A number of these texts have a parallel in Mark (see Mark

1.35; 3.13; 8.27; 9.2; 14.35, 39), but sometimes in these parallel texts there is no indication that Jesus prays. That shows that at this point Luke has enriched the tradition in his own way.

The praying Jesus is an attractive model for his disciples. That comes out well in 11.1. However, I want to point out that this is also the tenor of the scene on the Mount of Olives. The composition of this passage shows that clearly (Table 10).

Table 10: The composition of Luke 22.39–46

		22.39	Introduction
A	the disciples	22.40	Pray that you do not enter into temptation
B	Jesus	22.41	He… fell on his knees and prayed…
		22.44	And being in agony he prayed yet more urgently
		22.45	And when he arose from prayer…
A'	the disciples	22.46	Rise and pray that you may not enter into temptation

The healing of Peter's mother-in-law

Survey

We also have this narrative in triplicate. To make the comparison easier I shall put the three versions in columns side by side:

Matthew 8.14–15	Mark 1.29–31	Luke 4.38–39
14 And Jesus went to **the house of** Peter and saw his **mother-in-law** lying in bed <u>with fever</u>. 15 And he touched her <u>hand</u>, and **the fever left her**, and she <u>rose</u> **and she served** him.	29 And immediately when they had left *the synagogue*, they went to **the house of** *Simon* and Andrew, with James and John. 30 Now the **mother-in-law** *of Simon* lay sick <u>with fever</u>, *and they* immediately told him about *her*. 31 And he went to her, took her by the <u>hand</u> and <u>raised</u> her. **The fever left her, and she served** *them*.	38 When he had arisen from *the synagogue*, he entered **the house of** *Simon*. Now the **mother-in-law** *of Simon* was taken with a high fever, *and they* besought him for *her*. 39 And he stood at the head of the bed and rebuked **the fever**, and it **left her**. Immediately she arose **and she served** *them*.

The narrative in Mark

The question is whether the narrative in Mark is an original unit. Was the narrative written all of a piece or can we distinguish earlier and later layers in the text? A first support is provided by the fact that the text has the typical characteristics of a healing story.

1. Description of the sickness:	Simon's mother-in law has been laid low with a fever.
2. The request for healing:	this request is made indirectly in 'they told him about her'.
3. Deliverance (here by a gesture):	Jesus helps the sick woman to rise by grasping her by the hand.
4. Effect:	the fever leaves her.
5. The sick person is really cured:	she serves them.

We find all these characteristics in vv.30–31. These verses do not contain a single literary inconsistency. Together they present a complete healing narrative which Mark has taken from the tradition.[9] It was already in circulation before he wrote his Gospel and bears witness to the belief that Jesus brought salvation and healing to the sick.

Mark has not himself interfered with the formulation of the old account of the healing of Peter's mother-in-law. There is only one detail which indicates his hand, namely the word 'immediately' in v.30. This word is also used in v.29 and occurs often in the rest of Mark (41 times in all). Outside Mark we find this term in the New Testament only in Matthew (5 times), in Luke (once), in John (3 times) and in Acts (once). Given these frequencies, we can say that it is a favourite word of Mark's.

Verse 29 falls outside the series of typical characteristics of a healing story. Probably this verse was formulated by Mark himself. It forms a join between the healing narrative and the two narratives which precede it (1.16–20 and 1.21–28): 'when they had left the synagogue' refers back to the place where Jesus and his companions were in 1.21–28; Simon and Andrew and James and John are called by Jesus on the seashore to follow him.

The narrative about the healing of Simon's mother-in-law is part of a larger literary whole which extends from 1.21 to 1.39. We can mark this out by the indications of place and time:

1.21 They went to Capernaum; and immediately he went to the synagogue on the sabbath...

1.29 And immediately, when they had left the synagogue, they went to the house of Simon and Andrew

1.32 That evening, at sundown...

1.33 The whole city was gathered together at the door

1.35 And early in the morning, while it was still night... he went out to a lonely place

The successive pericopes take place within a period of twenty-four hours. The place of action is Capernaum and the immediate surroundings of the town. This context has been created by Mark. He has arranged various old stories which originally were circulating independently into a long sequence with a unity of place and time.

Thus Mark 1.29–31 displays a mixture of early and late elements. The healing narrative comes from the tradition. Mark has woven this narrative into a larger context. He has formulated v.29 with an eye to this. In the healing narrative itself, only 'immediately' indicates the hand of the redactor.

The narrative in Matthew

Matthew too knows this story. In his Gospel it appears in 8.14–15. If we compare his version closely with Mark, we come upon all kinds of differences. We can divide them into three categories: omissions, insertions and changes.

The most striking thing is that the narrative is much briefer in Matthew than in Mark. A number of elements have been omitted: (a) the twice-repeated 'immediately' has dropped out; (b) so too that Jesus leaves the synagogue; (c) Simon (now called Peter) is mentioned as the owner of the house, but does not play any further role in the narrative, nor do Andrew, James and John. The result of this that in Matthew only Jesus and the sick woman are mentioned; (d) this means that the request to Jesus to heal the woman has also disappeared; (e) it is not said that Jesus goes to the woman.

Matthew has two elements inserted: (a) at the beginning Jesus is mentioned by name; (b) we are told that he sees the woman (in Mark others have to draw his attention to the sick person).

Apart from omissions and insertions the two versions also differ in that some elements are formulated differently in Matthew:

Mark 1.29–31	Matthew 8.14–15
When they left the synagogue,	
they (plural) went	►Jesus went... (singular)
Simon	►Peter
Lay sick	Lying on the bed
Jesus took the sick woman by the hand	►He touched her hand
Jesus helped the woman to stand up	►The woman herself stood up
She served them (plural)	►She served him (singular)

The question now is where all these differences come from. Has Matthew used a source of information, a tradition, of his own, or has he taken over the narrative from Mark? The latter is most probable, since this would be the best explanation of why his narrative resembles that of Mark so strongly. The differences then derive from the fact that Matthew has thoroughly rewritten Mark's narrative. We can be certain that he has indeed done this if we can show that these differences have a redactional character, in other words that they fit Matthew's language and style and coincide with the views that he expresses elsewhere in his book.

Proving this is a quite technical matter. Here I shall content myself with a few observations. Matthew often mentions the name of Jesus in his book, in total around 150 times; the introduction of 'Jesus' in 8.14 is in fact presumably to be attributed to him. The replacement of 'Simon' with 'Peter' also indicates redaction. That Simon is given the name Peter is already mentioned in Matthew 4.18. Of more importance, the abbreviation of healing narratives is a phenomenon that we also find often in Matthew. He cuts out all kinds of details and is fond of reducing these details to a couple of key facts.[10] The many omissions in 8.14–15 by comparison with Mark fit this tendency. The result of this is that Jesus is alone with the sick woman. This is also reflected in the verbs in the text. Jesus is the subject of 'go', 'see' and 'touch'; the woman is the subject of 'rise and serve'. Action and reaction! In between comes 'the fever left her'. This event brings about a decisive change: the woman who first lay passive in bed stands up and becomes active again.

Matthew 8.14–15 is part of a series of three healing narratives. The first of these (8.2–4) takes place outside Capernaum; there Jesus heals a leper. The second (8.5–13) is about a centurion who asks for Jesus' help after he has entered the city. In the third narrative Jesus meets the sick woman at Peter's house. These three special cases are followed in 8.16–17 by a generalizing description ('Jesus healed all who were sick'), and rounded off with a fulfilment quotation which indicates that everything has to be seen in the light of Isaiah 53.4. The quotation from Isaiah runs as follows: 'He has taken upon himself our infirmities and borne our sicknesses.' Jesus takes the sicknesses and infirmities on his shoulders and carries them off in triumph out of the world without being bowed down by them.[11] Thus the context is quite different from that in Mark. There Jesus was in the synagogue before he entered Simon's house. No wonder then that 'when they left the synagogue' is dropped in Matthew. I should also point out that Matthew makes his narrative about Peter's mother-in-law correspond in some points with elements from the two preceding healing stories:

8.14 the woman is lying on the bed (Greek *beblēmenēn*)	8.6 the child is lying in bed paralysed (*beblētai*)
8.15 Jesus touches her hand	8.3 he touches the leper

All these facts point in one and the same direction: the many differences from Mark must be attributed to Matthew himself. So we need not appeal to a separate source of information. Matthew has reworded the narrative and in so doing added distinctive accents of his own which can be described as follows. The narrative is very much more sober. It is wholly concentrated on two characters, Jesus and the sick woman. Both appear actively in Matthew. Jesus himself sees what is wrong with the woman; he does not need to be told about her distress by others. The woman in her turn is more active than in Mark: she is now the subject of two verbs (not just of 'serve' but also of 'rise'). The saving gesture here is that Jesus touches her hand. In Mark Jesus acts differently: he grasps her by the hand. Touching seems lighter, indeed more playful, than grasping. The gesture is lighter, and at the same time the effect of it is much greater: in Matthew the woman rises herself, while in Mark she has to be helped to rise by Jesus.

In Matthew, does the narrative still purely have the character of a healing narrative? Certain elements would fit a call narrative very well.[12] Such a narrative is constructed as follows: Jesus sees someone in a particular situation; he calls this person, who stands up and follows him on his way (cf. Matthew 9.9). We cannot find all these elements in Matthew 8.14–16. But it is striking that it is expressly said that Jesus *sees* the woman, that she *herself* gets moving and that she serves *him* (this can mean that she becomes his disciple). Parts of the old healing story are here formulated in such a way as to move it in the direction of a call narrative. It is suggested that being healed and being called are in line. It is important that the person called here is a woman. The call narratives in the Gospels as a rule focus only on the call of men.

The narrative in Luke

We begin with a list of the differences from Mark. In Luke, too, the twofold 'immediately' is lacking. It is not said that Jesus was in the company of Simon and Andrew and of James and John. Only Jesus enters the house. But later it proves that others are also there: 'they called for his help'. This clause is a clarification of the indirect information in Mark 1.30 ('they told him about her'). Here we have a literary inconsistency (first a singular, later a plural subject) which indicates that the text of Luke has undergone a complex process of development and that the redactor has not smoothed out all the traces of it.

There are a few insertions. At the end it is said that the woman arose 'immediately'. That is surplus to Mark's purpose.

There are all the more changes. The departure from the synagogue is described as 'arose from' and not as 'left'. *Going* to the house of *Simon and Andrew* is replaced by *entering Simon's* house. The most changes are to be found in the description of the sickness, the request for healing and the deliverance that follows. The changes are probably to be attributed to Luke and show how he interprets the story. I shall survey them one by one:

- The woman's distress is heightened: she is not afflicted by fever but by a high (literally a great) fever, which is personified (at any rate Jesus addresses words to the fever). Because the sickness is much worse, the deliverance will be much greater.
- As has already been said, Luke clarifies the request for healing, which in Mark is given only indirectly. This explanation fits in with the story which preceded, in 4.38–39; there it has already proved that Jesus can overcome destructive forces.
- The action undertaken by Jesus is described in quite different words from those in Mark: Jesus goes and stands at the head of the bed and rebukes the fever. The place that Jesus chooses indicates that here he is lord and master of the situation. The verb used (in Greek *ephistēmi*) certainly comes from Luke: in the Gospels it occurs only in him (7 times), and in addition we find it 11 times in Acts, which Luke also wrote. Thus in total Luke uses this word 18 times. This is a high frequency, for in the entire New Testament we come across it only 21 times. The Greek term *ephistēmi* resembles the word *epistatēs* (= master), which occurs in the New Testament only in Luke and which is used by him to denote Jesus.[13]
- In Luke the deliverance does not take place with a gesture (as in Mark) but with a word of power: Jesus rebukes the fever. This term is used three times close together:

4.35 Jesus rebuked him: 'Be silent, and come out of him.'
4.39 He rebuked the fever
4.41 He rebuked them…

In 4.35 he is addressing an unclean, demonic spirit, and in 4.41 demons. Rebuke is a technical term which is often used in the case of an exorcism (the expulsion of a demon). We now find the same word in 4.39, where Jesus joins battle with the fever with which Simon's mother-in-law is afflicted. By means of this term

Luke makes clear the nature of her sickness: she is in the power of a demon. This implies that the healing narrative which Luke has taken over from Mark is transformed into a another kind of narrative, namely a narrative about the expulsion of an evil power. The change fits the context extremely well. Shortly before Jesus enters Simon's house he has freed someone in the synagogue from a demonic spirit, and immediately after his action in Simon's house we hear of a massive expulsion of demons.

• Jesus' powerful word has an immediate effect. 'Immediate' (in Greek *parachrēma*) is a favourite word of Luke's; it occurs sixteen times in Luke and Acts and only twice more in the whole of the New Testament (Matthew 21.19–20). The fact that the fever immediately takes flight shows that Jesus has special powers. In Luke 4.36 this is expressed as follows: 'With powerful authority he gives orders to unclean spirits and they go away.'

The narratives which frame Luke 4.38–39 are the same as in Mark. Both evangelists begin with the liberation of someone possessed in the synagogue of Capernaum. After that follows the deliverance of Simon's mother-in-law. Then towards nightfall large groups of the sick and possessed are delivered from their afflictions. Both authors conclude the series of narratives with Jesus' departure elsewhere. Luke has taken over this literary whole from Mark, but by small interventions he has clearly anchored the narrative about Simon's mother-in-law in the greater whole. In so doing he carries further a line which has already begun in Mark. Mark has put together stories that were originally going the rounds separately. Luke has forged them together even more strongly.

7

A text in duplicate

The parable of the stray or lost sheep

Survey

In paintings or sculptures the good shepherd is often depicted with a sheep on his shoulders. Seen in the light of the text of the Gospels that is a marvellous picture. In John 10 Jesus calls himself the good shepherd, while at the beginning of Luke 15 he speaks about a shepherd who puts a lost sheep on his shoulders. Artists have brought these two texts together to form a single whole.[1]

In reading the Gospels we are constantly exposed to the temptation to smuggle elements from one text into another. That danger of harmonization is particularly great with parallel texts. In a serious study we must try to suppress this tendency. We must not want to see more agreements than are really there.

The parable of the sheep does not occur in John and Mark. Only Matthew and Luke contain this text. It is wrong to call it the parable of the lost sheep in both cases. Only in Luke is it about a sheep which is lost. In Matthew the sheep is not yet lost, but has only gone astray. Hence the double title that I give to this section.

The two versions agree with each other word for word on a number of points. The verbal agreements are printed in bold in the translation below. Italics are used whenever there are small divergences in the (Greek) word order or when (in Greek) the same word is used, but not in precisely the same way. I have also set out the two texts in such a way that corresponding lines stand exactly opposite each other.[2]

This survey shows that Matthew 18.12a and 18.14 do not have a

Matthew 18.12–14

12. What do **you** think?
If it happens that a **man** has **a
hundred sheep**,
and *one of them* has gone astray,
will he **not** leave **the ninety-nine**
on the mountains
and *go* to look for **the** stray one?

13 **And** if it happens that *he finds it*,

Luke 15.4–7

4 What **man of you**, who has **a
hundred sheep**,
and has lost *one of them*,
does **not** leave behind **the ninety-
nine** in the wilderness,
and *go* after **the** lost one, until he
finds it?

5 **And** when *he has found it*,
he lays it on his shoulders, *rejoicing*, 6 and when he comes home,
he calls together his friends
and his neighbours and says,
'Rejoice with me,
for I have found my sheep which
was lost.'

truly **I say to you**,
he *rejoices*
over it more **than**
over the ninety-nine
that did not go astray.

7 **I say to you**,
So *there will be* (more) joy *in
heaven over* **one** sinner who
repents **than**
over ninety-nine righteous
persons who need no repentance.

14 **So** it *is* not the will of your Father
in heaven
that **one** of these little ones should
be lost.

counterpart in Luke; conversely there is no parallel to Luke
15.5b–6 in Matthew. But in neither of these cases can we speak of
pure special material. Note the following points of contact: (a) the
'you' from Matthew 18.12 corresponds to 'you' in Luke 15.4; (b)
that the shepherd rejoices is said both in Luke 15.5 and in Matthew
18.13; (c) Luke 15.7 resembles both Matthew 18.13 and 18.14.
The first survey has brought out many common elements. We can
rule out the possibility that the two versions are completely independent. But how then do they relate to each other? A direct
literary dependence of one version on the other (Matthew   Luke
or Luke   Matthew) is not obvious. The differences are too great
for that. It is more fruitful to think of an indirect literary relation-

ship: here Matthew and Luke both go back to an earlier source (Q).

Parables with the same structure

The two versions not only agree in containing the same words. There are also agreements which transcend that level.

In both cases we have texts of the same sort: a parable. Such a text consists of two components: (a) in a parable a picture is developed which is derived from the way we know things to be in nature or in everyday life; (b) that picture is applied to a deeper reality which escapes the usual perception and can only be illustrated by images. As a rule, the image used and the reality to which it refers are comparable on one point. When more details are given in this comparison, the text takes on an allegorical tendency.

The parable of the sheep has been constructed in the same way in the two versions: (a) the parable is introduced with a question which seeks to provoke a reaction from the hearers (Matthew 18.12; Luke 15.4); (b) there is a description of how joyful the shepherd is when he finds the sheep (Matthew 18.13; Luke 15.5–6); (c) the image is followed with an application which begins with 'so...' (Matthew 18.14; Luke 15.7).

It is also worth mentioning in this connection that the parable of the lost sheep is followed in Luke by the parable of the lost coin. These two parables display precisely the same pattern. German exegetes call such instances a twin parable (*Doppelgleichnis*). Such a duo need not always have existed. The parables could also have circulated independently. But that will not have been for long, since there is an established law that texts which closely resemble each other come to be coupled together at an early stage. The two parables were presumably already joined together before Luke included them in his book. It is also extremely likely that Matthew knew them both but used only the first of the two in his Gospel.

Differences

Before we say any more about the origin of the parable, we must first of all dwell on the differences between Matthew 18.12–14 and Luke 15.4–7. The differences are at least as numerous as the agreements. Here is a summary of some of them:

- In Matthew the sheep has gone astray, in Luke it is lost (the word is used three times!). But we must be on our guard here. Matthew also uses the verb 'lose', but only in the last verse, where the image is applied to the little ones in the community of faith. It is said of them that it is directly contrary to the will of God that they should be lost. Given the image used, Luke's choice of word seems the most obvious. A sheep that is parted from the flock must be regarded as lost, since it will never return of its own accord. Matthew too is familiar with this. He too speaks of lost sheep elsewhere in his book (10.6; 15.24).
- Matthew's version begins with two questions. After the question 'what do you think?' there follows a second question which we also find in Luke, put in other words. Luke's version contains only this one question.[3]
- Matthew 18.12 and 13 contain two conditional clauses ('if...'). In the original Greek text they both begin with *ean genētai* ('if it happens'). Here Luke opts for another sentence structure.
- In both versions the shepherd leaves the sheep unguarded during his search for the one sheep. This is a risky choice, since a flock without a shepherd is particularly vulnerable. In Matthew he leaves the ninety-nine remaining sheep alone upon the mountains, in Luke in the wilderness. This last location is not as strange as we might think, given the word 'wilderness'. In the Gospels this term denotes regions outside human habitation; in Israel wildernesses consist of limestone hills which after rainfall are temporarily fertile enough for sheep and goats to graze on.
- In Matthew the shepherd goes in search of the sheep. The chance of his finding it is not put as high as in Luke (see also the wavering beginning in Matthew 18.13: 'if it happens that he finds it'). Luke in turn emphasizes the finding. The shepherd goes after the sheep 'until he finds it', and then the text continues 'when he has found it'. There is no mention of his seeking it.
- A substantial part of Luke has no counterpart in Matthew: the shepherd puts the sheep which he has found on his shoulders; he does not go back to the flock in the wilderness but to the inhabited world, where he calls his friends and neighbours together and tells them that they must be just as overjoyed as he

is that he has found the lost sheep.
• Matthew connects the stray sheep with the position of 'the little ones', whereas Luke compares the sheep which has been found with a sinner who converts, and the ninety-nine other sheep with ninety-nine righteous who need no conversion. The point of comparison differs: in Matthew the main point is the search to be carried on with unceasing care, whereas in Luke the emphasis is on the unbounded joy which someone experiences when he or she has found something that is lost.

The context of the parable

Matthew 18.12–14 in context

In Matthew the parable is part of a long address by Jesus about the community (18.1–35). The audience for this discourse is the disciples. They are the ones meant when the second person plural is used in 18.12–14 (v.12: 'What do you think?'; v.13: 'I tell you'). The address is about mutual relationships in the community of faith. Problems are discussed which were topical in the last quarter of the first century, when the Gospel according to Matthew assumed its present form. The author makes Jesus, the main character in his book, discuss these questions. One of the problems was the precarious place of 'the little ones' in the community of faith as a whole. They are mentioned in the 'application' (v.14), but they are also named in the verse which precedes the parable (v.10: 'See that you do not despise one of these little ones, for I tell you that in heaven their angels always behold the face of my Father who is in heaven'). The parable is thus framed with a double statement about 'one of these little ones'.[4]

The title 'the little ones' shows something of the contempt in which they are held by other believers. However, it is evident from this address that they enjoy the sympathy of Jesus. They are people who put the advice of 18.3 into practice: in the perspective of the coming kingdom, followers of Jesus must become like children. That means that they must break with the prevailing pattern of values and voluntarily take the lowest place within the community. The little ones hear this call, but they encounter much hostility from people in their circle who do not make the same choice. The

contempt with which they are treated stands in sharp contrast to
the high respect which God has for them. At all costs, the Father
in heaven will see that they are not lost. His special concern for the
little ones must be a stimulus to the community to give their stray
members their rightful place.

Luke 15.4–7 in context

In Luke the parable is a sub-division of a textual unit which comprises the whole of Luke 15. It consists of three parts:

A vv.1–2	Jesus' dealings with toll collectors and sinners are criticized by the Pharisees and the scribes.	
B vv.3–10	To parry this criticism Jesus tells a twin parable: the lost sheep and the lost coin.	
C vv.11–32	After that he tells a fictional story about a father with two sons.	

In A, the Pharisees and the scribes grumble about Jesus' contacts
with sinners and toll collectors. We must keep this information at
the back of our minds on reading B and C. In these sections Jesus
strives to make his critics think differently.

To that end he tells two parables which run almost parallel. The
first is about a man, the second about a woman; the shepherd is in
the wilderness, the woman is at home in the inhabited world.
These details suggest that all, whoever and wherever they are, are
filled with joy when they find a lost object. The Pharisees and
scribes avoid this normal human rule. The parables make it clear
that the same rule is also observed in heaven (by God and the
angels). There too unbounded joy prevails whenever a sinner is
converted. The critics are thus not only opposing normal human
codes. Their criticism is also completely rejected by God!

In sub-division C Jesus adds one more extended narrative. The
two parables which have already been told have prepared the hearers thoroughly to be able to understand this complex narrative too.
The narrative again takes the form of a parable. This parable is not
about a course of events which is felt to be normal. It surprises the
audience and confronts them with unexpected perspectives.

Luke 15.11–32 is well known as the parable of the prodigal son.

That is the wrong title, since in that case the parable should end with v.24, in which the first part of the narrative is summed up as follows: 'My son was dead and is alive again, he was lost and has been found.' The parable goes on after that. After the return of the younger son, the elder son appears on the scene. He is put out by the festivities surrounding the return of his brother, to whom in a conversation with his father he refers as 'that son of yours'. He no longer regards him as his brother by blood. After the return of the younger son, the elder son risks being lost. So we could speak of the parable of the lost sons.[5] But that is an exaggeration. It is not at all certain that the elder son persists in his negative attitude. The only thing that we are told is that the father tries to make him think otherwise. He must give up his criticism and join in the festivities. Whether that also happens we are not told. The parable is broken off abruptly in v.32 with the call: 'We had to celebrate and be glad, for this your brother was dead, and is alive; he was lost, and is found.'

The chapter as a whole is open-ended as well: we are not told whether the Pharisees and the scribes give up their stubborn opposition either. The hearers and readers must fill in that gap for themselves. How the story ought to be concluded is clear. We have already seen three times how such a narrative must end: the lost sheep, the lost coin and the younger son are found again. The elder son, alias the Pharisees and scribes, must understand from this course of events that they have to stop their opposition. Otherwise they themselves will be lost.

Two redactors at work

Matthew's redaction

The text begins with a question (18.12: 'What do you think?') which stimulates the hearers to form a judgment on what they are going to hear. Apart from John 11.56, this question occurs in the New Testament only in Matthew. The question can be addressed both to a group (18.12; 21.28; 22.42; 26.66) and to an individual (17.25; 22.17). That is sufficient reason to speak of redaction here.

In 18.12–13 Matthew deliberately opts for 'stray' and not 'lose'.

In so doing he anticipates the application (18.14), for there it is evident that the little ones are not hopelessly lost. On the contrary, precisely that must be avoided. Hence the little ones are characterized as believers who go astray, who lose the way. That members of the community can easily land up in such a situation is expressed in the eschatological discourse (Matthew 24–25). This repeatedly speaks of internal tensions which are the result of the appearance of false messiahs and false prophets. These members will lead many astray (24.4, 5,11); by their signs and wonders they would lead astray, if possible, even the elect (24.24). 'Lead astray' means mislead, alienate from the community. In the original text the same word (*planaō*) is used here as in 18.12–13.

Matthew's hand is also visible in 18.14. Two combinations of words attract attention here. First, 'one of these little ones'. This expression has not been devised by Matthew himself. In 18.6 he has taken it from Mark (9.42), but soon afterwards, in 18.10 and 14, he speaks of the little ones again apart from Mark. This is a clear signal that their fate is close to his heart.

The second combination of words is 'your Father in heaven'. Matthew is very fond of this description of God (see 5.16, 45; 6.1; 7.11). The same is true of 'your heavenly Father' (5.48; 6.14, 26, 32; cf. also 23.9). Both expressions refer to the disciples' relationship to God. The same God is also the Father of Jesus. But at this point Matthew draws a sharp distinction between Jesus and the disciples. When Jesus speaks of his own relationship to God, Matthew always chooses '*my* Father in heaven' (7.21; 10.32,33; 12.50; 16.17; 18.10, 19) or '*my* heavenly Father' (15.13; 18.35). We also find this difference in the two verses which frame the parable of the stray sheep (18.10: '*my* Father in heaven'; 18.14: '*your* Father in heaven'). There is no doubt that this choice of words has a redactional character.

The result of this analysis is that Matthew has worked over the parable intensively and in so doing has been guided by problems within the church of his own time. I would want to compare what happens here with an old house that is being refurnished so that it becomes habitable for followers of Jesus from a later period.

Luke's redaction

At the beginning of the parable the second person plural is used ('What man of *you*'), as in Matthew ('What do *you* think?'). In both Gospels the audience are thus directly involved in the parable. In Matthew the disciples have to form a judgment on the parable; in Luke the Pharisees and the scribes must get under the skin of the shepherd: what would they do if they had a hundred sheep and one of them got lost? On the basis of the fact that Luke contains many other texts in which Jesus puts a question beginning with 'Which of you' (11.5, 11; 12.25; 14.5, 28; 17.7), we may assume that the beginning of 15.4 has been formulated by him.[6]

In Matthew it is far from clear whether the shepherd will see his quest crowned with success. He really does go in search of his sheep, and finds it purely by chance. Luke makes the shepherd head straight for the sheep. Three times it is said that he does find the sheep. However, that is not the end of the story. For Luke, the moment of finding forms the start of a sequel which is absent from Matthew: the shepherd puts the sheep on his shoulders and begins to make others share in his joy. He acts in the same way as the woman who has found her coin:

15.6	15.9
he calls together his friends and his neighbours, saying to them, 'Rejoice with me, for I have found my sheep which was lost.'	she calls together her friends and her neighbours, saying to them, 'Rejoice with me, for I have found my coin which was lost.'

The behaviour of the woman is completely normal; after all, she is in the inhabited world and while she is celebrating, the nine other coins cannot go missing. By contrast, the shepherd must first go home before he can let his neighbours and friends share in his joy. All this time the sheep which have been left are wandering around untended in the wilderness. It would have been more obvious for the shepherd to have returned to his flock without delay. This inconsistency betrays the fact that 15.6 found its way into the parable only later. That this verse has no counterpart in Matthew's version reinforces this suggestion. Probably Luke assimilated the parable of the sheep to the parable of the coin at this point; he formulated 15.6 on the basis of 15.9.

The concluding verse (15.7) deserves extended discussion. This verse mentions a sinner who repents, and righteous who need no repentance. Such a double explanation is unusual in a parable. As a rule the application is limited to one point of comparison. It would have been enough for 15.7 to have told us that the joy in heaven over a sinner who repents is just as great as the joy of a shepherd who has found a lost sheep. But the parable does not stop there. In passing another detail is filled in here: the ninety-nine sheep who are left behind stand for ninety-nine righteous who need no repentance. Here 15.7 takes on an allegorical slant. Furthermore it is striking that there is some incongruity between the application and the image that is developed. 15.7 speaks of 'repent' (an activity which is performed by sinners themselves: they return to the community), whereas 15.4 speaks of a shepherd who goes after the lost sheep and not of a sheep which finds its way back to the flock by itself. The parable (15.4–6) and the application (15.7) thus do not fit together quite seamlessly.

Probably Luke himself formulated an important part of 15.7. This verse contains words that flow easily from his pen. The clearest example of this is 'sinner'. This word fits the context admirably (15.1–2: 'sinners'; 15.18, 21: 'sin'). The parable is told to remove the offence at Jesus' contacts with sinners. In Luke 'sinner' occurs so often that we could say that it is one of the Third Evangelist's favourite words.[7] The sinner is expected to convert, and when that does happen, he or she receives forgiveness of sins. This process is expressed with three clusters of lexemes: (a) sin, sinner, a sin; (b) repent, repentance; (c) forgive, forgiveness. Table 11 lists those cases in which Luke combines at least two of the three clusters.

The closest parallel to 15.7 is 5.32. This verse runs as follows: 'I have not come to call the righteous but sinners to repentance.' The common points are the opposition between righteous and sinners and the combination of 'sinners' with 'repentance'. On the basis of all this it is certain that Luke himself had a hand in the formulation of 15.7.

Sin/sinner/a sin	Repent/repentance	Forgive/forgiveness
1.77		1.77
3.3	3.3	3.3
5.20–24		5.20–24
5.30–32	5.30–32	
7.36–50		7.36–50
11.4		11.4
13.1–5	13.1–5	
15.1–2, 7, 10, 18, 21	15.7, 10	
17.3–4	17.3–4	17.3–4
24.47	24.47	24.47

Table 11: Three word clusters in Luke

The conclusion of this analysis of Luke 15.4–7 is that in Luke, too, the original parable is hidden under a redactional layer.

In search of the Q text

We have found traces of redaction in both evangelists. The Q text has not been taken over unaltered by either Matthew or Luke. The question now is whether, starting from their versions and removing the redactional elements, we can put down on paper the basic text used by both of them.

In this connection we must pay attention again to Luke 15.7. Although this verse displays clear traces of redaction, the basic framework comes from the tradition. That is evident from the agreements with Matthew 18.13b:

Luke 15.7   I say to you... there will be joy... over... more than over ninety-nine... who not

Matthew 18.13b   I say to you... he rejoices... over... more than over ninety-nine... who not

It is important that in Luke these words belong to the application, whereas in Matthew they are part of the image developed. Which of the two has best kept the original place? Here we face a dilemma: it can be indicated as follows:

• Matthew has used elements from the original application of the Q parable in 18.13b, and that original conclusion still glimmers through in Luke 15.7;

or

• In 15.7 Luke provides us with an allegorically coloured exposition of a more original statement which has still been preserved in Matthew 18.13b.

With this dilemma we come to the limits of what we can reasonably know. Whichever solution we choose, the result is always highly hypothetical. Most exegetes prefer the first option.[8] For the sake of clarity I would point out that the parable within this variant was already accompanied by an application in Q. The remains of the original application are said to be preserved in Luke 15.7.

The alternative, the second option, is defended by J.Dupont.[9] In his view, the parable was not given an explanation in Q. Luke and Matthew have both added their own applications to the parable (Luke 15.7 or Matthew 18.14). According to Dupont, the parable itself has been best preserved in Matthew. The argument he gives for this is that the Greek text of Matthew 18.12–13 is stylistically far less polished than the version in Luke. In Matthew the parable (the developed image) consists of two parallel assertions which are introduced with 'if it happens' (*ean genētai*). The first of these relates to the seeking, the second to the finding of the stray sheep. Both assertions start from the same presupposition: that one sheep is worth more than the ninety-nine others. That is why the shepherd leaves his sheep behind untended, and that is why he rejoices more over that one sheep than over the rest of his flock. So there is a quantitative disproportion which can be expressed mathematically as $1 > 99$.

For a reconstruction of the parable in Q I shall follow Dupont's proposal. Beside it I have set once again the version of Matthew and Luke. I have indicated in bold the points at which they have kept the original.[10]

Matthew

What do you think? If it happens that a man has a hundred sheep, and one of them has gone astray, will he not leave the ninety-nine on the mountains and go to look for the stray one? And if it happens that he finds it, truly I say to you, he rejoices over it more than over the ninety-nine that did not go astray. So it is not the will of your Father in heaven that one of these little ones should be lost.

Q

If it happens that a man has a hundred sheep and he has lost one of them, will he not leave the ninety-nine on the mountains and go to look for the lost sheep. If it happens that he finds it, I say to you: he rejoices over that one more than over the ninety-nine which were not lost.

Luke

What man of you, who has a hundred sheep, and has lost one of them, does not leave behind the ninety-nine in the wilderness, and go after the lost one, until he finds it? And when he has found it, he lays it on his shoulders, rejoicing, and when he comes home, he calls together his friends and his neighbours and says, 'Rejoice with me, for I have found my sheep which was lost.' I say to you, So there will be (more) joy in heaven over one sinner who repents than over ninety-nine righteous persons who need no repentance.

In this survey it still has to be pointed out that the literary context in which we find the parable in Matthew and Mark has been created by the evangelists themselves. We can no longer discover what the context of the parable was in Q. All that is clear is that the parable of the sheep was already coupled with the parable of the lost coin at that stage.

So what we lack is information about the communicative situation in Q. At most we can expand the Q parable with 'Jesus said', but we have no way of discovering *to whom* he said it. Matthew and

Luke have embedded the parable in a narrative framework – each in his own way. Matthew makes the parable function within an extended instruction of Jesus to the disciples (viz. the community); Luke weaves it into a dispute with the Pharisees and the scribes.

However, I do not want to end with this cloud of ignorance as far as the Q text is concerned. The pains we have gone to in reconstructing the Q version would not be worthwhile if we could not go on to make any other meaningful statements about the presumed tenor of the Q version. A clear answer to this question cannot be given, but some interesting possibilities can be considered.

1. In Q, the parable functioned either as polemic or exhortation. By polemic I mean that the image of the shepherd and the sheep is applied to rebut critics. Their criticism is perhaps expressed in the taunt of 'this generation' which comes from Q, that Jesus is a glutton and a drunkard, a friend of toll collectors and sinners (Matthew 11.19; Luke 7.34). The original setting of the Q parable is still clearly visible in the narrative framework formulated by Luke (15.1–2). The critics, who are not identified in more detail in Q ('this generation'), are identified by Luke with the Pharisees and the scribes. However, we cannot exclude the possibility that the criticism in Q was also expressed by other persons or groups. By exhortation I mean that the parable in Q must be regarded as a challenge to 'the lost' (whoever they were: poor, sick, sinners, or others who were marginalized) to be aware that precisely because of their precarious situation they deserve special care and attention.

2. From whom are they to expect this care and attention? Here too we can give two answers. The first is that the parable shows God's care for the lost. In his eyes those who have been pushed aside as worthless are particularly valuable. The second possibility is that the quantitative disproportion which is expressed in the parable may be regarded as the compass by which Jesus travels in his indefatigable attempts to find people who are at the periphery of society or the community of faith and bring them home. These two answers are not mutually exclusive. Jesus makes God's concern his own agenda; or, his ministry shows how concerned God is for the lost.

The original tenor of Q proposed here is reworded by both

Matthew and Luke. The two evangelists make efforts to keep the parable 'readable' for later followers of Jesus too. In their re-reading they have remained faithful to the original without taking it over literally. Matthew emphasizes the function of the parable as exhortation and shows that God himself is specially concerned for the little ones in the community of faith. Luke emphasizes the polemical function of the parable more strongly and sees the pattern of behaviour described here becoming reality in Jesus' contacts with toll collectors and sinners.

8

John and the Synoptics

A bird's-eye view

John plays no role in the two-source theory. His Gospel is a separate narrative. In its present form it is later than the Synoptic Gospels. Usually its definitive redaction is dated between 90 and 100. However, we may not conclude from the late dating that this book contains material only from the period in which it came into circulation in written form. On the contrary, the Fourth Gospel is the fruit of a long process of growth, the roots of which lie far in the past. This Gospel is mediated by an authoritative figure, the beloved disciple, who may have belonged to the circle of Jesus' first followers.

After the prologue (1.1–18) the events related begin with the witness of John, who was baptizing in Bethany, on the other side of the Jordan. The book ends with appearances of the risen Jesus. From a global perspective the beginning and the end are the same as in the Synoptics. However, between the two extremes we find material which in many respects is totally different. That is immediately evident when we note the ordering of time and the topographical framework.

In the Synoptic Gospels Jesus is first active for some time in Galilee; after that he travels off to Jerusalem, where he is arrested within a week and crucified on the orders of Pilate. Because the feast of passover is mentioned only once, namely in the passion narrative, these Gospels give the impression that the whole public ministry of Jesus lasted only one year.

In John Jesus travels to Jerusalem four times (2.13; 5.1; 7.10; 12.12), each time on the occasion of a Jewish feast. Large parts of the narrative take place in this city (2.13–3.21; 5.1–47; 7.10–10.39; 12.12–20.29). In 2.13–3.21 and in 12.20–20.29 the passover is mentioned. In 6.2 the passover is mentioned once more, but then Jesus is by Lake Tiberias. So in total we have three passovers. The first takes place at the beginning of Jesus' activity, the last at the end of the book (a great deal of the book is devoted to this third passover). Because each time a year passes between two passovers, the total duration of Jesus' activity comes to around two years. In 5.1 a Jewish feast is mentioned without being specified more closely; if a passover is also meant here, the total activity of Jesus in John has a duration of around three years.

Already in a first survey of John we see that this Gospel contains a great deal of material that we do not find in (one of) the Synoptics. Technically speaking this is special material. The phenomenon in itself is not particularly striking, but its large scale is. The best-known examples include the wedding at Cana (2.1–11), the nocturnal conversation with Nicodemus (2.23–3.21), the dialogue with the Samaritan woman (4.1–42), the raising of Lazarus (11.1–46) and the extended farewell discourses in connection with the footwashing (13.1–17.26). Conversely we see that large parts of the Synoptics are missing from John. The Fourth Gospel contains no parables and only twice speaks of the kingdom of God (3.3,5).

Despite all the differences, some of the material from John does have a parallel in the Synoptics. Here I am referring to pericopes, not to detached verses (if we were also to count this last category, the number of parallels would come out much higher). I already remarked above that the Fourth Gospel too begins with the ministry of John. Another agreement with the Synoptic Gospels is that from the beginning of his activity Jesus is surrounded by disciples. The closer parallels include the cleansing of the temple (2.13–22), the feeding of the five thousand (6.1–15) and the miraculous crossing of the lake which is attached to that (6.16–21), Peter's confession (6.67–71), the anointing in Bethany (12.1–8) and the entry into Jerusalem (12.12–19). Reference can also be made to some incidents during the last gathering of Jesus with his disciples before his death (13.21–30: Judas will betray him; 13.36–38: Peter will deny him). The agreements are particularly great in the passion

narrative (18.1–19.42) and the group of stories about Jesus' resurrection and his appearances (20.1–29; in 21.1–11 an affinity can be
detected with Luke 5.1–11).

In this chapter I shall set two passages from John alongside related parts of the Synoptic Gospels. I have chosen the narrative of the
cleansing of the temple and the narrative of the women at the open
tomb. In my discussion each time I shall indicate the points at
which the text of John does or does not correspond with the
Synoptic versions. The comparison raises the burning question
how the Johannine text relates to the three other Gospels.[1]

Stories about the cleansing of the temple

John 2.13–22

13 And the Passover of the Jews was at hand, and Jesus went up to
Jerusalem. 14 In the temple he found those who sold oxen and sheep and
pigeons, and the money-changers at their business. 15 He made a whip of
cords and drove them all, with the sheep and oxen, out of the temple. And
he dashed the coins of the money-changers on the ground and threw
down their tables 16 and he said to those who sold the pigeons, 'Take
these things away! You shall not make my Father's house a house of
trade.' 17 His disciples remembered that it was written, 'Zeal for your
house shall consume me.'

18 The Jews then said to him, 'What sign have you to show us for
doing this?' 19 Jesus answered them, 'Destroy this sanctuary, and in three
days I will raise it up.' 20 The Jews then said, 'It has taken forty-six years
to build this sanctuary, and will you raise it up in three days?' 21 But he
spoke of the sanctuary of his body. 22 When therefore he was raised from
the dead, his disciples remem-bered that he had said this; and they
believed the scripture and the word which Jesus had spoken.

John 2.13–22: structure and meaning

The narrative consists of two parts (2.13–17 and 2.18–22).[2] The
first describes the action performed by Jesus, and in the second this
incident is the subject of a fierce discussion with 'the Jews' (in John
this term designates the enemies of Jesus; however, the word is also

used in a more neutral and even in a positive sense). One subtle detail is that 2.13–17 speaks of 'the temple' (in Greek *to hieron*, a designation of the whole complex of buildings), whereas in 2.18–22 this term is replaced by 'the sanctuary' (in Greek *ho naos*, a designation for the dwelling place of the deity, compare 'my Father's house' in 2.16). Both parts end with a remark about the disciples. According to 2.17 they already sense now that Jesus' action will result in his violent death (expressed with a quotation from Ps.69.10).[3] According to 2.22 it is only at a much later stage, after the resurrection, that the disciples began to sense what Jesus had meant by his cryptic assertion that he would raise up the sanctuary (see also 12.16). Now the readers are already told the true meaning of the statement that has been made (2.21): Jesus is himself the new sanctuary, the place where God dwells among us (1.14) and is worshipped in spirit and truth (4.23–24). By the reference to Jesus' suffering and death (2.17) and by the mention of his resurrection (2.22) the narrator anticipates the great drama with which he concludes his book in chapters 18 to 20. The story told here indicates in miniature something that will be played out at length there. Already the very first visit of Jesus to Jerusalem thus stands in the sign of the events which will take place on his last visit to the city, again on the occasion of a passover.

The second part of the narrative is constructed as follows: (a) the Jews put a question (2.18); (b) Jesus gives an ambiguous answer (2.19); (c) his conversation partners do not understand this answer because they take it literally (2.20); (d) the narrator informs the readers of the correct meaning of Jesus' statement (2.21). We repeatedly find this pattern, with the necessary variations, in John.[4] In a large number of texts we see how an ambiguous or metaphorical statement by Jesus is taken literally by his conversation partners (the Jews, but also the disciples, or an individual like Nicodemus, the Samaritan woman, Martha and Peter), whereas a deeper meaning is meant, which is then given by Jesus himself or the narrator.[5] The statements referred to here relate to Jesus' origin and his mission, and above all to the climax of his activity: his suffering, death and resurrection, which together are referred to as his exaltation or glorification. The intention is of course that the reader should pick up the deeper clue and not accept the more obvious, superficial meaning. In this sense the texts in which a misunderstanding is expressed serve as guides. They also indicate how the readers can guard against excessively obtuse attacks on their faith from outside.

John 2.13–17 and the Synoptic versions

The cleansing of the temple is also described in the Synoptic Gospels. However, there the literary context is completely different. In the Synoptics the incident takes place only towards the end of Jesus' life, and forms the direct occasion for his arrest (see Mark 11.18 and the parallel in Luke 19.47). In John the narrative stands almost at the beginning; it functions as an overture and indicates in a programmatic way Jesus' attitude to the authorities in Jerusalem. Despite his bold action in the temple area, afterwards Jesus can still show himself freely in the city. Only much later do the high priests and the Pharisees decide that he must die (11.47–53). The cleansing of the temple plays no role in that decision; the direct occasion is the raising of Lazarus. But John too makes a connection with Jesus' death: in the conversation following the cleansing of the temple he makes Jesus announce that his enemies will kill him.

In this connection it is also important to note that according to Mark Jesus pays a visit to the temple after his arrival in Jerusalem; there he surveys everything, but because it is already late, he leaves the city again to spend the night in Bethany. Only next day does the cleansing of the temple take place. In Matthew and Luke Jesus performs his action immediately after entering the temple on the day of his arrival in Jerusalem. In John's version, too, Jesus' arrival in Jerusalem and the action in the temple area follow directly after each other.

The next step is for us to make a detailed comparison of the four versions. We shall do that on the basis of a literal translation, which cannot take note of all the nuances of the original Greek text.

John 2.13–17

13 And the Passover of the Jews was at hand, and Jesus went up to Jerusalem. 14 In the temple he found those who sold oxen and sheep and pigeons, and the money-changers at their business. 15 He made a whip of cords and drove them all, with the sheep and oxen, out of the temple. And he dashed the coins of the money-changers on the ground and threw down their tables 16 and he said to those who sold the pigeons, 'Take these things away! You shall not make my Father's house a house of trade.' 17 His disciples remembered that it was written, 'Zeal for your house shall consume me.'

Matthew 21.12–13

12 And Jesus entered the temple and drove out all those who sold and bought in the temple, and he overturned the tables of the money-changers and [also] the seats of those who sold pigeons. 13 And he said to them 'It is written, "My house shall be called a house of prayer."' But you make it a den of robbers.'

Mark 11.15–17

15 And they went to Jerusalem. And having entered the temple he began to drive out those who sold and those who bought in the temple, and he overturned the tables of the money-changers and the seats of those who sold pigeons. 16 And he would not allow anyone to carry anything through the temple. 17 And he taught them, and said, 'Is it not written, "My house shall be called a house of prayer for all people"? But you have made it a den of robbers.'

Luke 11.15–17

45 And having entered the temple he began to drive out those who sold, 46 saying to them, 'It is written, "My house shall be a house of prayer"; but you have made it a den of robbers.'

All versions consist of a description of Jesus' action, followed by an elucidation given by him. John has a number of words in common with the other texts all along the line. The agreements are most numerous when we put John alongside Matthew (see Table 12).

lexemes	John	Matthew	Mark	Luke
the temple	X	X	X	X
those who sold	X	X	X	X
drive out	X	X	X	X
say	X	X	X	X
write	X	X	X	X
[God's] house	X	X	X	X
a house of...	X	X	X	X
the money-changers	X	X	X	
the tables	X	X	X	
those who sold pigeons	X	X	X	
Jesus	X	X		
all	X	X		
make (present tense)	X	X		
to Jerusalem	X		X	
TOTAL	14	13	11	7

Table 12: Verbal agreements between John 2.13–17 and the Synoptic versions

The comparison also shows that John 2.13–17 contains some details which are absent from the Synoptics: there is mention of oxen and sheep (2.14, 15); Jesus makes a whip of cords (2.15); he throws the coins on the ground (2.15); Jesus' words to those who sell doves begin with 'Take these things away!' (2.16);[6] the narrator mentions the effect of Jesus' action on the disciples (2.17).

The many agreements in vocabulary cannot be coincidental. There are two possible explanations: (a) in writing his narrative John made use of one of the Synoptic versions, probably Matthew; (b) John is going back to an oral tradition from which the Synoptic texts also originated.

Model (a) seems attractive, but this model gives no explanation of the extra details. If Matthew is John's only source, the extra details must be regarded one by one as elements which have been inserted by the redactor of the Fourth Gospel in order to make the narrative more lively. Model (b) offers more scope. The extra details fit admirably into the situation described (the commercial activity around the cult). Therefore we can assume that John drew them – or at least some of them – from oral tradition. If this is correct, it implies that he has preserved this tradition in a purer form than the Synoptics, who concentrate more on some main lines (this is most markedly the case in Luke's extremely sober version).

Parallels to John 2.18–22

The second part of the text (John 2.18–22) also contains points of contact with material from the Synoptics. The question of the Jews about a sign with which Jesus can legitimize his action (2.18) resembles the question about Jesus' authority ('With what authority do you do this? Who has given you the authority to do this?' See Matthew 21.23; Mark 11.28; Luke 20.2).

Even more interesting is Jesus' answer in John 2.19. This verse has a parallel in various other writings:

John 2.19	Destroy this sanctuary and in three days I shall raise it up.
Mark 14.58	We have heard him say: I shall destroy this sanctuary made with human hands and in three days build another which is not made by human hands.
Matthew 26.60	This man said: I can destroy the sanctuary of God and build it in three days.
Mark 15.29	Aha, you who destroy the sanctuary and build it in three days…
Matthew 27.40	You who destroy the sanctuary and build it in three days…
Acts 6.14	We have heard this man [= Stephen] say: Jesus the Nazorean will destroy this place…
Gospel of Thomas, logion 71	I shall destroy [this] house and no one will be able to build it up.

The formulations diverge markedly. All the texts have 'sanctuary' (in Greek always *naos*) except Acts ('this place') and Thomas ('this house'). Moreover Acts occupies a special position, in that it speaks only of destroying and not of building up. In all the other versions we find the combination of two contrasting verbs. In John this pair is given as 'destroy' and 'raise up'. He does not speak of building up because for him the statement must relate both to the temple and to the body of Jesus.

Diversity is also the word when we note the subjects of the two verbs. In John the Jews are the subject of 'destroy', while Jesus is the subject of 'raise up'. This division of roles is connected with the fact that the redactor of the Fourth Gospel has related the logion on the one hand to the death and on the other to the resurrection of Jesus. In Mark and Matthew Jesus is the subject of the two verbs, in Acts and Thomas Jesus is the subject of the verb 'destroy' only.

An extra complication is finally that the logion is in a different context in each case. In John it is directly connected with the cleansing of the temple. In Mark and Matthew the statement occurs twice, first in the narrative about the hearing before the Sanhedrin and afterwards in the narrative about Jesus' crucifixion. Luke has not included the logion in his Gospel but in Acts, where Stephen is accused by false witnesses of having said that Jesus would destroy the temple. In the last three authors the logion is to some degree left hanging.[7] It is quoted by speakers who claim that Jesus once made this statement ('he said' or 'we have heard him say') without indicating precisely when he said it.

If we survey these facts, the feeling comes over us that here we have a tangle which is almost impossible to sort out. However, I would venture to say something about the origin of the logion here. I shall put forward my proposal in three steps:

1. Given the distribution over divergent currents of tradition, a logion must have circulated at an early stage in which Jesus speaks of the destruction and restoration of the temple. It is uncertain whether he assigned himself an active role in this event. He could have announced the destruction and rebuilding of the sanctuary, while leaving open by whom that would be done.

2. The original setting of this logion has been best preserved in John, where the logion is still connected with Jesus' short but fierce

action in the temple area, which in fact involved a disturbance in the normal process of offering sacrifice. His action could easily be understood as a frontal attack on the whole activity of the temple.

3. In Christian communities the logion took on different connotations at an early stage. It was related to Jesus' death and resurrection. At this stage the statement was given an indication of time ('in three days'). The original meaning continues to echo in texts in which the logion is quoted by speakers other than Jesus himself in order to accuse him or to mock him.

Redactional emphases in John 2.13–22

There are still many questions about the origin of John 2.13–22. But it is certain that the narrative has old roots. In creating his narrative the author of the Fourth Gospel has had recourse to oral tradition. We find traces of that in the extra details in 2.13–17 and in the temple logion in 2.19. In addition he may have been inspired at some points by the written texts of the Synoptic Gospels, in particular by Matthew's version.

However, it is most interesting that the redactor has put his own stamp on the facts that he uses. In his case deep reflection on the old material has led to new perspectives. He has put the old story of the cleansing of the temple at the beginning of his book. In so doing, from the beginning he indicates that the authority of Jesus is far greater than that of the temple authorities in Jerusalem.

Another sign of redaction is that the narrative contains a quotation from Psalm 69.10. This quotation is part of the narrator text. In the Synoptic versions we find two quotations from Isaiah.56.7 and Jeremiah.7.11 combined; these quotations are spoken by Jesus. In the Johannine text Psalm 69.10 functions as an early announcement of Jesus' suffering and death. The tenor of the quotations in the Synoptic versions is quite different. They show that Jesus' action must be understood along the line of the Old Testament prophetic criticism of the actual functioning of the temple. The texts from Isaiah and Jeremiah do not announce the end of sacrifice but argue for a purification of it (hence Jesus' action is usually referred to as the cleansing of the temple).

The redactor of the Fourth Gospel is not particularly interested in the eschatological function of the temple but allows himself to be guided by a christological interest. This is also evident from his thorough working over of the temple logion in 2.19. The original and literal meaning of this statement still glimmers through in the reaction of Jesus' conversation partners. They understand his words as a reference to the temple complex rebuilt by Herod. In the eyes of the redactor this is an inadequate interpretation, a mis-understanding. According to him the logion has deeper connota-tions; it refers to the person of Jesus, to his death and resurrection. In 2.22 the author himself says that this is a new interpretation which saw the light in the period after the resurrection and was the fruit of deep reflection in the circle of 'the disciples'. By already mentioning this new interpretation at the beginning of his book he indicates that his Gospel must be read throughout in the light of the Easter faith. For the circle around the author, the Jerusalem temple has lost its significance. The original and literal interpreta-tion of the temple logion is held only by enemies of the Johannine community (here called 'the Jews'). For the community itself the person of Jesus stands in the foreground: he is the true temple, he is God's abode on earth; the zeal of the Father is his only driving force, his ministry is crowned in his death and resurrection.

Stories about the women at the open tomb

In all the canonical Gospels we find a narrative about women at the open tomb. First I shall discuss the versions of Mark (16.1–8), Matthew (28.1–10) and Luke (23.56–24.12); then I shall ask how the parallel from John relates to this trio.[8]

Mark 16.1–8

The Gospel of Mark originally broke off with the report in 16.8 that the women fled from the tomb and told no one about their experiences. Towards the beginning of the second century the book was enlarged with 16.9–20, which speaks of the appearances of Jesus. This passage has been added to assimilate the conclusion of Mark to that of the other Gospels.

Mark 16.1–8 consists of three parts: the women go to the tomb (16.1–4), they enter the tomb (16.5–7), and they flee from the tomb (16.8). The second part forms the heart of the narrative: in the tomb the women hear from a young man clothed in white that Jesus has been raised to life by God and that the disciples will see Jesus again in Galilee. This shining message is anticipated in the first part, which says that the sun had already risen and that the stone at the entry to the tomb had been rolled away. In the last part the readers hear to their amazement that the women tell no one anything about their special experiences.

The story told by Mark goes back to an earlier tradition. In the rendering which follows I have put the elements taken from the tradition in italics.

> 1 And when the sabbath was past, *Mary of Magdala, Mary of James, and Salome* bought spices, so that they might go and anoint him. 2 And *very early on the first day of the week they went to the tomb*, when the sun had risen. 3 And they were saying to one another, 'Who will roll away the stone for us from the opening of the tomb?' 4 And looking up, they saw that the stone was rolled away – it was very large. 5 *And entering the tomb, they saw a young man sitting on the right side, dressed in white, and they were very alarmed. 6 But he said to them, 'Do not be alarmed; you seek Jesus of Nazareth, who was crucified. He is raised to life, he is not here. See the place where they laid him.* 7 But go, tell his disciples and Peter, "He is going before you to Galilee; there you will see him, as he told you."' 8 *And they went out and fled from the tomb; for fear and dismay had come upon them*; and they said nothing to any one, for they were afraid.

If we assume that the young man is a heavenly messenger (his clothing points in this direction), then the tradition used has the characteristics of an epiphany. Fixed ingredients of such a narrative are: the sudden appearance of a heavenly figure to people who are terrified by it; the heavenly being proclaims a message which is accompanied with a sign; the recipients of the message are very alarmed. In this case the message relates to Jesus' resurrection from the dead. This event is discussed by means of a fixed formula which the earliest Christian communities used when expressing their belief in Jesus (see for example I Corinthians 15.3–5). The resurrection itself is not described. This silence expresses the feeling that this event escapes normal perception.

Mark has connected the narrative taken from the tradition with the narrative about Jesus' suffering and death. Some elements from 16.1–2 can be understood from this perspective. The indication of time at the beginning of 16.1 ('when the sabbath was past') recalls the fact that Jesus was buried shortly before the beginning of the sabbath (15.42). The purchase of the spices makes a connection with the purchase of the linen cloth by Joseph of Arimathea (15.46). The fact that the women want to go to anoint Jesus recalls the story about the anointing of Jesus by an anonymous woman (14.3–9). The rising of the sun (16.2) contrasts with the darkness which had covered the whole land for some hours shortly before Jesus' death (15.33). Probably all these elements are redactional.

The remarks about the stone in 16.3–4 have been inserted by Mark on the basis of 15.46 (Joseph seals the rock tomb with a stone). The discovery that the stone has been rolled away is the direct preparation in the narrative as we now have it of the special experiences of the women after they have entered the tomb.

The command in 16.7 to go to Galilee similarly points to redaction. Here the young man repeats the words of Jesus from 14.28 ('after my resurrection I shall go before you to Galilee'). It is interesting that the movement mentioned here (from Jerusalem to Galilee) is the opposite to the movement in 10.32 (from Galilee to Jerusalem); both according to 10.32 and according to 16.7, Jesus goes out before his disciples. The redactor has developed the end of the narrative (16.8a: the women flee in terror from the tomb) with the report that they tell no one anything because they are afraid (16.8b). In combination with 16.7 this note gives a particular picture of the women: they do not carry out the task that they have been given. Thus Mark emphasizes that the women display the same behaviour as the disciples earlier in the book. As a rule the disciples, too, do not live up to expectations (see above all 4.40; 6.51b–52; 8.17–21). By bringing this out again now, at the end of his Gospel, Mark lays a heavy burden on the readers: they have to react differently from the characters from the book and without delay go after the risen Jesus.

Matthew 28.1–10

Matthew reports the message to the women in the same way as Mark. In the rest of his narrative he goes his own way. For the sake of clarity I give the two versions side by side, marking in italics the wording which the two have in common (in the Greek).

Mark 16.1–8

1 And when *the sabbath* was past, *Mary of Magdala, Mary* of James, and Salome, bought spices, so that they might go and anoint him. 2 And very early *on the first day of the week* they *went* to the tomb, when the sun had risen. 3 And they were saying to one another, 'Who will *roll away the stone* for us from the opening of the tomb?' 4 And looking up, they saw that the stone was rolled away – it was very large. 5 And entering the tomb, they saw a young man *sitting* on the right side, dressed in *white* robe, and they were very alarmed. 6 And he said to them, 'Do *not* be alarmed; *you seek Jesus* of Nazareth, *who was crucified. He is raised to life, he is not here. See the place where* they laid him. 7 But go, *tell his disciples* and Peter, "*He is going before you to Galilee; there you will see him*, as he *told you*." 8 *And they went* out and fled *from the tomb*; for fear and dismay had come upon them; and they said nothing to any one, for they were *afraid*.

Matthew 28.1–10

1 After *the sabbath*, towards the dawn of *the first day of the week*, *Mary of Magdala* and the other *Mary* went to look at the tomb. 2 And behold, there was a great earthquake; for an angel of the Lord descended from heaven and came and *rolled away the stone*, and *sat* upon it. 3 His appearance was like lightning, and his raiment was *white* as snow. 4 For fear of him the guards trembled and became like dead men. 5 But the angel said to the women, 'Do *not* be afraid; for I know that *you seek Jesus who was crucified. 6 He is not here*; for *he is raised to life*, as he said. Come, *see the place where* he lay. 7 Go quickly and *tell his disciples*, "He is raised from the dead, and behold, *he is going before you to Galilee; there you will see him*." Behold, I have *told you*.' 8 *And they went* quickly *from the tomb* with fear and great joy, and ran to tell his disciples. 9 And behold, Jesus met them and said, 'Hail!' They went to him, took hold of his feet and knelt before him. 10 Then Jesus said to them, 'Do not be *afraid*. Go and tell my brothers to go to Galilee; there they will see me.'

The differences indicate that Matthew has thoroughly rewritten the narrative and enriched it with new perspectives.

The four indications of time in Mark 16.1–2 have been reduced by Matthew to two temporal statements: 'after the sabbath, towards the dawn of the first day of the week'. In place of three women he has only two appearing, both of who are called Mary (the same two are mentioned in 27.61). They go to *look* at the tomb. This element suggests that Jesus' death is not the bitter end; the women are still reckoning with a sequel. Matthew drops the statement that the women buy spices and want to go to anoint Jesus, and he also leaves out the women's question who will take away the stone. Matthew uses the fact that the stone at the entry to the tomb was particularly large in Matthew 27.60 (there Mark speaks simply of 'a stone').

A new element in 28.2–3 is that the women are confronted with a great earthquake. Jesus' death is also accompanied by this natural phenomenon: an earthquake made the rocks split, so that many dead could leave their tombs (27.51–54). In the Bible earthquakes are often mentioned in connection with the dawn of the end-time. With Jesus' death and resurrection salvation is definitively breaking through. The young man in Mark is changed into an angel from heaven. Matthew also has an angel appear at the beginning of his Gospel to make it clear that human history is under the direction of heaven (1.20,24; 2.13,19). The angel rolls away the stone and goes to sit on it. So he is outside the tomb (not in the tomb, as in Mark). Matthew first describes the appearance of the angel (cf. Daniel 10.6) and then his clothing (cf. Daniel 7.9). The order is the same as in 17.2, where it is said of Jesus that his face began to shine like the sun and that his garments became as white as snow. As in Mark, the event of the resurrection is not described. The angel removes the stone not to give free access to Jesus; he does so to show the women that Jesus is no longer in the place where Joseph of Arimathea had laid him in their presence.

Verse 4 has been inserted by Matthew. The content refers to facts from the context which are also peculiar to Matthew. On the cross Jesus was guarded by soldiers (27.54). The high priests and Pharisees put a guard on the tomb and seal the stone (27.62–66).

They take these measures to prevent Jesus' followers from taking away his body and going to tell the people that he was risen from the dead. In 28.11–15 the guard is ordered by the high priests and the elders to spread the rumour that the disciples have stolen the body of Jesus from the tomb while they were sleeping. In exchange for this mission they are paid a substantial sum of money. Matthew does not conceal the fact that this anti-story was still going the rounds in his time. He tries to defuse it by setting his own story over against it: the message about the resurrection of Jesus has not been made up by Jesus' followers, but is based on a heavenly revelation.

In 28.5–7 the angel speaks to the women, not to the guards. They must not be afraid, while the guards are seized with fear. Matthew reverses the order of the two statements in Mark 16.6 ('he is raised, he is not here'). He first mentions that Jesus is no longer in the tomb. The opposition also starts from this assumption: at any rate to explain that phenomenon, the Jewish notables make the soldiers spread the rumour that the body has been stolen. Matthew gives a completely different explanation: Jesus has been raised to life by God. The angel draws attention to the fact that Jesus had already announced this ('as he has said', cf. 16.21; 17.23; 20.19). That Jesus has been raised from the dead is repeated once again in 28.7. The women have to go to tell the disciples that they will see Jesus again in Galilee (this rendezvous takes place in 28.16–20). Peter is not mentioned by name, while in Mark 16.7 he is. The angel insists that the women go and perform their task quickly (see also 28.8: they went quickly from the tomb). He does not end his words with a reference to a saying of Jesus (as in Mark 16.7: 'he has told you') but with a reference to his own authority ('I have told you'); this brings out once again that the message of the resurrection is of heavenly origin and cannot be dismissed as human fraud (27.64).

Matthew 28.8 diverges strongly from Mark 16.8. The women go away from the tomb without it needing to be mentioned that they go out, since Matthew has not taken over the remark in Mark 16.5 that the women entered the tomb. The women are afraid, but at the same time filled with great joy. In Mark they are utterly distressed.

The most important difference is that in Matthew the women in fact obey the angel's command and go quickly to convey their message to the disciples.

Matthew has expanded the narrative with an appearance of Jesus to the two women (28.9–10). This part is probably redactional. Jesus repeats the words of the angel from 28.7. The positive reaction of the women to their encounter with the risen Christ (they grasp his feet and kneel before him) takes up the positive tones in 28.8. In Matthew, kneeling down is an expression of respect for Jesus which occurs often (in 28.17 the eleven male disciples fall on their knees before him).The narrative about the appearance confirms that the testimony of the angel is correct: by appearing, Jesus shows that he has indeed been raised from the dead.

In his retelling Matthew puts much emphasis on the reunion of Jesus with his disciples (announced in 26.32 and in 28.7,10 and in fact brought about in 28.16–20). Apart from a heavenly revelation, the belief in Jesus' resurrection is based on the experience of the disciples that Jesus is again in their midst (28.20: 'I am with you always, to the consummation of the world').

Luke 23.56–24.12

Luke is also based on Mark 16.1–8. The elements which are in agreement are printed below in italics.

Mark 16.1–8	Luke 23.56–24.12
1 And when *the sabbath* was past, *Mary of Magdala, Mary of James*, and Salome bought *spices*, so that they might go and anoint him. 2 And very early *on the first day of the week they went to the tomb*, when the sun had risen. 3 And they were saying to one another, 'Who *will roll away the stone* for us from the opening of *the tomb*?' 4 And looking up, they saw that *the stone* was *rolled away* – it was very large.	56 On *the sabbath* they rested according to the commandment. 1 But *on the first day of the week*, at early dawn, they *went to the tomb* taking the *spices* which they had prepared. 2 And they found *the stone rolled away* from *the tomb* 3 and *entered*, but they did not find the body of the Lord Jesus. 4 While they were perplexed about this, behold, two men stood by them in dazzling apparel. 5 And as

5 And *entering* the tomb, they saw a young man sitting on the right side, dressed in white, and they were very alarmed. 6 But he said *to them*, 'Do not be alarmed; *you seek* Jesus of Nazareth, who was crucified. *He is raised to life, he is not here.* See the place where they laid him. 7 But go, tell his disciples and Peter, "He is going before you *to Galilee*; there you will see him, as *he told you*."' 8 And they went out and fled *from the tomb*; for fear and dismay had come upon them; and they said nothing to any one, for they were afraid.

they were frightened and bowed their faces to the ground, the men said *to them*, 'Why do *you seek* the living among the dead? 6 *He is not here*, but *he is raised to life*. Remember how *he told you*, while he was still in *Galilee*, 7 "The Son of man must be delivered into the hand of sinful men, and be crucified and on the third day rise."' 8 And they remembered his words, 9 and returning *from the tomb* they told all this to the eleven and to all the rest. Now it was *Mary of Magdala* and Joanna and *Mary* the mother *of James* and the other women with them who told this to the apostles, 11 but these words seemed to them an idle tale, and they did not believe them. 12 But Peter rose and ran to the tomb; stooping and looking in, he saw the linen cloths by themselves, and he went home wondering at what had happened.

In mentioning the most important differences I shall first point out the changes. Luke 24.1 ('the spices which they had prepared') follows on closely from 23.56 ('they prepared spices and balsam'). The indication of time 'very early' in Mark is changed to 'at early dawn'. The names of three women are given; that happens only in 24.10. Mary of Magdala and Johanna have already followed Jesus from Galilee (see 8.2–3). Mark's young man is changed into 'two men' (cf. Acts 1.10), who suddenly stand before the women. The women's reaction of terror is formulated differently from in Mark. The two men rebuke the women for seeking the living among the dead: there is no such rebuke in Mark 16.6. The order of the two statements in Mark 16.6 ('he is raised to life, he is not here') is changed round by Luke (here there is an agreement with Matthew

28.6). The most incisive change is to be found in 24.6–8. There is no mention of a future reunion in Galilee. Instead, the women are reminded of what Jesus said earlier in Galilee (cf. 9.22). This reference is connected with the composition of Luke-Acts: the Third Gospel begins in Galilee and ends in Jerusalem, while Acts begins in Jerusalem and ends in Rome. So at the end of his Gospel Luke cannot refer to an appearance in Galilee; the encounters with the risen Jesus all take place in Jerusalem or in its immediate environs (24.13–35, 36–49; in 24.49 Jesus impresses on his followers that they must remain in the city until they are endowed with power from above; according to 24.53 they observe this command). The last change is that the women obey the command of the two men and give an account to the eleven and all the others. The mention here – as in 24.13, 33 – of a wider circle is connected with the beginning of Acts, where a successor to Judas is chosen from this company.

Some elements have been omitted by Luke. The conversation on the way about the stone has dropped out. This is connected with the fact that there is no mention in 23.53 that the tomb has been closed with a stone. The remark in 24.2 ('they found the stone rolled away from the tomb') thus hangs completely in the air.

There are also a couple of insertions. In Luke Jesus is called 'the Lord' thirty-six times; in 24.3 'the Lord Jesus' is used for the first time. Thus the narrator gives Jesus a new status (this new name occurs fifteen times in Acts!). The women do not find Jesus' body in the tomb. That this confuses them is understandable, given that they were the witnesses to his burial (23.55). Another new element is that the women recall the earlier words of Jesus (24.8). Finally, the narrative has been expanded with the disbelieving reaction of the apostles (this term occurs six times in Luke and twenty-eight times in Acts), and is rounded off by a visit of Peter to the tomb.

Some lines become evident in the differences from Mark. Luke emphasizes that the women from Galilee were eyewitnesses to Jesus' death and burial; they are also the first to hear that he is alive. The discovery that Jesus' body is not in the tomb does not lead the women to believe in the resurrection. The change takes place only when the women remember the words that Jesus spoke during his lifetime. Luke here provides the Easter faith with a new foundation: it is based on words of Jesus. In connection with this it is said in 24.25–27, 44–47 that it is based on all that can be found about Jesus in the scriptures.

John 20.1–18 and the Synoptic versions

1 On the first day of the week Mary of Magdala went to the tomb early, while it was still dark, and saw that the stone had been taken away from the tomb. 2 She ran to Simon Peter and the other disciple, the one whom Jesus loved, and said to them, 'They have taken the Lord out of the tomb, and we do not know where they have laid him.'

3 Peter and the other disciple went towards the tomb. 4 The two were running together, but the other disciple outran Peter and reached the tomb first. 5 He stooped to look in and saw the linen cloths lying there, but he did not go in. 6 Simon Peter came, following him, and went into the tomb; he saw the linen cloths lying, 7 and the napkin, which had been on his head, not lying with the linen cloths but rolled up in a place by itself. 8 Then the other disciple, who had reached the tomb first, also went in, and he saw and believed, 9 As yet they did not know the scripture, that he must rise from the dead. 10 Then the disciples went back to their homes.

11 But Mary stood weeping outside the tomb. And as she wept she stooped to look into the tomb; 12 and she saw two angels in white, sitting where the body of Jesus had lain, one at the head and one at the feet. 13 They said to her, 'Woman, why are you weeping?' She said to them, 'Because they have taken away my Lord, and I do not know where they have laid him.' 14 Saying this, she turned round and saw Jesus standing, but she did not know that it was Jesus. 15 Jesus said to her, 'Woman, why are you weeping? Whom do you seek?' Supposing him to be the gardener, she said to him, 'Sir, if you have carried him away, tell me where you have laid him, and I will take him away.' 16 Jesus said to her, 'Mary.' She turned and said to him in Hebrew, 'Rabboni!' (which means teacher). 17 Jesus said to her, 'Do not hold me, for I have not yet ascended to the Father; but go to my brethren and say to them, "I am ascending to my Father and your Father, to my God and your God."' 18 Mary of Magdala went and said to the disciples, 'I have seen the Lord'; and she told them what he had said to her.

This narrative corresponds in a number of points with the Synoptic versions (see Table 13).

John	Matthew	Mark	Luke
Mary of Magdala	28.1	16.1	24.10
she goes to the tomb	28.1	16.2	24.1
early		16.2	24.1
on the first day of the week	28.1	16.2	24.1
the stone before the tomb has been taken away/rolled away	28.2	16.4	24.2
Jesus has been taken away from the tomb/stolen	28.11–15		
Peter runs to the tomb			24.12
stoop (20.5, 11)			24.12
the beloved disciple/Peter sees the linen cloths			24.12
(from) the dead	28.7		24.5
rise			24.7
go back home			24.12
	angels/an angel		28.2, 5
two			24.4
sitting	28.2	16.5	
clothed in white	28.3	16.5	
the body of Jesus			24.3
the angels address Mary	cf.24.5–7	cf. 16.6–7	cf.24.5–7
Jesus appears to Mary	28.9		
she does not immediately recognize Jesus (24.16,37)			
Jesus repeats the words of the two angels/ the angel	28.10		
seek	28.5	16.6	24.5
hold/touch Jesus	28.9		
Jesus calls the disciples his brothers	28.10		
Mary has to perform a task	cf.28.7, 10	cf.16.7	
Mary gives an account to the disciples			cf.24.10

Table 13: Agreements between John 20.1–18 and the Synoptic versions.

In addition to this list I want to point out two subtle agreements. (a) In John Jesus appears to Mary only on her second visit to the tomb, and not on her first visit. This last corresponds with the versions of Mark and Luke: there too the women go to the tomb without seeing Jesus. (b) From the moving of the stone Mary concludes that Jesus has been taken out of the tomb (20.2, 13, 15). In 20.2, 13 she thinks of more than one perpetrator ('they'). We also find in Matthew that Jesus has been taken out of the tomb. In both cases we encounter a polemic against the idea that the emptiness of the tomb can be explained by the theft of the body. In the case of Matthew that is clear from 28.11–15. In the case of John we can point to 20.6–7: the linen cloths are still there, but the napkin which had covered Jesus' head is not lying with the other cloths but has been rolled up and is lying quite separately. These details function as an argument against the idea that robbers have hastily made away with the dead body.

The many agreements indicate that there is a relationship between John 20.1–18 and the Synoptic versions. The relationship can be indirect or direct. Indirect: John 20.1–18 derives from traditions which have also been used in the Synoptics. Direct: the redactor of John 20.1–18 has used the Synoptic versions (above all Matthew and Luke are relevant here).

Redactional emphases in John 20.1–18

Mary goes to the tomb for the first time when it is still dark (20.1). In John, darkness is connected with the absence of Jesus (see also 6.17).

Mary goes to the tomb by herself. That originally at least two women were mentioned still glimmers through in 20.2, where Mary uses the plural ('*we* do not know'). If this observation is correct, the redactor has adapted the tradition at this point: he has eliminated the other woman (women) and given Mary a special position.

The introduction of Simon Peter and the other disciple in 20.2 serves to prepare for the narration in 20.3–10. Here too traditional material is used. In it Peter appears by himself (cf. Luke 24.12).

This is confirmed by the fact that the verb at the beginning of 20.3 in the Greek text is in the singular (*exēlthen*). According to the tradition used here Peter himself is said to have paid a visit to the tomb after the return of the women, but from the phenomena which he perceived there he did not draw the conclusion that Jesus had risen from the dead. The redactor has adapted the tradition by making Peter appear in the company of 'the disciple whom Jesus loved', a character who was also already a witness to the death of Jesus (19.26; see further 13.23; 18.15 (?); 19.35; 21.7,20; elsewhere too the beloved disciple is often mentioned in combination with Peter). There was some rivalry between these two. We also see that here. The beloved disciple is the first to reach the tomb, but Peter is the first to enter. It is reported at length what exceptional phenomena Peter perceives in the tomb (20.6–7), whereas it is said of the beloved disciple that after entering the tomb he 'saw and believed' (seeing without an object is already enough to lead him to believe). Thus the Fourth Evangelist makes the beloved disciple react in a more adequate way than Peter. This is connected with the fact that for him the beloved disciple is the foundation of the community for which he is writing his Gospel.

The connections between 20.1–18 and the narrative about the raising of Lazarus also point to redaction. The most striking of these is the mention of the napkin which had covered Jesus' head (cf. 11.44: Lazarus comes out, his feet bound with bandages and his face wrapped in a cloth). The connection also suggests a contrast: Jesus removed the shroud himself, while Lazarus has to be freed from it by others. We also find connections with 11.1–44 in 20.1 (Mary goes to Jesus' tomb; 11.38: Jesus goes to Lazarus' tomb) and in 20.11, 13, 15 (Mary stands weeping; the same word is used in connection with her namesake from Bethany: 11.31,33).

The two angels, their white clothes and their seated position come from tradition. We find similar details in the Synoptic versions. In the Synoptics the women learn from the heavenly figure (or figures) that Jesus has been raised. In John the angels ask only why Mary is weeping so. Here Mary learns from Jesus himself that he has overcome death.

After her conversation with the angels Mary comes to see Jesus himself. In Matthew we see the same sequence of events: after the women have been instructed by the angel, they have an encounter with Jesus, who repeats the command given by the angel ('Go and tell my brothers...'; the term 'my brothers' also occurs in John 20.17!). However, the comparison again draws attention to a remarkable difference: in Matthew it is the angel who speaks of Jesus' new mode of existence ('he is raised from the dead'). This part of his words is not repeated by Jesus in Matthew 28.10. In John, Jesus repeats the question of the two angels why Mary is weeping so, whereupon she once again expresses her suspicion that Jesus has been taken from the tomb; but in this version it is Jesus himself who draws Mary's attention to his new position (20.17).

The description of Jesus' new status is given completely in Johannine terms: he is ascending to the Father. This description corresponds to the vocabulary of the farewell discourses (John 13–17). The formulation indicates redaction.

At the end it is reported that Mary in fact carries out the task which is given to her. Here the text is directly opposed to the report in Mark 16.8, but is along the lines of the versions of Matthew and above all of Luke. In Matthew it is not explicitly reported that the women indeed carried out their task, but in view of 28.16–20 we may assume that they in fact did so. Luke says explicitly that the women went to tell 'the eleven and all the others' everything. He adds that in the eyes of the apostles the women's story is nonsense and that they did not believe them. This last statement is absent from John: the reaction of Jesus' brothers is not mentioned there.

Conclusion

The agreements indicate an indirect or direct relationship with the Synoptics. The differences can be explained one by one in terms of the particular interests of the redactor. It is not necessary to attribute the divergent elements to an old tradition which would be separate from the Synoptics. Surveying all the evidence, I think it probable that John has used the Synoptic narratives about the women at the empty tomb and rewritten them from his own theological perspective.

Part III
The window of intertextuality

9

Intertextuality and the Gospels

With this chapter we get into quite a different channel: we now move on the almost infinite sea of intertextuality. This word comes from the Latin (*intertexere* = interweave, weave with something) and denotes the fundamental interweaving of texts. They are linked by all kinds of threads. Together they form a fabric which time and again changes colour when a new text is added to the existing arsenal.

No one can survey the whole of this gigantic network. In that sense it is unreadable. We see parts of the network when we steep ourselves in a concrete text. A text speaks about things which are also mentioned in other texts. In reading it we compare the content of the text with the content of other texts. Those who write texts also do this. In reading and writing we are continually in dialogue with other texts in one way or another.

These general remarks also apply to the Gospels. The mere fact that there are four of them in the New Testament leads us to compare them with one another. A particular characteristic of the Gospels is that they constantly refer to Old Testament texts. In this chapter I shall investigate whether the theory of intertextuality which has recently been developed gives us a new view of this phenomenon.

The theory of intertextuality

Two camps

In the last twenty-five years a good deal of attention has been paid in literary theory to the concept of intertextuality. It was introduced by Julia Kristeva to indicate that every text functions in a colossal universe which includes not only the total corpus of literary texts but also the social and cultural order in which that corpus is embedded.[1] Other theorists hastened to tame this wild concept. To avoid the danger of readers losing themselves in arbitrary and subjective connections which are far from being under control, they limited the concept to connections deliberately made by the author when setting down the text on paper. Readers must allow themselves to be led by these more or less compelling relationships and must not all too quickly get involved in connections which lie outside the author's field of view.

This split is the reason why intertextuality in biblical exegesis is still in its infancy.[2] Kristeva's broad view is not very attractive, since her description is not intended for the analysis of concrete texts. Nor can too limited an idea of intertextuality arouse enthusiasm, for in this case intertextuality is no more than a new label for investigations which have long been carried out in biblical exegesis: we are back to the author and his use of earlier texts and traditions. Fortunately there is still a broad channel between these two extremes which I shall now attempt to map.

A profile of intertextual study

An intertextual study is focussed on the relations between text A (in our case a text from the Gospels) and one or more texts from other books. The comparison of texts from the same book does not fall under intertextual investigation. In the comparison we must take account of the position of the texts on the chronological axis. A later text can never influence an earlier text. In principle an intertextual analysis can start with either the earlier text or the later text; in the first instance we are investigating what traces the text has left in later texts; in the second case we are studying how far the later text contains echoes of earlier texts.

Whether there is in fact a relationship between the texts of which we want to make an intertextual analysis need not be established from the start. The aim of the analysis can also be to answer this question with a yes or a no in a reasoned demonstration. If this question were not put regularly, we would uncritically limit ourselves to texts which already at first sight clearly refer to texts from another book.

An innovative fact is that the comparison relates to textual units. Here it emerges that an intertextual study to some degree has a synchronic slant. Each of the texts to be compared has the extent of at least a pericope; of course it is also possible to combine larger textual wholes. Comparative studies sometimes sin against the synchronic perspective expressed here by being exclusively focussed on similar elements of two or more texts (identical words or similar clauses and sentences). This overlooks the fact that agreement always also implies difference. Even though two texts contain precisely the same elements, in text A they have a different meaning and function from that in text B, since in both cases they are also determined by the surrounding text.

An intertextual study does not lose itself in hypothetical reconstruction of texts and traditions which we cannot with any certainty show really to have existed on paper. The comparison always relates to texts that really exist, and in their final redactional form.

An intertextual study deals more with the differences than with the agreements between texts. In the case of a mechanical repetition the intertextual relationship is extremely weak. The connection is intensive when the texts make differing statements about something that they are both about. This is also the source of the phenomenon of intertextuality. A text has a particular claim to truth. A text makes a statement with the claim that this statement is valid. Precisely because of this, such a text provokes a response which is again expressed in a new text that denies, qualifies, supplements, broadens, limits, applies what is stated. If the new text only confirms old statements, there is little reason for its existence. This means that the term 'transformation' is a basic one in an intertextual analysis.

Intertextual network

From the start the Gospels are part of a particular intertextual network. In describing this we can distinguish ever wider circles. The first circle which surrounds the Gospels is formed by the rest of the biblical writings. The Gospels have in common with the other books of the New Testament that they speak of Jesus. That speaking is determined to the depths by texts from the Old Testament. Thus the Bible is itself an intertextual fabric within which later texts elaborate on earlier texts.

The Bible is in turn surrounded by a second circle, but the boundaries of this are already to some degree fluid. Within this cluster I include the early Jewish and early Christian writings which have not been included in the Bible. A number of them give an independent version of material which can also be found in the Bible; the majority of them, however, have sprung from the Bible itself and give an exposition of texts from this literary corpus.

This second cluster is in turn embedded in an even more comprehensive circle: the literature of the ancient Near East and the literary products of the Graeco-Roman world. At this third level we find material which is related to material from the two clusters mentioned earlier. Here we also come upon literary conventions which were widespread and have also left traces in texts from the first and second clusters.

Of course this intertextual network can be extended even further, but that does not make sense at this point. I shall return to the first circle, since we have not yet said everything about the Bible as an intertextual fabric.

The Gospels and the Old Testament

The name 'the Old Testament' is of Christian origin. The evangelists referred to this literary corpus as 'scripture'. At the time of Jesus and the evangelists the limits of scripture were not yet completely fixed. The Torah and the Prophets already enjoyed great authority; the Writings were also highly respected, but the extent of this group was still a matter of discussion.

The Old Testament was written in Hebrew. Our modern translations of the Bible are from the Hebrew text. We consequently tend to read the Gospels as a response to the Hebrew Bible. However, that is too simplistic. When the evangelists refer to scripture, they usually did not have the Hebrew text in mind. They made much use of the earliest Greek translation of the Old Testament, the Septuagint, which saw the light in the period between 250 and 100 before the beginning of our era. This translation was originally intended for Greek-speaking Jews and later became very influential in the earliest Christian communities.[3]

Thus scripture circulated in both Hebrew and Greek. Now a translation is never a precise replica of the original. At all events, the translation of Hebrew into Greek gave rise to differences in text and interpretation. The same Old Testament passage can in fact occur in two versions in the New Testament. One example of this is Isaiah 53.4. The rendering of this in Matthew 8.17 ('he has taken our sicknesses upon himself and borne our infirmities') is close to the Hebrew text, whereas I Peter 2.24 ('he has borne our sins') takes up the Septuagint.

The picture becomes even more complicated when we include the Targums in our consideration. A Targum is a translation of the Hebrew Bible into Aramaic – often a paraphrase. The roots of this lie in the synagogue, where during worship texts from scripture were read out in Hebrew and simultaneously translated into Aramaic by a 'translator'. This became necessary when knowledge of Hebrew declined and Aramaic had become the vernacular. The translators did not strive for an extremely literal rendering; the liturgical setting stimulated them to intersperse their translation with interpretations and updatings, also with a view to the sermon which followed the readings from scripture. All this is important for the Gospels, since in their rendering of Old Testament texts they may have been influenced by the traditions of the synagogues. Certainly we must be cautious here. At any rate, for our knowledge of the Aramaic translation – apart from some fragments from Qumran – we are dependent on written sources (the Targums) which are later than the Gospels.

What has been said leads to a clear intertextual maxim: excessively narrow lines between the Gospels and the Hebrew Bible must be avoided, for when the Gospels came into being, scripture was also circulating in other textual versions. Often the Septuagint is a link between the Hebrew text and the Gospels. We must also

remember that the Gospels are not the only or oldest interpretations of Scripture. In their exposition they are also influenced
by the contemporary Jewish exegesis of the Hebrew Bible.

Quotations

Quotations represent a specific form of intertextuality which is
very much present in the Gospels and deserves a separate discussion.

A quotation is the inclusion of a segment of text A in text B. The
quotation can extend from a single word to complete sentences. In
present-day literary texts such borrowings are put in quotation
marks and they correspond word for word with the source text. In
the Gospels their presence is marked by the writer only in a limited
number of cases, by an introductory formula. These formulae
display a great variety. Sometimes they mention the part of
scripture referred to ('Moses' or 'the Law' or 'the Prophets') or the
book of the Bible from which the quotation comes ('the prophet
Isaiah', 'the prophet Jeremiah', 'the Psalms'), but they can also be
limited to the report that the authority of scripture is involved ('it
is written'; 'God has said'; 'have you not read that...?', 'this word
of scripture must be fulfilled'). In a number of passages the
Gospels contain quotations which are not provided with such a
marking. It is then up to the readers themselves to discover that a
quotation is involved here; whether they succeed depends on their
knowledge of the Old Testament and their feeling for sudden
transitions to another vocabulary or differences in style. Finally,
there are many cases in which there really is no quotation but at
most an allusion (there is a link in content with a segment of the
Old Testament, though the formulation is completely different).

In the Gospels 'quotation' is blurred term. On the one hand
there are quotations with a maximal possibility of recognition
(explicit quotations); on the other there are quotations with a
minimal possibility of recognition (implicit quotation). In between
there are all kinds of transitional forms that we cannot name precisely because our conceptual apparatus is not sufficiently refined.

Even explicit quotations seldom coincide exactly with the source
text in one of the versions of the Old Testament known to us. As a

rule some words are added, omitted or changed, with the obvious intention of making the quotation suitable for the function which it has to fulfil in its new literary context. This is true to an even greater degree for more implicit quotations; the divergences from the source text are so great here that they are not immediately recognizable as a quotation.

An explicit quotation functions as a powerful signal that parts of an earlier text have been used in the text. I like to compare such a quotation with the tip of an iceberg. The quotation is immediately visible. There is a good chance that other more hidden references to the text from which the quotation has been made can be found in the vicinity of that quotation.

An important function of a quotation is to bring about a reciprocal effect between the Old Testament text from which it comes and the text from the Gospels in which it is used. A quotation is an old and well-known voice in new company. By being included in a new context the old words take on a new meaning and function. In other words, a transformation takes place in the meaning that these words and sentences had within their own original context. Despite its integration into a new context, the quotation still preserves characteristics of the meaningful unit within which it originally belonged. A quotation makes a text polyphonic.

This provides an important rule for an intertextual analysis. We may not limit ourselves to an analysis of the meaning and function of a quotation in its new literary setting. No, to get a clear view of the transformation that has come about we must also investigate what the segment quoted meant in its original setting. That brings the distinctive colouring of the Gospels to light all the better. In this way we also allow the Old Testament texts to retain their own evocative force and do not burden them with meanings which they received only by being included in the Gospels.

Intertextual aspects of Matthew 4.1–11

I shall now discuss some passages from the Gospels with an Old Testament background. The first example is Matthew 4.1–11, the narrative about Jesus' tempting by the devil.

4.1 Then Jesus was led up by the Spirit into the wilderness to be tempted by the devil. 2 And he fasted forty days and forty nights, and afterwards he was hungry. 3 The tempter came and said to him,

> 'If you are the son of God, command these stones to become loaves of bread.'

4 And he answered,

> 'It is written: "Man shall not live by bread alone but by every word that proceeds from the mouth of God."'

5 Then the devil took him to the holy city, and set him upon the pinnacle of the temple, 6 and said to him,

> 'If you are the son of God, throw yourself down; for it is written, "He will give his angels charge of you," and, "On their hands they will bear you up, lest you strike your foot against a stone."'

7 Jesus said to him,

> 'Again it is written, "You shall not tempt the Lord your God."'

8 Again, the devil took him to a very high mountain, and showed him all the kingdoms of the world and the glory of them; 9 and he said to him:

> 'All these I will give you if you will fall down and worship me.'

10 Then Jesus said to him,

> 'Begone, Satan, for it is written, "You shall worship the Lord your God and him only shall you serve."'

11 Then the devil left him, and behold, angels came and ministered to him.

This text derives its coherence largely from the four explicit quotations which are used in it. They are all introduced by 'It is written'. Three of these are spoken by Jesus in reply to the devil. They are taken from the book of Deuteronomy, but in turn the sentences quoted from Deuteronomy point back to incidents in the book of Exodus, so that we can speak of an intertextual link:

Matthew 4.4 ➤	Deuteronomy 8.3 (see 'the manna') ➤	Exodus 16
Matthew 4.7 ➤	Deuteronomy 6.16 (see 'as in Massa') ➤	Exodus 17.1–7
Matthew 4.10 ➤	Deuteronomy 6.13 (or 10.20)	➤ Exodus 32 as a clear example of the opposite

In their formulation the quotations in Matthew take up the Septuagint, which shows some small differences from the Hebrew text. The freest is the quotation in Matthew 4.10: the 'worship' used here is an echo of the words of the devil in 4.9 and goes against the Hebrew text and the Septuagint, which speak of 'fear' (= be in awe of).

That the original context of a quotation leaves traces in the New Testament text can well be illustrated in this case from the quotation from Deuteronomy 8.3. In the surrounding verses it says that God *led* the people of Israel *forty* years through *the wilderness*, *put* them *to the test*, made them *suffer hunger* and brought them up as someone brings up his *son*. The words in italics recur at the beginning of the narrative in Matthew. Obviously this narrative about Jesus must be read as a haggadic midrash, a narrative exposition of the narrative about Israel's stay in the wilderness: Jesus goes the same way as Israel. The agreements make the differences stand out all the more sharply: the people is put to the test by God, while Jesus is tested by the devil; Israel failed (it put God to the test), while Jesus brilliantly withstands the test.

In Matthew 4.6 the devil uses an explicit quotation from Psalm 91.11a, 12 (v.11b has been omitted, otherwise the quotation is identical with the Septuagint version). He quotes the psalm to seduce Jesus into an audacious piece of trust in God. The text quoted by the Satan is defused by Jesus' reference to Deuteronomy 6.16. The validity of the psalm is thus put up for debate by a text from the Torah. At the end of the narrative the psalm text does come true, but not in the way meant by the devil: angels indeed come to Jesus to serve him.

In 4.3, 6 ('if you are the son of God...') the devil takes up the explicit reference to Psalm 7 made by God in 3.17 ('this is my beloved son'). The satan is out to force Jesus to make a wrong interpretation of his divine sonship. Under the surface Psalm 2 has a major role in Matthew 4.8–10 without being explicitly quoted. In his third test the devil twists the words of the psalm. His perverse interpretation can be clarified as follows:

The devil offers Jesus lordship over the world	God gives his son, the messianic king, lordship over the whole earth (Psalm 2.8).

| Jesus has to kneel in worship before the devil | The people must serve God and be subject to his son (Psalm 2.11–12). |

The relations referred to in the psalm are restored in Matthew 28.16–20, the closing passage of the First Gospel. Like 4.8–10, this conclusion also takes place on a mountain. Jesus declares to his disciples that all power has been given to him in heaven and on earth. He has received this rule, which far surpasses the offer made by the devil, from God, the only one who according to Psalm 2.8 can give it. In 4.9 Jesus is invited by the devil to fall in worship before him; in 28.17 the disciples fall on their knees before Jesus and thus show him the reverence which according to Psalm 2 is due to him. The closing scene in Matthew thus corrects the wrong interpretation of the psalm given by the devil.

On the heels of Elijah: Luke 7.11–17

11 Afterwards he went to a city called Nain, and his disciples and a great crowd went with him. 12 As he drew near to the gate of the city, a man who had just died was being carried out, the only son of his mother, and she was a widow, and a large crowd from the city was with her. 13 When the Lord saw her, he had compassion on her and said to her, 'Do not weep.' 14 And he came and touched the bier, and the bearers stood still. And he said, 'Young man, I say to you, arise.' 13 And the dead man sat up, and began to speak. And he gave him to his mother. 16 Fear seized them all; and they glorified God, saying, 'A great prophet has arisen among us!' and 'God has visited his people!' 17 And this report concerning him spread through the whole of Judaea and all the surrounding country.

The trained reader will immediately connect this brief narrative with a similar narrative in I Kings 17.17–24, in which Elijah raises a dead child. The agreements and differences are indicated in Table 14.

I Kings 17.17–24	Luke 7.11–17
The narrative takes place in Zarephath, which comes under Sidon, and does not have any other characters than Elijah, the mother and her child.	The narrative is set in Nain in Galilee. Jesus is in the company of his disciples and a large crowd; the cortege consists of many people from the town.
The dead child is the only son of a widow. She rebukes Elijah for being the cause of the death of her child. In his prayer Elijah rebukes God for letting the child die.	The dead child is the only son of a widow. Jesus has compassion on her. No rebuke is expressed.
Elijah puts the boy on a bed in the upper being room, where he is alone with him.	The boy lies on a bier and is taken out of the town, surrounded by many people.
Elijah prays to God and then stretches himself upon the child three times, meanwhile asking God to restore the spirit of life to the child. In the Septuagint it says that he breathes on the child three times.	Jesus touches the bier and says to the dead child, 'Arise'.
The boy is restored to life. In the Septuagint he utters a cry.	The boy man sits up and begins to talk.
Elijah gives the child to his mother (in the Septuagint *kai edoken tei metri autou*).	Jesus gives the child to his mother (in Greek *kai edoken tei metri autou*).
The story ends with the recognition by the woman that Elijah is a man of God and that God really speaks through his mouth.	The narrative ends with the recognition by the crowd that Jesus is a great prophet and that God has visited his people.

Table 14 Two narratives about the raising of a dead child

Here we encounter a special form of intertextuality: the two narratives belong to the same kind of text (the raising of a dead person). That explains why they have the same pattern. In addition they have a few details in common: the dead person is the only son of a widow; the young man brought to life utters a cry or begins to talk. The most striking thing is that the Septuagint formulation in I Kings 17.2b ('he gave him to his mother') recurs word for word in Luke 7.15b. The agreements here are such that we can speak of a quotation. They show that the narrative has been created by Luke in the image and likeness of the narrative about Elijah. This sheds a specific light on the concluding reaction of the crowd. That Jesus is a great prophet can only mean that he is put in a line with Elijah, who is himself described as a man of God.

The intertextual relationship is also combined with some transformations. In Luke the action is transferred to the land of the Jews, to Galilee, while the narrative from I Kings takes place in the region of Sidon, beyond the frontiers of Israel (see Luke 4.25–26, where there is a reference to I Kings 17.1–16). The town of Nain is not far from Shunem, where Elisha, Elijah's successor, raises a child to life (II Kings 4.18–37). In I Kings the raising takes place in complete privacy, before preparations are made for the burial, while the incident in Nain has a public character and the story about Jesus's action spreads like wildfire over the whole region. There are great differences in the way in which the raising of the dead itself is described. In the case of Elijah the child revives only after the prophet has performed a threefold action. From the combination of his action with prayer it is evident that God is the real giver of life. The Septuagint underlines this by using *enephusēsen* (he breathed: I Kings 17.21), which occurs in Gen.2.7 in connection with the creation of a human being by God. In the case of Jesus the action remains limited to a simple gesture (touching the bier), which is accompanied with just as simple a word, 'arise'. This term is chosen with an eye to the combination of quotations in Luke 7.22 ('the dead are raised up') with which Jesus answers John's question whether he is the expected bringer of salvation. From the reaction of the crowd it is nevertheless evident that God's life-giving power also forms the background to Jesus' successful intervention.

An implicit quotation in John 18.19–24

In John 18.19–24 Jesus is interrogated by Annas before being sent to Caiaphas and Pilate. The interrogation is about the disciples and the teaching of the man who has been arrested. In 18.20–21 Jesus answers as follows:

20 'I have spoken openly to the world; I have always taught in synagogues and in the temple, where all Jews come together, and I have said
nothing secretly. 21 Why do you ask me? Ask those who heard what I
have said to them; they know what I have said.'

This reply contains an implicit quotation from Isaiah 45.18–19.
Such an almost unrecognizable allusion can establish a very
intensive intertextual relationship, as I hope to show here. First I
shall give a translation of the sentence from Isaiah to which I am
referring:

18 Thus says YHWH,
who created the heavens – he is God –,
who formed the earth and made it – he established it –,
who did not create it a chaos, but formed it to be inhabited:
    'I am YHWH and there is no other.
    19 I did not speak in secret, from a place in a land of darkness,
    I did not say to the offspring of Jacob:
        "Seek me in chaos."
    I, YHWH, speak what is right and proclaim what is righteous.'

The prophet introduces this passage with 'Thus says YHWH', but
before God himself speaks he is characterized three times from his
work of creation: he is the creator of the heavens, the maker of the
earth and the one who has seen that the earth is habitable.[4] The
God who has created the world has also formed Israel, Jacob's seed.
This last is expressed in the embedded direct speech (vv.18e–19).
The words of God have a clear structure: they begin and end with
'I... YHWH'; these sentences frame two other sentences, both of
which begin with a firm denial ('I did not'). In the two outermost
sentences God states that he alone is God, and no one else. The
sentences introduced with 'I did not' argue this by fixing attention
on the place where God has spoken to Israel. He has not spoken in
the hiddenness of the underworld and he has not invited Israel to
seek him in chaos. No, God's word to Israel has resounded quite
publicly, in world history.

In his reply to Annas Jesus takes elements from this text. This is
clearly signalled by Jesus' contrast between 'openly' and 'secretly'.

In John, too, these terms indicate the place where the statements are uttered. The public order is coloured further within the text: Jesus has spoken 'to the world' (this domain is opposite to the chaos of the underworld from Isaiah) and 'in synagogues and in the temple, where all Jews [to be compared with Jacob's seed] come together'.

The contrast between 'openly' (or in public) and 'secretly' extends further than the scene in which Jesus is facing Annas. This scene is framed by 18.15–18 and 18.25–27, in which Peter, one of Jesus' disciples (do not forget that the interrogation by Annas is also about the disciples!) has to answer questions about his relationship with Jesus, who has been arrested. His fearful reaction contrasts sharply with the frank and free stance of Jesus. Peter tries to conceal the fact that he indeed belongs to the circle of Jesus' followers. So we could say that Peter opts for the sphere of the hidden, for the chaos which God keeps away by his word of creation. If this observation is tenable, we see how the implicit quotation used in 18.20 also leaves traces in the direct context of these verses, indeed itself determines the composition of 18.15–27.

In Isaiah God says that he is speaking what is right and proclaiming what is righteous. These words have no counterpart in John 18.20–21, but they are echoed in 18.23, where Jesus speaks to the servant who has struck him in the face as follows: 'If I have spoken wrongly, bear witness to the wrong; but if I have spoken rightly, why do you strike me?' Here too the text from Isaiah is an influence. Here it should also be noted that the words of God in Isaiah function in the framework of a legal case that relates to the peoples, whereas in John we have an interrogation in preparation for the trial of Jesus, which takes place before Pilate. A striking agreement in the situation described!

If we survey these findings, we are forced to conclude that Jesus uses words which in the Old Testament passage are in the mouth of God. By applying this intertextual procedure the narrator subtly indicates that Jesus is no usual prisoner but can lay claim to the completely unique position which according to the Isaiah text is due to God. Perhaps this is still put too weakly. We cannot exclude the possibility that the narrator also hears at work in Isaiah

45.18–19 the Logos to whom he gives voice in the prologue of his own book. Thus in the Isaiah text he does not hear the words of God but those of the Logos, who is very closely associated with God. Just as God can be characterized as the creator of heaven and earth, so too it is said of the Word that everything has come into being through him and that without him nothing has come into being (John 1.3). And just as God has spoken to Israel in the public of world history, so Jesus has spoken openly, before the whole world, to all Jews.

This example is particularly instructive. It shows that an intensive intertextual relationship is not bound up with a long and explicit quotation which is clearly marked by an introductory formula, but can also derive from a hidden allusion. For readers who can place this allusion, the New Testament text takes on a clear surplus of meaning.

Matthew 5.21–26 and the halakhah

What has been said above refers to relationships between texts from the Bible. The picture would not be complete if no reference were made to connections between texts from the Gospels and the broad stream of the oral Torah. There is a good example of this in Matthew 5.21–22: 'You have heard that it was said to the men of old, "You shall not kill; and whoever kills shall be liable to judgment." But I say to you that every one who is angry with his brother shall be liable to judgment.'

Here a reference is made to one of the Ten Commandments: 'You shall not kill'. In the Decalogue, this prohibition is formulated so pointedly that we are left with many unanswered questions. No wonder that the prohibition is the subject of extensive halakhic discussions. Many traces of them can be found in early Jewish literature, in which traditions are used which go back to the first century, the time of Jesus and Matthew. Matthew's Jesus takes part in this debate and expresses standpoints related to statements by some Jewish teachers of the law.

How does this appear from the text of Matthew? 5.21 combines a literal quotation from the Decalogue with another statement:

'Whoever kills shall be liable to judgment.' The second statement adds a sanction to the prohibition: a murderer must be brought to justice. This sanction is absent from the Decalogue itself. Certainly the Old Testament contains some texts which indicate what must happen to a murderer – but these occur outside the Decalogue. According to Exodus 21.2 and Leviticus 24.17 such a person must also be put to death. In Numbers 35.12, 30 we find a mitigation of this harsh sanction: a murderer must face the community and a statement by witnesses is required. Deuteronomy 17.8–13 also prescribes that a legal statement is required in the case of murder. The texts of Numbers and Deuteronomy want to avoid a murderer being done away with without any form of trial. Matthew 5.21 stands in the perspective of this more humanizing regulation. But the formulation is not precisely the same as in the texts from scripture which have been mentioned.[5]

A surprising new light is shed on the vocabulary of Matthew 5.21 if we put this verse next to the commentary on Exodus 21.12 in the tractate Nezikin from the Mekilta, an old midrashic collection on the book of Exodus. This word states that the sanction mentioned in Exodus 21.12 may be only carried out on the authority of the court (*beth din*). That this is the purpose of Exodus 21.12 is argued from Numbers 35.12, but in the last mentioned text the term *beth din* used by the Mekilta does not occur. That indicates that the Mekilta is bringing Numbers 35.12 up to date in the light of later forms of jurisprudence. The point now is that the *krisis* (= judgment, court) used in Matthew is an exact parallel to the term *beth din* in the Mekilta. Therefore we can assume that Matthew 5.21 not only refers back to the prohibition from the Decalogue, but in the same breath also adds a later halakhic standpoint there.[6] Thus what is said to those of old includes not only the written Torah but also the way in which this is interpreted within the oral Torah.

In his further commentary Jesus goes into the meaning of 'kill' (5.22). He equates being angry with someone else or making someone else out to be a fool with murder. This is evident from the fact that in 5.22a the same sanction is mentioned as in 5.21 ('liable to judgment'). Jesus' interpretation is in line with current developments in oral teaching. According to Jewish sources, too, someone is already a murderer if he bursts out in anger or puts another to shame, at least if this happens without any reason or in public.[7] It is striking that there are no such qualifications in Jesus' exposition. By comparison with parallels from Jewish sources his statements are more unconditional in character.

In 5.23–26 attention is shifted to positive activities (being reconciled with someone, trying to reach an agreement with someone). This is about disturbed relations between two individuals: Jesus admonishes reconciliation. But to whom is his admonition directed: to the one who has caused the split or to the injured party? The text speaks of 'a brother who has anything against you'. This expression also occurs elsewhere (Mark 11.25; Revelation 2.14; cf. also Acts 24.19). From these passages it emerges that person A has something against person B because B has done something wrong, or at least is suspected of that. This means that probably the words in Matthew 5.23–24 are also addressed to person B, to the one who caused the conflict. The perpetrator, not the victim, must take the initiative in healing the breach. The reconciliation commended here enjoys a higher priority than making a sacrifice, fulfilling cultic obligations. The mention of sacrifice confirms the reference at the beginning of the Ten Commandments, where God's honour is central. To honour him clearly calls for relations with others to be optimized.

Intertextuality: never complete and never perfect

Intertextual Bible reading is an attractive but also a risky business. It is attractive because texts become deeper when we read them alongside other texts. It is risky because not everything can be compared with everything else. To keep the material under control, each time a difficult choice must be made: what text do we relate to what text, what phenomena are involved in the comparison and what are not? Possibilities always remain undiscussed which would have been worth while discussing.

An intertextual study must be judged by the results that it produces. Has the comparison been carried out with the necessary care? Or is the analysis spoilt by things which have a subjective and arbitrary character? These questions can be put to any exegetical study. The assertions must rest on demonstrable facts in the text. It is fatal for any exegete to see that he or she is reading more into the texts than is in them.

An intertextual study can easily go off the rails, above all through a lack of knowledge and through uncritical presuppositions. A lack of knowledge of the literary genres represented in the Bible corrupts the comparison of texts with one another. So-called agreements can in fact just as well be differences because text A belongs to a different genre from text B. A lack of knowledge of the history of the development of scripture is equally fatal. That Genesis cannot contain a quotation from Mark but that the opposite can be the case will be clear even to the beginner in Bible reading, but what is to be done with complicated intertextual chains to which texts belong when it is not irrefutably clear how they relate chronologically to one another? However difficult this problem sometimes is to solve, we certainly must not deny it, for in that case we are handing ourselves over to the pernicious idea that in the Bible everything is connected with everything else and that we are completely free in making connections.

Uncritical presuppositions can also play tricks on us. An intertextual study loses its credibility if it is based on an all too fixed idea about the relationship between the Old Testament and the New. How this relationship is to be seen is the precise object of study. Here great caution is called for, since Christians all too readily see the Old Testament as an incomplete herald of the New. Everything that comes clearly to light in the New Testament is said already to lie hidden in the Old Testament.[8] In this typical Christian view the relationship between the two Testaments is fixed in the scheme of prophecy (or prefigurement) and fulfilment. This scheme has two disadvantages: (a) it does not leave enough room for the distinctive meaning of Old Testament texts; (b) it takes no account of a distinctive Jewish reading of the Tenach.

Intertextuality draws attention to the phenomenon that already in the Bible we are confronted with shifting meanings. The dynamic of this process is determined by the fact that the historical and social-religious context keeps changing. Earlier texts must constantly be re-read in the light of a new context. The tradition never becomes outdated because it constantly rejuvenates itself. So we have a never-ending recontextualization. This process is not concluded with the coming into being of the Tenach or the Christian Bible. The Jewish community and the Christian churches try to keep alive the literary heritage from the past and to renew it by relating it to new circumstances. Intertextuality is on their agenda daily.

10

Five women by Jesus' cradle

Matthew begins his Gospel with a genealogy of Jesus. A better way of surveying large parts of the Old Testament in a short space is hard to think of. The many proper names recall as many stories. This is attractive material for an intertextual study, not least because in the genealogy of Jesus five women appear among forty-two men. In this chapter I shall concentrate on these five.

I am integrating into my discussion some results of exegetical women's studies: what light is shed on the text if they are read through the eyes of women?[1] The nomenclature 'exegetical women's studies' is broader than the term 'feminist exegesis', which until recently was used very widely and gave the impression that the prime concern was to develop a separate method alongside other approaches in biblical studies. A distinctive method results in a high profile, but the disadvantage is that its influence on exegesis as a whole is quite small. The new term 'exegetical women's studies' indicates an aim which goes far wider: the feminist questions must have a place on the agenda of every exegete, no matter what method he or she is using. In the exegesis of biblical texts the masculine is often tacitly elevated to be the norm for the human; in this way feminine aspects are negated or sidelined. Not only exegesis suffers from this evil; this mechanism is also at work in the texts themselves. Women's studies make use of different reading strategies to bring out the positive images of women that lie hidden in the Bible; they also criticize images of women which are one-sidedly based on masculine ideas about women and their place in society. Because the concept of 'intertextuality' puts so much emphasis on the dialogical relationships between texts, it is particularly appropriate for this exercise.

The problem

Mention of Mary in Matthew 1.1–17 is not surprising, because she is Jesus' mother.[2] But why does the author mention four other women: Tamar, Rahab, Ruth and the wife of Uriah (Bathsheba)?

Various answers are given to this question. Usually exegetes look for a characteristic which the four Old Testament women have in common, but which does not apply to Mary. One explanation that used to be popular is that the four women are sinners who indulged in dubious sexual activities and that they were included in the family tree in order to make clear that Jesus was born to liberate people from their sins (1.21).[3] This interpretation is a classical example of an androcentric exegesis which associates women with sexuality, which connects sexuality with sin, and which shuts its eyes to the far from irreproachable reputation of many men in the genealogy.

A different explanation, which still appears frequently today, is that the four women are all of foreign origin.[4] Ruth is a Moabite, Rahab is from Canaanite Jericho, and Bathsheba's husband, Uriah, is Hittite. That Tamar is also of foreign origin is deduced from early Jewish literature. The presence of these non-Jewish people points in a universalistic direction: Jesus has alien blood in his veins. He has indeed sprung from the people of Israel, but Matthew makes it clear at the very beginning of his book that Jesus is also important for the Gentiles. This view has the drawback that it attributes to Tamar and Bathsheba a characteristic which in the Hebrew Bible is clearly applicable only to Ruth and Rahab.

These two explanations do not apply to Mary, since Mary is not a pagan woman, and the exegetes who emphasize that the Old Testament four were sinners do not go as far as to accuse Mary of sinful behaviour. The two explanations referred to are sensitive only to the contrast between Mary and the four other women.

In my opinion, we should search for correspondences, rather than contrasts, between Mary and the four other women. This too

has been done before. Different answers have already been given to
the question whether the five women possibly have something in
common. R.E.Brown speaks of 'something extraordinary or irreg-
ular in their union with their partners', a deviation from the usual
pattern; the five women show that God brings about the fulfilment
of Israel's history precisely through eccentric individuals.[5]
F.Schnider and W. Stenger speak of 'a fathering by a third agent
in another's sphere': Tamar and Bathsheba have a child by someone who is not their husband, Rahab and Ruth become mothers by
entering into a bond with someone belonging to another
people, and Mary's child is not the biological descendant of
Joseph, although Joseph is explicitly mentioned as her husband.[6]
According to J. Schaberg, what the four Old Testament women in
Matthew 1.1 – 17 have in common is that all of them have for some
time occupied a position outside the context of the patriarchal
family: each of them became the mother of a child that was open to
the suspicion of having been born as the result of an illicit affair.
Mary's pregnancy should likewise be understood against this
background. Matthew takes a stand against the suspicion that Jesus
had been fathered not by Joseph but by another man.[7]

My thesis is that Mary continues a role which Tamar, Rahab,
Ruth and Bathsheba already played in the stories from the Hebrew
Bible. I shall work this out in three stages. The first step is an
analysis of Matthew 1.1–17 and Matthew 1.18–25. In these two
passages, Mary's position is described much more fully than the
position of the four other women. What is told here about Mary is
also of importance in dealing with the question why Matthew
has included four more women in his list of Jesus' ancestors. As a
second step I shall briefly discuss some frequently forgotten
elements in the Old Testament stories about Tamar, Rahab, Ruth
and Bathsheba. These stories show that Israel's history would have
been cut short prematurely had these women not seen it as their
task to map out alternative routes to the future. The way in which
this group of four operates also sheds some light on Mary's
position. As a third step, I shall try to find a common pattern in the
stories about the five women.

Jesus' origin according to Matthew 1.1–17

The best start is the text itself. So I shall quote Matthew 1.17
below in a quite literal translation.

> 1 Book of the origin of Jesus Christ, son of David, son of Abraham.
>
> 2 Abraham fathered Isaac, Isaac fathered Jacob, Jacob fathered
> Judah and his brothers, 3 Judah fathered Perez and Zerah from Tamar,
> Perez fathered Hezron, Hezron fathered Aram, 4 Aram fathered
> Amminadab, Amminadab fathered Nahshon, Nahshon fathered
> Salmon, 5 Salmon fathered Boaz from Rahab, Boaz fathered Obed
> from Ruth, Obed fathered Jesse, 6 Jesse fathered king David. David
> fathered Solomon from the wife of Uriah. 7 Solomon fathered
> Rehoboam, Rehoboam fathered Abijah, Abijah fathered Asaph, 8
> Asaph fathered Jehoshaphat, Jehoshaphat fathered Joram, Joram
> fathered Uzziah, 9 Uzziah fathered Jotham, Jotham fathered Ahaz,
> Ahaz fathered Hezekiah, 10 Hezekiah fathered Manasseh, Manasseh
> fathered Amos, Amos fathered Josiah, 11 Josiah fathered Jechoniah
> and his brothers at the time of the exile in Babylon. 12 After the exile
> in Babylon: Jeconiah fathered Shealtiel, Shealtiel fathered Zerubbabel,
> 13 Zerubbabel fathered Abiud, Abiud fathered Eliakim, Eliakim
> fathered Azor, 14 Azor fathered Zadok, Zadok fathered Achim, Achim
> fathered Eliud, 15 Eliud fathered Eleazar, Eleazar fathered Matthan,
> Matthan fathered Jacob, 16 Jacob fathered Joseph, the husband of
> Mary, and from her Jesus was fathered, who is called messiah.
>
> 17 So in total from Abraham to David were fourteen generations,
> from David to the exile in Babylon fourteen generations, and from the
> exile in Babylon to the Messiah fourteen generations.

The genealogy (1.2–16) is framed by two sentences (1.1 and 1.17),
in which the narrator provides the list with a commentary. In 1.1
he mentions the three most important figures: Jesus, David and
Abraham. These three figures in 1.1 reappear in reverse order in
1.17: Abraham, David, the Messiah. According to this verse, the
genealogy consists of three series of fourteen generations: the
starting point is Abraham; fourteen generations later David forms
a high point; fourteen generations later still the exile is a nadir; and
after another fourteen generations the history of Israel reaches its
climax in Jesus.

The first verse stands out as a title above the whole passage:

what now follows is 'the book of the origin of Jesus Christ, son of David, son of Abraham'. The word 'origin' (in Greek, *genesis*) comprises far more than someone's birth; it also points to his coming into being, his origin or descent. Here we have the origin of Jesus Christ.

The genealogy mentions a large number of males who are linked together by the word 'fathered', repeated thirty-nine times. The repetition suggests continuity, an unbroken line. In most cases (thirty-five times) we encounter the following formula: A (a man) fathered B (also a man). Mothers and daughters remain anonymous in this summary of fathers and sons. Unexpectedly the monotonous cadence is interrupted: four times the formula is expanded with the mention of a woman:

1.3 Judah	fathered	Perez and Zerah	from Tamar
1.5 Salmon	fathered	Boaz	from Rahab
Boaz	fathered	Obed	from Ruth
1.6 David	fathered	Solomon	from Uriah's wife.

The four women are not themselves the subject of 'fathering'. They are connected with this verb by means of the preposition 'by'. The women are not mentioned until the end of the sentence: first the fathers and their sons are mentioned, and only then the mothers.

With the introduction of the four women, an entirely new pattern emerges to interrupt the old one. This new pattern is interrupted in its turn in v.16. Here Jesus is mentioned, the person whom this is all about. The text reads: '... Joseph, the husband of Mary, and from her Jesus was fathered'. All of a sudden the focus switches from Joseph to Mary. The active verb form ('fathered') is replaced by a passive form of the same verb ('was fathered'). Whereas with most of Abraham's descendants only the father is mentioned, and with only four of them a mother as well as a father, the last in the list is said to be descended from a mother who has a husband, but whose husband is not Jesus' biological father.

The special position occupied by Mary and Jesus according to 1.16 has been prepared for by the fourfold mention of women from the Old Testament. They build a bridge between the thirty-five children of whom only the father is explicitly mentioned, and the child introduced in 1.16 of whom only the mother is mentioned. The last of the four especially ('the wife of Uriah') paves the way for the introduction of Mary. Just as Solomon was not the child of Uriah, Bathsheba's husband, but of another man, King David, so too Jesus is not the biological son of Joseph, Mary's husband, but the son of..., well, of whom exactly? Readers have got used to the male subjects of 'fathering' and in fact ask themselves curiously who the father of Jesus can be. We must not prematurely silence that question by reading 'was fathered' as a periphrasis for the action of God.

Jesus' origin according to Matthew 1.18–25

Matthew's genealogy hasn't entirely explained Jesus' origin. This subject comes up again in 1.18–25. Literally translated, this passage runs as follows:

> 18 The origin of Jesus Christ was like this. His mother Mary was betrothed to Joseph, and before they came together she was found to be pregnant from the Holy Spirit. 19. Joseph, her husband, was a just man. Because he did not want to put her to shame, he decided to divorce her quietly. 20 While he was considering this, an angel of the Lord suddenly appeared to him in a dream, and said, 'Joseph, son of David, do not be afraid to take Mary as your wife, for what is fathered in her is from the Holy Spirit. 21 She shall bear a son, and you must give him the name Jesus, for he will save his people from their sins.' 22 All this took place that what the Lord had spoken by the prophet might be fulfilled: 23 *'Behold, the virgin shall conceive and bear a son, and they shall give him the name Emmanuel*, which means, *God with us.*' 24 When Joseph woke from sleep, he did as the angel of the Lord commanded him. He took her as his wife, 25 but did not have intercourse with her before she bore a son. He gave him the name Jesus.

That this passage elaborates on the genealogy can be seen by the fact that both sections are provided with a heading (which is in part the same):

1.1   Book of the origin of Jesus Christ
1.18   The origin of Jesus Christ was like this.

The connection is also evident in two other ways. (a) The passive form of 'father' which we know from 1.16 occurs again in 1.20 (b) The preposition *ek* in the Greek text of 1. 3, 5, 6, 16, is used again in 1.18, 20: In the English translation of these verses the somewhat strange 'from' is used because in the original Greek text the same preposition (*ek*) is always used:

1.3   Judah fathered Perez and Zerah from Tamar
1.5   Salman fathered Boaz from Rahab
       Boaz fathered Obed from Ruth
1.16   Joseph, the husband of Mary, and from her Jesus was fathered.
1.18   She was found to be pregnant from the Holy Spirit.
1.20   For what is fathered in her is from the Holy Spirit.

What is the meaning of 'from the Holy Spirit'?[8] Is the Holy Spirit then by any chance the father of Jesus? Is he the tacit subject of the passive verb form in v.16? We must not draw that conclusion too hastily. The Holy Spirit does not fulfil the role of the father; he is on the side of the mother. That is evident from the fact that the preposition 'from' recurs in 1.18,20, but there is combined with the Holy Spirit. His role is thus described in the same terms as that of Mary and the other four women. The Holy Spirit is not Jesus' father, but Jesus is fathered from Mary (1.16) and from the Holy Spirit (1.18,20).

The preposition 'from' makes a connection between 1.18, 20 (the Holy Spirit), 1.16 (Mary) and 1. 3, 5, 6 (the four other women). It can be inferred from 1.18, 20 that the motherhood of Tamar, Rahab, Ruth and Bathsheba was also something special. In their case, too, the influence of God's spirit manifested itself.

However, there is also a striking difference. The four women are flanked by men who are the biological fathers of their children. In Mary's case this very point, too, comes under pressure. This new aspect emerges on two different levels: (a) it is communicated by an angel to Joseph (1.20–21), who draws the appropriate conclusion from this announcement (1.24–25); (b) it is referred to by the narrator in sentences that function purely in communication with the readers (1.18,22–23).

Let's consider Joseph first. In 1.18–25 he plays an important role. The story is also told from his perspective. By contrast, Mary is not portrayed in the text as an individual acting independently. She is only the subject of the conversation; the text does not give us any definite information about what Mary knows, thinks, or does. This type of narration links up with 1.1–17, a text in which the attention paid to the active role of men in the course of Israel's history is likewise disproportionate. When Joseph comes on to the scene in 1.19, he is wrestling with the problem of what he, the male partner, must do now that he has discovered that his wife is pregnant. He can account for Mary's pregnancy only by presuming that her child has been fathered by another man. His wife still lives in her father's house, and he sees her pregnancy, with which he has had nothing to do whatsoever, as a reason for not taking her into his own house. Must he publicly repudiate her, or quietly put an end to the relationship that has already been legally sealed? Joseph is helped to solve this problem by an angel, who draws his attention to the creative role of the Holy Spirit. Joseph, convinced by the words of the angel, takes Mary into his house. By giving her child the name indicated by the angel he acknowledges fatherhood in a legal sense and recognizes Mary's child as his. Through Joseph, who is himself a son of David (1.20), Jesus can be considered a legitimate descendant of David.

The readers are supplied with more information. They clearly have an advantage. On the basis of the genealogy, they already know that women time and again were able to map out alternative routes to the future. Even before the readers learn anything about Joseph's inner struggle, they learn from the narrator the answer to the question that arose in 1.16. As early as 1.18 the narrator informs the readers that Mary is pregnant 'from the Holy Spirit'. This view is confirmed in 1.20 by the angel of the Lord and thus corroborated by a double authority. So readers must have very good reasons not to adopt this view.

In 1.22–23 the narrator interrupts his story for closer reflection on the history he is telling. These two verses also function exclusively as part of the communication between the narrator and his readers. The readers are here provided with information which is withheld from Joseph. They perceive that they must understand Jesus' origin in the light of Isaiah 7.14, a text which also speaks of a woman.

Readers who are aware of the differences between the Hebrew text of Isaiah 7.14 and the Septuagint version will be surprised again. In the Hebrew Bible this verse runs as follows: 'Behold, the young woman shall conceive and bear a son, and she shall give him the name Emmanuel.' The Septuagint here reads: 'Behold, *the virgin* shall conceive and bear a son, and *you* [= king Ahaz] shall give him the name Emmanuel.' The formulation in Matthew corresponds to the Septuagint version. By interweaving Isaiah's text with his own story, Matthew shifts the original meaning of the sentence he is quoting. The Septuagint speaks of a young girl who is still virgin (unmarried) at the moment when Ahaz receives a sign from God, but in the near future that girl will know a man and bring a son into the world. Matthew applies this text to Mary, but she is already betrothed. The quotation must make it clear that her pregnancy, which came about after she was betrothed to Joseph, was not caused by a man, whether by Joseph or by another man.

The assumption that Jesus is a special child is now sustained by scripture, indeed by the words of God himself, for in Matthew it is God himself who utters the saying from Isaiah 7.14 (1.22: 'what the Lord had spoken'). Later the same voice will be heard again. In Matthew 2.15 God speaks of Jesus as his son, 'Out of Egypt I have called my son' (quotation from Hosea 11.1). And in Matthew 3.17 a voice from heaven explains, 'This is my beloved son, in whom I am well pleased.'

At this point, all the riddles which puzzled the readers when they were first confronted with Matthew 1.16 are solved. Jesus is not Joseph's biological son, yet he can justly and rightly be called 'son of David' (1.1), because Joseph, a legitimate descendant of David, has acknowledged Mary's child as his own. It is not necessary for the reader to conclude from 1.16 that Jesus is an illegitimate child. Joseph initially got this notion into his head, but the narrator disproves the idea by all the means at his disposal.

First, he brings his own authority to bear (1.18); next, he has his announcement repeated by an angel of the Lord (1.20); finally, he refers to scripture to demonstrate that Jesus is the embodiment of God's presence in our midst (1.23: Emmanuel), indeed that he is the son of God (2.15; 3.17). Only then is Jesus' origin fully explained.

Old Testament narratives

The genealogy of Jesus is really one great intertextual web. Behind a number of names lie great stories that we can read in the Old Testament. That also applies to Tamar (Genesis 38), Rahab (Joshua 2 and 6), Ruth (Ruth 1–4) and Bathsheba (II Samuel 11–12; I Kings 1–2). In Matthew, each of these women is presented only in her role as mother. The Old Testament stories are much broader, and they also show other facets of these women's creative contribution to the building up of the house of Israel. Here is a short review of the main facts.

Tamar

In Genesis 38, Judah leaves his birthplace and goes to Adullam, where he marries a Canaanite woman. The couple have three sons: Er, Onan, and Shelah. Judah marries his eldest son to Tamar, and after Er's untimely death he has Onan take Er's place. According to the levirate law (see Deuteronomy 25.5–10), Onan, Tamar's brother-in-law, has to father a descendant for his brother who has died childless, but he shirks his duty. Thereupon God takes his life, too. Judah then sends Tamar back to her father's house; he no longer wishes to be bound by the demands of the levirate law, because he suspects that Tamar is the cause of the death of two of his children, and he does not want to risk the life of his third son.

Tamar takes active steps to ensure that the law runs its course. To secure a descendant for Er, she veils herself and goes to sit by the roadside. There she is met by her father-in-law, who thinks she is a prostitute and makes love to her. When Tamar's pregnancy becomes visible, she is charged with adultery and sentenced to the stake by Judah. Tamar confronts her father-in-law with conclusive evidence that he himself has slept with her. Judah then admits that she is a righteous woman (38.26: 'She is more righteous than I, since I did not give her to my son Shelah'). The birth of Perez and Zerah rounds off the story. In Matthew 1.1–17 and other genealogies, Tamar's two children are considered Judah's descendants.

Tamar's role can be summarized thus: by making creative use of the levirate law, she manages to keep the history of Israel from coming to a dead end with Judah.

Ruth

In Ruth 4.12 Perez is named as the son of Tamar and Judah. According to Ruth 4.18–22, Perez is David's forefather. The ten names in the genealogy with which the book of Ruth ends also occur in Matthew 1.3–6.

The mention of Tamar in Ruth 4.12 indicates that the book of Ruth and the story of Tamar are connected.[9] The story of Ruth is even stranger than that of Tamar. Ruth is a Moabite woman who experiences the early death of her husband, a man of Judah. Like Tamar, she is left childless, but while Tamar still fell under the provisions of the levirate law, this is out of the question for Ruth. Her only brother-in-law, Chilion, and her father-in-law, Elimelech, have both died. Nor can the family be continued through Naomi, Ruth's mother-in-law, since Naomi is getting on in years. A great deal of resourcefulness will be required to overcome this predicament.

Naomi and Ruth succeed through a united effort. Together they leave Moab and return to Bethlehem. This is possible only because Ruth resolutely takes sides with her mother-in-law, Naomi, her people and her God. In Bethlehem the two women fall outside the social order. In turn they take initiatives to change this situation. The initiative initially lies with Ruth: she goes gleaning and manages to attract the attention of Boaz, a distant kinsman of her mother-in-law. Naomi takes her cue from this and sends Ruth to the threshing floor where Boaz will be spending the night. This scene is sometimes used to blacken Ruth's reputation. She is supposed to have let Boaz make love to her on the threshing floor, catching him in her nets by this unfair ruse. The text itself is not so clear on this point; as the story progresses, it suggests that Ruth and Boaz have intercourse only when their relationship had been legally sealed. Anyway, Ruth succeeds in getting Boaz to act as redeemer (a redeemer watches over the family property; he must buy back land which has already been lost or threatens to be lost to the family; he also fulfils the duties which stem from the levirate law). Actually, Boaz has that duty only with regard to Naomi. An additional problem is that there is a nearer kinsman who precedes Boaz in the obligation to fulfil that duty. However, that kinsman withdraws when he learns from Boaz that he not only has to redeem Naomi's family property, but has also to marry the young Moabite woman. Ruth and Boaz marry and have a child, who is given the name Obed. The narrator ends the story with a genealogy from which it emerges that David is the grandson of Obed.

This story, too, shows women taking risky steps to build up the house of Israel. The special aspect of this story is the powerful collaboration between a Moabite woman and a woman from Judah. Together they manage to earn themselves a position in the social upper class of Bethlehem. Thanks to this pair Obed is born, the grandfather of David.

Rahab

According to Matthew, Rahab is the wife of Salmon and the mother of Boaz. Nothing can be found in the Old Testament to substantiate this assertion; the stories about Rahab in Joshua 2 and 6 speak neither of her marriage nor of her motherhood. What is more, she lived at the time of the entry into the promised land, whereas Boaz lived at the time of the judges (Ruth 1.1).

In Joshua 2 and 6 Rahab is a Canaanite woman who works as a prostitute in Jericho, where she lives detached from her clan, in a house of her own against the city wall. At the risk of her life, she takes the two Israelite spies into her house. She ignores the king's command to give the two men up and makes sure that they get away safely. Her motives for this brave action are dwelt on at length. The accounts of Israel's fortunes in the wilderness have convinced her of the special position of the God of Israel. In 2.9 she repeats the words that were previously spoken by God himself. In 1.2-3, 6, 11, 13, 15, God has announced that, true to his promise, he will give the land to Israel. Rahab's assertion in 2.9 that God has given the land to Israel is also in keeping with the creed of the author of the book. Later on in the story this same view is expressed by the spies and by Joshua (2.14, 24; 6.16). Thus Rahab, a Canaanite woman, reveals herself as someone who seeks to adopt the faith of Israel.

The two men who owe their lives to Rahab promise in turn to spare her and her entire family when Jericho is destroyed. In Joshua 6 they fulfil their promise and save Rahab and her family. According to the narrator, her family 'dwells in Israel even to this day' (6.25). This indicates that long after the entry of the Israelites, the country still had a mixed population of Israelites and Canaanites. The narrator has his own view of this historical fact. For him, it is because of Rahab's merits that the Canaanites have been able to retain their place in the country dominated by Israel. Matthew brings in this notion when he includes Rahab in the genealogy of Jesus.

Bathsheba

The three women I have discussed so far played a highly active role in Israel's history and found God on their side. Does this also apply to Bathsheba?

Stories about Bathsheba are to be found in II Samuel 11–12 and I Kings 1–2. Bathsheba is the daughter of Eliam, and is probably a member of Jerusalem's aristocratic upper class. She is married to the Hittite Uriah, who occupies a prominent position in David's army. The stories about Bathsheba picture her rise to the centre of power at the royal court. Whether she was bent on acquiring this position from the start, however, is not so clear. In the stories of II Samuel 11–12, the initiative is explicitly David's. While the army is in the field, his eye falls on her as she is bathing in order to cleanse herself after her monthly period. This last detail is not communicated to us until after David has had her brought to his palace, where he has intercourse with her. It makes it clear that the

pregnancy of which she sends word to David some time later
cannot have been caused by Uriah. Since she can now easily be
charged with adultery, she is in a very vulnerable position:
although she is still married to Uriah, she is expecting the king's
child.

Soon afterwards, David contrives Uriah's death. Perhaps Uriah
had got wind of what had happened from stories told by the
servants.[10] As soon as Bathsheba is out of mourning, David takes
her into his harem. Not until then does the narrator disclose God's
displeasure in what has happened: 'What David had done was evil
in the eyes of the Lord' (11.27). This concluding sentence of
chapter 11 is preliminary to the next chapter, in which God sends
Nathan the prophet to censure David. It is abundantly clear that
the guilty one is not Bathsheba but David. She is the victim, not
the offender. David is the sole offender. He has seized someone
else's ewe lamb. That is why here Bathsheba is always referred to
as 'the wife of Uriah' (12.9, 10, 15; cf. 11.3, 26), a designation
which we also find in Matthew 1.6.

David's adultery with Bathsheba and the murder of Uriah form
the beginning of the decline of his kingship. God causes the death
of the child born of the sexual contact between David and
Bathsheba when Uriah was still alive. After the child's death,
David and Bathsheba have intercourse again, and then she gives
birth to Solomon. The narrator asserts that God loved this child.

The text of II Samuel 11–12 does not give us any idea of
Bathsheba's feelings. It is never indicated that from the start she
was intent on placing her child on the throne. That changes in I
Kings 1–2. At that point, David is dying, and Adonijah, one of his
children from another relationship (II Samuel 3.4), proclaims
himself king. At the instigation of Bathsheba and Nathan, David
appoints Solomon his successor. Somewhat later, Bathsheba is
involved in another palace intrigue. She manages to induce
Solomon to have Adonijah done away with, since his half-brother
continues to covet the throne. In these two chapters Bathsheba
plays an active role in the turbulent period of the succession. It is
ultimately thanks to her that David's kingship is eventually passed
on to Solomon.[11]

A common pattern

The concrete details of the narratives about Mary and the four Old
Testament women differ greatly. All the same, it is not difficult to
discover some common elements.[12] I shall concentrate on five facts
and provide each with an elucidation.

1. All the texts about these women speak of a number of legal
provisions or presuppose that these provisions are known to the
reader. The legal provisions refer to sexual intercourse between
men and women, or to the rights and obligations which are connected with membership of a particular family, clan or people.
   Elucidation: In Genesis 38 and in Ruth, the levirate law plays a
role. Genesis 38 also presupposes that the reader is familiar with
the regulation that a man may not have sexual intercourse with his
daughter-in-law (Leviticus 18.15). In the stories about Tamar and
Rahab, the attitude of men towards prostitution is somewhat
ambivalent: on the one hand, they tolerate prostitution as an ordinary social phenomenon; on the other hand, a prostitute is treated
with contempt (see Leviticus 19.29; Deuteronomy 23.17a). In II
Samuel 11 David sins against several of the Ten Commandments:
he covets someone else's wife (against Exodus 20.17), he commits
adultery (against Exodus 20.14) and he kills Uriah (against Exodus
20.13). Because Mary is already betrothed to Joseph, she may not
have sexual relations with a third man (Deuteronomy 22.23–24).
The reader is also aware that the rape of a virgin who is already
betrothed will be severely punished (Deuteronomy 22.25–27).

2. The narratives start from a situation in which the women occupy
a protected position within their family, clan, or people in
accordance with legal provisions or with customary law.
   Elucidation: Tamar becomes Er's wife and subsequently Onan's,
and so is part of Judah's family. Naomi is initially married
to Elimelech, a male member of the prominent family of the
Ephrathites from Bethlehem. Ruth is married to Mahlon, who
comes from Judah. Bathsheba is the wife of Uriah the Hittite, and
Mary is betrothed to Joseph. Although Rahab is unmarried, she too
occupies a firm position within her own clan. She no longer lives in

her parents' house (Josh.2.18) but has a house of her own, where she is in frequent contact with both fellow citizens and foreigners. She enjoys the confidence of the inhabitants of Jericho: not for a moment is there any doubt about the credibility of her reports to the king of Jericho or to the men pursuing the two Israelite spies (Joshua 2.4–5).

3. The women find themselves in a precarious situation as a result of a special event or unusual combination of circumstances. It is precarious because they are no longer protected by the law, or can be accused of breaking the law and possibly even incur penalties under the law.

Elucidation: After the deaths of Er and Onan, Tamar, who is still childless, finds herself deprived of the benefits provided for her by the levirate law. When after some time she proves to be pregnant, her father-in-law condemns her to the stake. By helping two spies Rahab runs the risk of being accused of high treason. Naomi and Ruth are two childless widows. Because of Naomi's advanced age the levirate law does not help her and this law does not apply to Ruth, who is much younger. As long as Uriah is still alive, Bathsheba can be charged with deliberate adultery. Mary, because of her pregnancy, is an easy prey for rumours that she has had sex with another man, or has been raped after her betrothal to Joseph.

4. In this new situation the women come upon unexpected possibilities of making a contribution to the progress of Israel's history. Here some of them take advantage of ambiguities and lacunas in existing legislation. They sometimes find support and sometimes resistance from men around them.

Elucidation: In Genesis 38 Tamar is the only one to make efforts to ensure that Er has a descendant after all; she achieves her goal by taking advantage of complications in the law. Rahab knows that it is useless to resist the Israelites because God himself will give them the land. She cleverly uses the readiness of the two spies to spare her and her family in exchange for the protection that she has offered them. Ruth prefers an uncertain life at Naomi's side in Bethlehem to the security of life in the midst of her own people. By the striking initiatives that Ruth takes on arrival in Bethlehem, her

mother-in-law also awakens from her lethargy. By their concerted
action, the two women succeed in persuading Boaz to meet his
obligations with regard to Elimelech, Naomi's deceased husband.
In Bathsheba's case, it is initially uncertain whether she was aiming
at a place at the royal court. The assumption that she deliberately
aspired to become David's wife goes against the thread of the story
in II Samuel 11. In her young days she was the object of David's
sexual desires, but many years later, when the king is on his
deathbed, she takes control. Mary is not as active as the other
women. Matthew does not mention a single activity that she
undertakes. Whereas the other women are very active in improving
their lot, in Mary's case the active role is assumed by an angel of the
Lord who prevents Joseph from carrying out his plan of re-
pudiating his wife publicly or sending her away quietly. However,
there is no doubt whatsoever that Mary too is of great importance
to the house of Israel. Jesus, her child, is depicted in Matthew
1.1–17 as the culmination and fulfilment of Israel's history.

In the five stories under discussion, some men deal differently
with the law from women. Onan and Judah assume a lax attitude
and refuse to do what might be expected of them according to the
levirate law. Naomi's next of kin wants to acquire the land that
belonged to Elimelech, but he shrinks from marrying the young
woman from Moab. By recalling Uriah to Jerusalem and exhorting
him to go to his home and lie with his wife, David tries to wipe out
the traces of his adultery. When David's plan fails, he arranges for
Uriah to be killed at the siege of the city of Rabbah.

There are also men who dedicate themselves to observing the
law. When Judah receives the report of Tamar's pregnancy, he
condemns her to the stake. In II Samuel 12 Nathan tells David a
parable, making it clear to him that he has broken the law. Joseph
is a law-abiding individual who wants disciplinary measures to be
taken against his wife for becoming pregnant by someone else.

5. The stories about the five women all turn out well: the women
are again accepted into their family, clan or people, or at the end of
the story they obtain a position in a society to which they had not
belonged before. Retrospectively, it becomes clear that the women

were within their rights, and in their fortunes a power has been revealed that neither men nor women could themselves deploy: the power of God or of his Spirit.

Elucidation: Tamar gives birth to Perez and Zerah, and her two children are regarded as Judah's legitimate offspring. Rahab succeeds in saving herself, her parents and her family from death when Jericho is destroyed. According to the narrator, 'her family has lived in Israel to this day' (Joshua 6.25). It is impossible to find fault with her choice to be loyal to the Israelites, because God himself has promised the land of Canaan to Israel. The book of Ruth shows how a Moabite woman and a woman of Judah together manage to earn themselves a position in the aristocratic upper class of Bethlehem to which Naomi originally belonged. At the beginning of I Kings, Bathsheba has become an influential woman at the royal court. And against all expectations, Joseph takes Mary as his wife and acknowledges her child as his own.

Retrospect

Apart from the intertextual relations between the book of Ruth and Genesis 38, within the Old Testament we cannot discover any connections between the stories about Tamar, Rahab, Ruth and Bathsheba. Yet I have set the stories about these women side by side. This comparison is suggested by Matthew's listing of these women together in his genealogy of Jesus, where they are connected not only with each other but also with Mary, Jesus' mother.

My intertextual analysis showed a double movement: (a) first I argued that what is said in Matthew about Mary sheds a specific light on the four Old Testament women; (b) then I tried to show that Matthew's story about Mary in turn fits into the basic pattern that emerges from the Old Testament stories about Tamar, Rahab, Ruth and Bathsheba.

The result of my intertextual analysis can be summed up as follows. Despite or precisely because of their tragedy these four women in the Old Testament have been assigned a heroic role. They contribute towards the continuation of Israel's history or to a decisive turn in it. Matthew also assigns such a role to Mary.

Artistic texts in the light of the Gospels

The two previous chapters were devoted to intertextual networks within the Bible. That by no means exhausts the concept of intertextuality. Just as texts from the Gospels are the product of earlier texts, so they themselves stand at the origin of later texts. Down the centuries they have been taken up in exegetical and theological commentaries, in sermons, hymns and catechetical narratives. To this series must be added texts from secular literature which borrow material from the Gospels. This chapter discusses some examples of this. First I shall show how Jesus is presented in a modern novel; after that come some poems in which themes and motifs from the Gospels can be heard.

Jesus in a modern novel

In 1991 the Portuguese writer José Saramago startled the world with a novel in which he draws an eccentric and sometimes bizarre portrait of Jesus. It was called 'The Gospel according to Jesus Christ'.[1] I shall give the main outline of the book and then subject it to an intertextual analysis.

The Gospel according to Jesus Christ

After a prelude, which anticipates Jesus' crucifixion, the novel begins on the night when Joseph and Mary (he is twenty, she is not yet sixteen) make love and Mary becomes pregnant. Four weeks later she has a fleeting encounter with a beggar. He calls himself an angel and appears to know that she is pregnant. Mary had not yet told Joseph anything. She anxiously begins to ask herself who really is the father of her child.

Around passover, when Mary's baby is due, on the orders of the emperor Augustus the young couple have to go to Bethlehem to be registered. Mary gives birth to her first child in a cave outside the village. He is given the name Jeshua, Jesus. In the birth she is helped by Zelomi, a midwife. Three shepherds come to pay a visit, and Mary recognizes one of them as the beggar whom she had met earlier. On the eighth day after his birth the baby is circumcised in a synagogue. Thirty-three days later the young family goes to the temple for the purification of the mother.

Meanwhile Joseph has found employment as a carpenter in the building of the temple, which is already far advanced. There one day he hears a couple of soldiers telling each other that Herod has ordered them to kill all the children in Bethlehem under three. Joseph does not know the motive behind this decision. However, the readers hear that Herod is being tormented at night by a dream in which the prophet Micah tells him that someone *has come* from Bethlehem who will rule over Israel. A priest who is summoned in haste makes a connection with the passage in the book of Micah which says that someone *shall come* from Bethlehem who will rule over Israel. Herod sees that this prophecy has been fulfilled and gives orders for the massacre of the children.

So Joseph is by chance informed of the painful event that Bethlehem is to expect. He hastens to the cave to rescue his child. Soon after his arrival the death cries of the children in the village can already be heard. Because the soldiers do not inspect the caves in the neighbourhood, the two-months-old Jesus escapes death.

Before Joseph and Mary travel back to Nazareth with their child, the beggar alias the shepherd appears once more to Mary. He indicates that Joseph has the death of the children from Bethlehem on his conscience. He should have warned the village. In a dream Joseph sees himself as one of the soldiers, on the way to Bethlehem to kill his own son. This dream continues to torment Joseph for years, until at the age of thirty-three, by a bizarre combination of circumstances, he is nailed to the cross with thirty-nine rebels.

That happens in Sepphoris, a centre of Galilean opposition to the Romans, which is near Nazareth. After Joseph's wretched death Jesus inherits his father's dream. He sees Joseph coming after him as one of Herod's soldiers, with the firm intention of killing him, his son. This nightmare plays a key role in the novel. Finally it will be God, Jesus' true father, who inflicts death on his son.

Joseph and Mary have nine children in all, seven sons and two daughters. Shortly after Joseph's death, Jesus, who is then thirteen, leaves his parents' house. He travels via Jerusalem to Bethlehem, where he meets Zelomi, who shows him the cave where he was born. There he meets a shepherd, who is called Shepherd and says that he is an angel. The young Jesus enters into his service. Gradually it becomes clear that Shepherd is a fallen angel, the devil in person. Jesus is not deterred from his Jewish way of life by Shepherd. So at passover he goes to Jerusalem to fulfil his religious obligations, but at the last moment he refuses to sacrifice the lamb that he has obtained on the way. Three years later the lamb, which has by now grown into an adult sheep, wanders off into an inhospitable region south of Jericho. The moment that Jesus finds the lost sheep he sees a pillar of smoke and the voice of God resounds from a cloud, telling him that he will have to die in exchange for power and glory. To seal the covenant that God makes with him, Jesus must immediately sacrifice the sheep. His own fate is reflected in that animal: as a child he is saved from death, but once he is grown up he will have to shed his blood.

After this encounter with God, Jesus is thrown out by Shepherd. He goes through the Jordan valley to the Sea of Galilee, where he comes into contact with some fishermen, the brothers Simon and Andrew and the sons of Zebedee. Through Jesus' action the fishermen see their catch increase enormously. Jesus travels to his parents' house via Magdala. In Magdala a gaping wound in his foot is lovingly tended by one Mary, a local prostitute, with whom he sleeps for about a week. Really she comes from Bethany, where her twin sister Martha and her brother Lazarus still live. Arriving home, Jesus finds no faith in his mother and his brothers and sisters when he tells them that he has seen God. Disappointed, he goes back to Mary of Magdala, and from that moment they form an inseparable pair. This Mary takes him at his word. Jesus' mother is the next to be enlightened about the special role of her child. She learns from an angel that God mixed his seed with that of her husband in the night when she first became pregnant. The messenger further confirms that Jesus really has seen God.

The next part of the novel gives a picture of Jesus' activities by the seashore. He performs a number of miracles which are presented as 'house and garden and kitchen miracles, mere conjuring tricks':[2] he stills a storm, provides wine at a wedding in Cana, heals Peter's mother-in-law, liberates a possessed man from a host of demons, curses a barren fig tree, and provides a great crowd of people with food. These deeds show that he is an instrument of God. The demons themselves say that he is God's son. In this phase the encounter which Jesus has with God and the devil in the midst of the misty lake is decisive. God appears in the form of an old man with a long beard. He confirms that Jesus is his son and reports that Jesus, the lamb of God, will die on a cross, like Joseph. This cruel death is necessary, for in this way God, who has always been the God of the small Jewish people, will spread his power over the whole world. By dying as a martyr Jesus will win praise and glory. He will be the figurehead of the church. The whole of later history will be an endless story of murder and killing. God sums up in alphabetical order the many names of those who will be martyred for Jesus' sake. The Crusades and the Inquisition are also expressions of the world-embracing kingdom that God will found. Jesus beseeches his divine father that this cup may pass by him, and the devil too makes a desperate attempt to change God's mind, but finally they have to abandon their opposition, since God requires blind obedience. Jesus is a necessary pawn in God's chess game, and the devil too is indispensable in the scenario which is going to take place, since God and the devil are twins: good cannot exist without evil.

Still totally confused, Jesus sets out to perform the task that is imposed on him. He gathers twelve disciples around him, whom he initiates into his destiny and his identity as son of God. He now also begins to announce the nearness of God's kingdom and to call for repentance. After a long stay in Galilee he travels with Mary to the village where she was born, Bethany. Lazarus is healed by Jesus of a chronic disease, but when later he suddenly dies, Mary stops her brother being raised to life for, she says, he has not deserved to have to die twice. Jesus hears from two of his disciples that a certain John on the banks of the Jordan is trying to persuade the people to be baptized. Jesus hastens to the preacher of repentance and has himself baptized by him.

Now events follow one another in rapid succession. Jesus has already attracted the attention of the high priest by a short but fierce action in the temple area. When John is beheaded, it is clear that the end of Jesus' life is also near. In sight of the end, he resolves to thwart God's plan. If he dies as son of God, he will cause death to many others. Just as Joseph was responsible for the death of twenty-five children from Bethlehem, so Jesus will be responsible for the death of millions of people. Jesus thinks that he can oppose God's plan by recanting his statement that he is God's son and instead giving himself out to be a political rebel, the king of the Jews. The disciples think that this is a bad choice for someone who was predestined to become king of the whole world. Jesus finds a supporter only in Judas: Judas is ready to tell the authorities in Jerusalem about Jesus' plan. After that, Jesus is arrested and brought before the high priest. Before him Jesus denies that he is the son of God. Because he so stubbornly calls himself the king of the Jews, the high priest puts the case before the Roman procurator. Jesus is condemned to die on a cross. His last wish is for Pilate to put a placard on the cross containing the words *Iesus Nazarenus Rex Iudaeorum*. Shortly before Jesus dies, God appears again and cries with a resounding voice, 'You are my beloved son, in you I am well pleased.' Jesus understands that he has been lured into the trap and his last words are: 'People, forgive Him, for He does not know what He has done.'

Analysis

Saramago's book is 387 pages long and is written in a difficult style: it contains long sentences in which narrator and character text go into each other almost imperceptibly. The author calls his novel a gospel; given that Luke 1.1–4 forms the motto of his book, he joins the circle of hagiographers. The claim of the novel is that now at last the one real Gospel is on the table. The material for the book is largely drawn from the four canonical Gospels, which are reproduced in a harmonizing way. In addition, here and there it contains fragments which have been taken from non-canonical texts. The greater part of the novel has sprung from Saramago's own imagination; here in detail he shows a certain knowledge of history and the institutions of Judaism in the first century.

The novel extends from the beginning of Jesus' life to his crucifixion. The reader is offered a consecutive account in chronological order with hardly any gaps. We can follow the main figure from year to year, often even from day to day. The time shortly before and after Jesus' birth fills almost one hundred pages; this contrasts sharply with the scanty reports about this in Matthew and Luke. The childhood years of Jesus and his growth to adulthood are described at length.

In reproducing and adapting the material Saramago makes use of certain procedures. He limits himself to specific parts of the Gospels. In this selection words of Jesus play a lesser role than narratives about his fate; the Synoptic Gospels are used more readily than John.[3]

When we set out the material taken from the Gospels, we see a zigzag movement through the sources used. In terms of content, this gives rise to a number of new causal relations and new connections. The order of the separate episodes is quite different from that in the original writings (thus John the Baptist becomes active only shortly before Jesus' death). Well-known sentences are rendered in a different way (Saramago changes 'Father, forgive them, for they do not know what they are doing' from Luke 23.34 into 'People, forgive Him, for He does not know what He has done'). To increase the vividness, Saramago expands the original narratives with new details. The poorer the original narrative, the richer is the novelist's retelling. He introduces new characters on stage like Ananias and Chua, Joseph and Mary's neighbours. Characters who have a subordinate role in the Gospels and there hardly have a face of their own grow in the novel into independent figures who make their own contribution to the development of the plot. Joseph is such a person. In the Gospels he plays a role only at the beginning of Matthew and Luke; later he is mentioned only incidentally, without appearing on the scene himself (Luke 4.22; John 1.45; 6.42). Precisely because so little is told of him, he provokes the reader's curiosity. Saramago plays on this by developing Joseph into a dynamic character whose career shows in anticipation the later fate of his oldest son.

The supplementary details are sometimes inspired by the Christian tradition. This can be illustrated by Mary of Magdala. Her role as witness to the resurrection is left aside in the novel. But she is depicted as a prostitute. That cliché is based on the identification of Mary of Magdala with the woman who was a sinner in Luke 7.36–50. Moreover Saramago fuses her with Mary of Bethany. At that point he is following a centuries-long tradition of the Western church,[4] but he expands this tradition with the idea that Mary was the sexual partner of Jesus (which is equally unoriginal).

The effect of all these procedures is that there are marked shifts in meaning, but that is precisely Saramago's concern. With his book he wants to offer a new interpretation, one which even goes against the grain. The author fits into the modern tradition, in which material from ancient authors is sometimes reworked so intensively that the original meaning is almost completely reversed.

In short, Saramago's interpretation amounts to this. The human world is dominated in a magical way by two non-human figures, God and the devil. Of these two, God is the real villain. In the novel he is a maniac for power who after his centuries-long rule over the small Jewish people wants to extend his territory to the whole world, with the intention of submerging it in evil. To carry out that godless plan he has let his eye fall on Jesus, an apparently ordinary Jewish young man who step by step attains to the role which God has intended for him. In a brutal way God has preprogrammed him for his role from the earliest beginnings: Jesus is born of God's own seed. This purely biological interpretation of texts about the divine sonship of Jesus is extremely functional within the novel. As son of God, Jesus cannot make any choice of his own: he is totally delivered over to the tyrannical will of his father. The implementation of this is as it were in his genes!

This image of Jesus is based on something that the evangelists could not yet have known, but is well known to Saramago, the new evangelist: the church, which in the meantime has come to be almost two thousand years old, has left a bloody trail. This one-sidedly negative picture of church history contains a clear message: people must take responsibility for their lives in complete freedom; they must cast off God, the devil and even Christ, for these are evil projections which provide an excuse for one's own failure. Or, in the words of Saramago himself: 'the only possible history is made up of earthly affairs'.[5]

Poets and the Gospels

After Saramago's portrait of Jesus, painted with much critical sensitivity, I now turn to some poems in which the main emphasis is on a more positive reception of material from the Gospels. The selection is quite arbitrary. I have chosen some examples in which the connections with texts from the Gospels do not remain all too implicit. In succession I shall present poems originally written in Dutch by Ed Hoornik, Guillaume van der Graft, Jan Willem Schulte Nordholt, Gerrit Achterberg and Ida Gerhardt.

I AM THE LITTLE DAUGHTER...

I am the little daughter of Jairus.
I lie here on a bier which is far too big.
Death sits in my eyes and in my hair,
which, now the curls are gone, has no grace.

I miss my doll, who now she is no longer here,
sleeps as I sleep, fingers clasped.
I know that two and two make four,
but now I'm dead that is no longer true.

Why was it that I was sad just now?
A man, a magician, ought to have come
to make me better, but then he didn't come.

The people on the roof and in the trees
went home, but I keep dreaming of him.
Tomorrow I shall be the first to see him.

Ed Hoornik[6]

This sonnet is related to Mark 5.21–43. The clearest signal is the
name Jairus (this is absent from the parallel versions in Matthew
9.18–26 and Luke 8.40–56). In Mark, the story of Jairus' daughter
is combined in a sandwich composition with the story about a
woman who had been suffering from haemorrhages for twelve
years (A: 5.21–24; B: 5.25–34; A' 5.35–43). In A, the girl, who
doesn't have a name of her own either in Mark or in Hoornik, is
seriously ill; in the following part of the narrative (B) Jesus' saving
action encounters delay, so that he does not arrive until the girl has
already died (A'). We find this transition from being sick to being
dead in the sonnet, too: the dead girl says that a man ought to have
come who could make her better. The fact that he did not come is
stated in a quite matter-of-fact way by the girl; in Mark it is
explained by the event sketched out in part B.

The novelty of the poem is that the text is put completely in the
mouth of the girl. In Mark she does not say a word. In the retelling
of biblical material it often happens that a character comes more
sharply into the limelight than was the case in the original text.
The special feature is not only that we hear more about the girl herself, but also that the whole poem is presented from her perspective. The choice of the first-person form requires the language
to be childlike and simple all the way through. Nevertheless, the
quite complicated rules which a sonnet must observe are fully
respected in the original Dutch text (but impossible to reproduce
in an English translation without losing the simplicity and natural
quality of the original). The sonnet breaks off before the child has
really been raised from the dead. The public who had rushed to
satisfy their curiosity, watching out from the roof (cf. Mark 2.4)

and the trees (cf. Luke 19.4), have all gone home, but the girl has not yet given up hope. She compares her state with sleep (cf. Mark 5.39), continues to dream of the man who should come, and is certain that she will see him when she wakes up in the morning.

ASKING

I asked the birds
   the birds were not at home
I asked the trees
   haughty trees

I asked the water
   why they do not say anything
   the water gave no answer

if even the water gives no answer
although it has so many tongues
what is it

   what is it
it is only a fisherman

who carries the water
under his feet
who carries a tree
on his back
who carries on his head a bird.

Guillaume van der Graft[7]

In this poem the references to the Bible remain somewhat implicit. The title is taken up in the thrice repeated 'I asked'. The question is put in succession to the birds, the trees and the water. These natural elements give no answer. Only then is the content of the question given: 'what is it'. The only thing left to us is 'a fisherman', a designation which refers to early Christian depictions of Jesus as a fish.[8] The fisherman's answer to the question of meaning turns the world that is familiar to us upside down. This is subtly expressed in the reversal at the end. The natural elements return here, but in reverse order.

In the last part of the poem various texts from the Gospels play a role. They are combined by 'carry' (three times). Seen from the perspective of scripture this verb fits the tree best, where the reference is to the cross (think above all of John 19.17: 'he himself carried the cross'; in the Synoptics Simon of Cyrene is compelled to carry the cross). In the poem Jesus also carries the water (under his feet), and he carries a bird on his head. It is as if carrying the cross is extended here to other episodes in his life: the cross permeates the whole of his existence. Carrying the water alludes to the stories in which Jesus walks on the sea (Matthew 14.23–33; Mark 6.45–52; John 6.16–21). The bird on his head recalls the descent of the holy Spirit as a dove after Jesus' baptism in the Jordan (Matthew 3.16; Mark 1.10; Luke 3.22). In John 1.32–33 it is very strongly emphasized that the Spirit abidingly rests on Jesus: the poem also makes this suggestion.

Next I shall discuss a poem by Jan Willem Schulte Nordholt in which the fisherman's answer forms the starting point for new questions.

A JEWISH MAN

I

A Jewish man from year zero
who at the age of barely thirty-three
died for our guilt
when we were still Batavians.

Who even more, once he was dead
and hidden in a deep rock
is said to have risen large as life,
body and soul one spring morning.

Who was seen, heard, touched
and then ascended to heaven
where He reigns in eternity.

Who one day will surprise us like a thief
who knows after how many thousand years,
who knows, tonight. He knows the time.

II

What kind of a story is that, this Jewish man,
miraculously born of a virgin,
who bears our guilt on his shoulders,
like beams of a cross, as if that were possible?
And then, why? That implies a god
who first creates us and after that rebukes us
for being only human, and with death
punishes us, and then he does not, and then he lays our fate
and all that the poor world suffers
on the back of a doomed Jew.

Jan Willem Schulte Nordholt[9]

The first part teems with references to New Testament texts. They
are concentrated into pithy sentences which recall formulae from
the later Christian creed. Four elements are surveyed: Jesus' death,
resurrection, ascension and coming again. His death at the age of
'barely thirty-three' (cf. Luke 3.23: 'around thirty years of age') is
given a theological interpretation ('for our guilt'; cf. I Corinthians
15.3: 'for our sins'), which returns in line 3 of Part II and forms the
core problem in the whole of that second part. Before we reach that
point, here are some other core elements. 'Hidden in a deep rock'
(line 6) requires the modern reader to be familiar with the custom
of laying a dead body in a tomb that has been hewn in a rock (Mark
15.46). The poet emphasizes the bodily resurrection of Jesus
('body and soul', line 8). The following line refers to the appearance stories in Matthew (28.9–10, 16–20), Luke (24.13–49)
and John (20.11–29), and possibly also to the appearances in the
secondary conclusion to Mark (16.9–20); the ascension recalls
Luke 24.50–53 and Acts 1.9–11. That the parousia takes place
unexpectedly is stated with the image ('like a thief... who knows,

tonight') used in the New Testament ('as a thief in the night': I Thessalonians 5.2; II Peter 3.10; Revelation 3.3; 16.15). That this event may have to be awaited for 'who knows... how many thousand years' was also already known to the author of II Peter (3.8). The concluding sentence of Part I ('he knows the time') is in tension with Jesus' statement that the day and hour are hidden even from him (Mark 13.32).

Part II is the most attractive. After the story in Part I has been further enriched with a reference to his miraculous birth from a virgin (Matthew 1.18–25; Luke 1.34–35), the questions arise which we, descendants of the Batavians, put to such a story today. The poet doubts whether vicarious suffering is possible ('as if that were possible') and then in the next line asks about its meaning ('and then, why?'). The implication would be that there is a god who has let things go so far that he irrationally loads all guilt and suffering on the back of 'a doomed Jew' who must serve as scapegoat. The capriciousness of God is indicated with the help of material from the stories of the beginning (Genesis 1–3). New Testament stories about 'a Jewish man' are here criticized on the basis of Old Testament texts about God. In the background there is also the sense that a connection between creation and reconciliation certainly is not strange to Christian theology and that in the course of history Christianity has often exalted itself at the expense of Judaism.

Now follows a poem by Gerrit Achterberg with a strong biblical slant. For the sake of clarity I shall present the poem here together with a selection of the New Testament passages which play a role more or less explicitly.

A TRAVELLER 'DOES' GOLGOTHA · · · · · · · Matthew 27.33;
Mark 15.22; John 19.17

I
Without asking Him
whether He could bear it,
they have nailed him to a cross. · · · · · · · Luke 23.33

And when he hung there suffering
– a nail is an ugly thing –
He said: Father, forgive them.   Luke 23.34

He said: They know not what they do.   Luke 23.34
For they were longing
to see what He would do now!   Luke 23.35–37

So He still prayed for them,
and in His dying He gave them
an excuse for their consciences.

And I stood in the distance talking humbug   Luke 23.49 (Matthew
to a couple of needless, simple soldiers.   27.55; Mark 15.40)
They were doing what they could not
avoid doing anyway.

But He commended himself to the very last:
the hands of His Father; – still before   Luke 23.46
Passover I had to hasten to my ship in Jaffa.

II

Then I read in the newspaper
– it was on Cyprus:
J of N called Christ,
after being crucified three days previously,
as our esteemed readers know,

was not found in His tomb: it was open.   Stories about the open
Stubborn rumours are going the rounds   tomb
that His disciples stole up on the guards   Matthew 28.11–15

when they were asleep, and stole the body.
However, exalted women supposed   Matthew 28.9–10;
that they saw Him walking through the   John 20.11–18
meadows;

Mary must have stammered: Lord!   John 20.16 ('rabboni')
There are also fishermen who assert: John 21.1–14 (above all
He ate with us by the lake.   v.13)

But this is contradicted by the authorities.	Matthew 28.11–15
Do not believe that the moon is made of cheese.	

III

Rome – The anchor falls. We are home.
I hasten to the baths, am purged
of travel and carousing and in my own house
sitting with wife and fire and radio,
I soon forgot Christ and cross.
… Then an SOS went through my soul:

'My Spirit is being poured out on all flesh.	Acts 2.17
Who is not for Me is against Me,'	Matthew 12.30;
signals a Secret Transmitter white and hoarse.	Luke 11.23

Again under sail, over the solitudes
of oceans which separate me from You,
Christ, might You appear to me
on the far horizon.

Gerrit Achterberg[10]

The 'I' figure in this long poem is a shipowner who travels from
Jaffa via Cyprus to Rome, where he has his home port. On his
journey, by chance he is confronted with an execution on
Golgotha. He describes this event in a quite laconic tone, as if it
were a tourist attraction (see also the title), but the use of capital
letters in the personal and possessive pronouns betrays from the
start that the seaman has respect for the crucified man. He is
intrigued by the fact that the executed man asks for forgiveness for
his executioners and at the last talks about 'his Father's hands'
(because the onlooker is standing at a distance, he catches only
scraps of what is said). A slight note of criticism can be found in the
fourth strophe: by his prayer for forgiveness the crucified man is
unburdening the conscience of his executioners. The indication of
time 'before Passover' best fits the Johannine detail that Jesus is
crucified on a Friday, 14 Nisan, on the day of preparation for the

Passover, thus the day before the feast; the Synoptics similarly put the event on a Friday, but opt for 15 Nisan, the first day of Passover. It is even more probable that here the poet is taking up the later Christian distinction between Good Friday and the celebration of Easter on the following Sunday.

The name of the executed man appears only in Part II: 'J of N, called Christ'. Reports about him pursue the shipowner on his way home. During a stopover on Cyprus he reads in the newspaper (an anachronism, like the radio and the SOS message in III) about events which are said to have taken place three days after the crucifixion but which have meanwhile been strongly denied by the authorities. In this part we find an attractive anthology from the resurrection and appearance stories in the Gospels.

After his arrival in Rome the 'I' figure is confronted even more directly with the figure whom he has seen die at Golgotha. The contact comes about through an SOS message: given the 'I' figure's profession, that is an excellent choice. Although he feels miles away from Jesus ('oceans which separate me from You'), on his new voyage he begins passionately to long for Christ to appear to him. The Spirit has taken possession of his driven soul. From being a nonchalant observer at a distance the 'I' figure has grown into someone who allows himself to be moved by Jesus in his new mode of existence.

EASTER

A deep sorrow that has come over us
can sometimes, after bitter tears, unexpectedly,
be assuaged. I went along through Zalk,
on Easter morning, still very early in the day.
Where under the dyke there was a little vegetable garden
adorned with rustic rows of primulas,
I saw, in Sunday best, a child standing.
It pointed and pointed and looked at me radiantly.
The March rain had done it overnight:
there stood his baptismal name, sown in cress.

Ida Gerhardt[11]

The indications of time in the title ('Easter') and in the fourth line ('on Easter morning') stimulate the reader to look for connections with material from the Gospels. At first sight we are far removed from the stories told there. The poem is set in Zalk, a village on the IJssel, west of Zwolle in the Netherlands. But the text contains all kinds of quite implicit references to the stories about the women at the open tomb (Matthew 28.1–10; Mark 16.1–8; Luke 24.1–11; John 20.1–18). This implies that the 'I' figure of the poem is a woman, although that is not said explicitly. It is still very early in the day, a Sunday (cf. Mark 16.2: 'on the first day of the week, very early'). Below the dyke there is a vegetable garden (cf. John 19.41: Jesus is buried in a garden; in 20.15 Mary thinks that she has met the gardener). In the child in 'Sunday best' we recognize the young man from the story in Mark, who is clothed in white. The young man points out to the women the place where Jesus was laid; so too the child looks with a radiant gaze to the place where shortly beforehand it had sown fast-growing cress seeds and where now the young plants are putting their heads above the ground. The baptismal name refers to the custom of administering baptism on Easter Eve. It is interesting that the plants must have shot up in the night under the benevolent influence of the March rain (here an early date for Easter is presupposed). The event itself has not been perceived by the child; in excitement it points to the new life that has shot up in the garden. So too the moment of the resurrection is out of sight in the Gospel stories; only traces can be seen which indicate a fundamental change.

In this poem the Easter event is depicted by the process of growth in nature. The poet may also have been influenced by the way in which Jesus speaks of his death in John 12.24: 'unless a grain of wheat falls into the ground, it does not bear fruit; it has to die, only then does it bring forth abundant fruit'.

The Bible and literature: a gold mine?

To conclude this chapter I shall look for an answer to two questions: is the Bible a gold mine for literature, and do modern literary texts contribute to a better understanding of scripture?

The first question has been answered in the affirmative by Northrop Frye. He regards the Bible as the great code of Western (Christian) culture.[12] For centuries writers have drawn on this enormous reservoir and followed the style and composition of biblical writings. The same idea has been put more vividly by I.de Wijs: '...anyone who wants to do away with the Bible would do best to throw in half Dutch literature'[13] (and the same can be said of English literature). The other side of this statement is that such texts are only half understood if they are not related to the biblical material used in them. The reader and the literary critics must be thoroughly familiar with the Bible if they want to analyse contemporary literary texts.

The next question is whether the reverse is also true: must readers of the Bible and exegetes steep themselves in modern literature to gain access to the Bible? That is certainly useful, but not necessary. Biblical texts are not fixed to the exposition that they are given in texts from a later time. Whether the later interpretations come from exegetes or writers and poets, they always remain subject to the criticism of them that can be made in the light of the original. However, knowledge of modern literature is certainly useful. It shows how biblical texts – often detached from the interpretative schemes of churches and theologians – are read today, the questions they raise, where they are provocative and at what points they can also be ridiculed in a modern interpretation. The adaptations by modern writers and poets are at least in part also provoked by typical characteristics of the original Bible text. Their creativity is mobilized by dark or ambiguous passages in the Bible: they try to channel the meaning of these in a particular direction. Characters which play a subsidiary role in scripture are often assigned a main role in literary texts, while the chief characters in the Bible are pushed into the background. This rearrangement can open our eyes to the way in which characters in the original are arranged in relation to one another and to the meaningful effects of this. One fruit of new developments is that the fates of figures from the Bible are subjected with a degree of eagerness to a psychological interpretation which drives away the original theological interpretation. The truth and trustworthiness of the biblical view of God, human beings and the world is illuminated in an idiosyncratic way, from an original perspective. That brings about a dialogue between the wisdom of the past and present-day views about values and norms. As a result of this modern literature becomes an attractive Eldorado for lovers of the classic text that the Bible still is.

Part IV The window of history

Jesus as a character and as a historical figure

In studying the Gospels we have different methodological perspectives at our disposal. At that level we are particularly richly blessed: never before has the diversity of approaches been as great as it is now. This book has mapped out the main ways. The panorama developed raises an urgent question: how do the stories relate to history? Has the historical Jesus been removed from our field of view for ever, or through the paper witnesses can we still catch a glimpse of the human being of flesh and blood who was so deeply rooted in Judaism and who stood at the origin of Christianity?

This is an old question, which recently has again become very important and has gained sharpness from the present-day emphasis on synchronic and intertextual models of reading. In this chapter I shall first survey modern investigation into the historical Jesus. Then I shall scrutinize a number of sub-questions. What sources are available to the investigator? What is their genre? What criteria play a role in the quest for the Jesus of history? I shall end the chapter with a global sketch of Jesus as a historical figure.

The modern investigation of Jesus

The first wave

In the modern investigation of Jesus we can distinguish three phases.[1] The first extends from 1778 to 1906 and is called the 'first quest' or the 'old quest'.[2] In this period people began to put historical-critical questions to the canonical Gospels. This resulted in two new insights: (a) the historicity of narratives from the Gospels must be seriously put in doubt; (b) the Gospels are historically conditioned documents; they are the outcome of a long and complicated history of development.

Doubting their historicity means that the Gospels are no longer regarded as a trustworthy historical account of Jesus' activity. Texts from the Gospels are steeped in interpretations by believers which come from Jesus' earliest followers and by no means always correspond with Jesus' own intentions. Can the life of Jesus still be detached from the faith of the first Christians? Full of optimism, many researchers from the first wave thought that this was indeed possible. They thought that they were in a position to write a biography of Jesus, a *curriculum vitae*, which would put the real facts on the table and show that there is a marked difference between the historical Jesus and the church's pictures of Christ.

The starting point of the investigation was that the *earliest* sources lend themselves best to statements about the historical Jesus. Historical criticism (who was Jesus?) thus went hand in hand with literary-historical investigation (which sources stand closest to Jesus?). The Gospel according to John quickly dropped out. According to D.F.Strauss (1808–1874), this book is so strongly coloured by later theological ideas that it has little to offer as a source of historical information about Jesus.[3] In any case, it has less to offer than the Synoptic Gospels. The investigation into the Synoptics was given a new impulse by the rise of the two-source theory (which is now widely accepted): Mark is the earliest Gospel; Matthew and Luke have used Mark independently of each other; in addition they used a second source which exclusively contained sayings (logia) of Jesus and therefore is called the Logia source (abbreviated as Q). The consequence was that Mark and Q became the springboard for historical statements about Jesus. People borrowed the outline of a Jesus biography from Mark, whereas Q was regarded as a source from which one could reconstruct the authentic statements of Jesus.

That did not last long, at least for Mark, since already in 1901 William Wrede made it clear that this Gospel, too, contains traces of a christology which was developed only after Jesus' death.[4] Something similar was also to be said of Q. But by then the first wave was already over. In 1906 Albert Schweitzer wrote a critical study of the many new schemes (for example Jesus was a rebel/ he was someone with a lofty ethic/ he was focussed above all on the inner life) and came to the conclusion that researchers often projected their ownmost ideas and ideals back on Jesus.[5] From their work there emerged a Jesus who was created in their own image and likeness. That is sound criticism. However, it is notable that Schweitzer did not subject his own picture of Jesus to the criticism which he practised on others. He depicted Jesus as a prophetic-apocalyptic figure whose life and teaching were totally dominated by the expectation that the end of the world would dawn during his lifetime or soon afterwards; because the time still remaining was so short, Jesus taught a quite demanding interim ethic.

The second wave

According to the chroniclers of the study of Jesus, the second wave – also called the 'new quest' – did not come until 1953. In that year Ernst Käsemann gave a lecture which has become famous, in which he issued a clarion call for new investigation.[6] The years between Schweitzer and Käsemann have been called the period of the 'no quest'. This term is extremely unfortunate, for two reasons. The first is that the trio 'old quest –no quest – new quest' gives the wrong impression that after years of calm the new quest took up the threads at the point where the first wave had stopped. The second is that even during the time of the so-called 'no quest', Jesus stood high on the scholarly agenda and work continued to be done indefatigably within a historical paradigm. Certainly the positivistic idea that the bare facts of his life were still directly accessible had lost all meaning as a result of the depressing results of the first wave.

The period between 1906 and 1953 roughly coincides with the heyday of form criticism. The application of this model to the Gospels was given a powerful stimulus by Rudolf Bultmann. The emphasis came to lie on the history of the traditions in which Jesus is mentioned. The literary forms which can still be recognized in the Gospels were said to have been created with much freedom and creativity by the earliest Christian communities, and to have been deeply influenced by their belief in Jesus' resurrection from the dead. The Gospels therefore primarily have the character of a testimony of faith. They are windows on the life of the earliest community inside and outside Palestine. Given the genre of the Gospels – they are not biographies or historical chronicles but documents of faith – they cannot be used as a springboard for historically reliable statements about Jesus' life. Jesus himself has disappeared behind the faith of the church. What we are left with are the many pictures of Jesus developed by the earliest Christian communities.

Bultmann replaced the purely historical interest of the old quest of the earthly Jesus with a purely theological interest in the heavenly Christ, Christ as he is proclaimed by the primitive community. Gradually his scepticism about the possibility of developing a historically reliable picture of Jesus increased, and even more, he thought such knowledge almost completely irrelevant for the study of the New Testament kerygma. Only one fact is important for Bultmann: that Jesus once existed (otherwise faith would be based on a myth); in his view faith needs no further facts.

Opposition to this came from the circle of Bultmann's former pupils. In 1953 Käsemann threw down the gauntlet. By that I do not mean that he came out with his own new sketch of the historical Jesus. He continued to put the emphasis on the Christ of faith, but in order to prevent that faith from running wild he sought a connection between the kerygmatic Christ and the historical Jesus. He sought to emphasize that the beginnings of the kerygma of Christ are to be found in the pre-Easter preaching of Jesus.

So there was a search for a bridgehead on the other side of the river of Easter! According to Käsemann, that bridgehead is formed by sayings of Jesus, not by narratives about his actions. But by no means all sayings go back to him, certainly not in their present form. So we must first reconstruct the earliest form of logia contained in the Gospels. Then the question arises whether the oldest version that we can attain indeed goes back to Jesus. A strict criterion is necessary to assess the question. The criterion runs as follows: the earliest formulation of logia from the Gospels probably goes back to Jesus if this formulation cannot be derived from the Judaism of the time and cannot be attributed to early Christianity. This criterion is called 'the criterion of discontinuity' for short.

With this programme Käsemann breathed new life into the investigation of Jesus. He became the torchbearer of the new quest. Very soon, however, it proved that the criterion proposed is extremely debatable. On the one hand the criterion must give access to Jesus as a historical figure; on the other it begins from the presupposition that Jesus was so completely unique and original that he really stands outside history. Application of it produces only a picture of Jesus who is detached from his Jewish roots and his influence on his followers. Another disadvantage is that the criterion can be applied strictly only if we have a complete picture of Judaism at the time of Jesus and a thorough knowledge of early Christianity. Therefore the desire to search for 'authentic' sayings of Jesus quickly began to decline, and at the beginning of the 1970s it died a silent death.

The third wave

Since the beginning of the 1980s investigation of the historical Jesus has blossomed again like a rose. This time English-speaking authors, above all from North America, are in the lead. The new wave is known as the third quest. There are many positions under this one roof. There are still scholars who are completely devoted to detecting authentic sayings of Jesus. A famous and notorious example of this is the Jesus Seminar, established in 1985, a changing group of between fifty and seventy-five New Testament scholars who with the help of a four-point scale try to indicate how probable it is that sayings of Jesus from the four canonical Gospels and the Gospel of Thomas in fact come from Jesus himself.[7] In the wake of the work they have undertaken, John Dominic Crossan has argued that Jesus was an illiterate Galilean peasant who led an itinerant existence as a preacher (comparable to the philosophical school of the Cynics) and by his stress on the equality of all men brought hope and consolation to the lowest classes of society.[8] According to Marcus J.Borg, Jesus was a charismatic figure led by the Spirit, who had special magical powers.[9] Among others we find images which were also revered earlier: according to E.P.Sanders Jesus was the eschatological messenger of God,[10] while Gerd Theissen presents him as a social and political activist.[11]

Despite the diversity of pictures of Jesus, the third quest does have some general characteristics. Generally, Jesus is explicitly put within the Judaism of his time; here account is taken of influences from Hellenistic culture. After the un-Jewish – and therefore often also anti-Jewish – perspective of form criticism and the new quest it is a positive development that Jesus is now so consistently illuminated from the world of Jewish faith. Full attention is also paid to the influence of Jesus on early Christianity. Later interpretations of faith are not suspected a priori: they often form a trustworthy reflection of what Jesus himself said and did. Against this background it is not surprising that the criterion of discontinuity is now used only with caution. It is steadily being replaced by another criterion which Gerd Theissen and Annette Merz have formulated as follows: 'What is plausible in the Jewish context and makes the origin of primitive Christianity understandable may be historical.'[12]

The third quest has a multi-disciplinary approach, within which archaeology and the social sciences play a major part. Apart from a few late flowerers, the one-sided fixation on sayings of Jesus has been overcome. His words are again related to the narratives about his actions. The explicit preference for the canonical sources has also been broken through. A great openness to non-canonical texts like the Gospels of Peter and Thomas can be detected.

The window of history

From my survey is evident that time and again the window of history is provided with new glass. During the first wave it may be said after the event that people were fond of using mirror glass, so that the investigators kept finding themselves in the picture of

Jesus that they sketched. Form criticism opted for ground glass: by the use of this sort of glass the historical Jesus was largely withdrawn from the eye of the investigator. The third wave has a preference for stained glass: the sketches are particularly colourful and unanimity is hard to find.

The 'historical Jesus' does not coincide with the Jew from Nazareth of the same name who lived at the beginning of our era. The greater part of the life of this figure is inaccessible to the historian, simply for lack of sources. The historical Jesus is the Jesus of the historian: it is the Jesus whom we can sketch out by making use of the scholarly instruments of historical research. So really the historical Jesus has 'existed' only since scholarly historical investigation was undertaken into him. In this search the investigator's historical context plays a major role. Present-day historians are fully aware that they themselves also have a historical context and that they do not hover above history as neutral observers.

Up till now I have always spoken of the historical Jesus in the singular. Perhaps we must even use the plural. From the beginning historical investigation has produced different sketches. Within the third wave diversity has even almost become a norm.

Present-day investigation of Jesus sees itself faced with a number of methodological questions which were already put in the past, but which can now be answered in a new way. I shall discuss the following questions: what sources are available to researchers today, to what genre do the Gospels belong, and what criteria are being used at present to arrive at a critical sifting of the source material?

The sources

Jesus himself set nothing down in writing. For knowledge of his life we are dependent on texts by others. A further complication is that all the texts in which he is mentioned were formulated by his followers, with the exception of some Jewish and Roman sources.[13] The number of written sources has been extended in our century by new discoveries. Our knowledge of Judaism has increased substantially as a result of the discovery of the Dead Sea Scrolls.

Indirectly these writings also shed new light on Jesus, since the context in which he lived can now be described in more detail.[14] Just as spectacular was the discovery in 1945 of Coptic manuscripts in the Egyptian town of Nag Hammadi, including a complete copy of the Gospel of Thomas.

About half of the 114 sayings of Jesus contained in the Gospel of Thomas have a parallel in the Synoptics. According to some scholars, Thomas is here directly dependent on the Synoptic Gospels; according to others material has been used in the Gospel of Thomas which goes back to the oral tradition in the pre-Synoptic phase and is related to the sayings of Jesus in Q. The discussion of this question is so fierce because it involves the more general question of the relationship between canonical and non-canonical writings. The classical standpoint that only the books included in the canon are important for the historical investigation of Jesus is increasingly being abandoned. We can distinguish between earlier and later layers of tradition in non-canonical texts, too, and it cannot be excluded a priori that these older layers bring us near to the historical Jesus.

The genre of the Gospels

One question which is studied intensively is the genre to which the Gospels belong. In resolving this question we must steer a middle course between two extremes. One extreme is that the Gospels offer a completely reliable account of Jesus' words and actions; the other is that they are of little value as a historical source because they are utterly steeped in the faith of the earliest communities. In the one case the Gospels offer too much historical information; in the other too little. The correct insight of form criticism is that the Gospels are indeed no historical biographies in the modern sense of the word. However, to say that they are pure confessions of faith is a gross exaggeration; it does not explain why the earliest Christians chose so clearly to express their faith in Jesus through an orderly narrative about his life.

According to David Aune, a comparison with literary products of the Graeco-Roman world offers a way out.[15] He establishes that the evangelists were guided by a theological agenda, but he points out that in their narrative about Jesus we find the characteristics of the genre of the Graeco-Roman biography. The writings which belong to this genre are called *bioi* ('lives') in Greek and *vitae* in Latin. These books are about memorable figures from the past who are thought to be of lasting significance. The special character of such a person is expressed by a narrative of his life in chronological order, from cradle to grave. The public activity of the hero is developed broadly within this whole. The *bioi* are a kind of framework narrative within which all kinds of other literary forms with varying historical content are included. The authors of an ancient biography present their main character as a shining example worthy of being followed. By seeking to attach themselves to this genre, the evangelists show that they want to give an account of what in their view had really happened. We find repercussions of this in the third wave. The historical reliability of the Gospels is again established, but without scholars falling back into the old idea that the Gospels have the character of a factual account from a to z.

Much-used criteria

The investigation of the historical Jesus calls for clear and objective criteria; otherwise subjective preferences become normative.[16] Clear and objective does not mean that the criteria are established once and for all. The results of the investigation can make it necessary for the criteria to be readjusted. Here I shall present some much-used criteria. This gives me the opportunity to bring out a few facets of Jesus as a historical figure.

1. In my description of the second and third waves I referred to the criterion of discontinuity: a saying which cannot be derived from the Judaism of the time and/or early Christianity comes from Jesus himself. This rule has only limited value. The criterion focusses so one-sidedly on the differences that at most some dozen texts can be found that satisfy the criterion. One example of this is that according to Jesus the disciples do not need to fast (Mark 2.18–22 and parallels), since this statement goes against both Jewish and early Christian practice. The criterion may not be

turned round: it is not claimed that words which agree with Jewish and/or early Christian traditions *per se* may not be attributed to Jesus.

2. One sound criterion is that of multiple attestation. This implies that something can withstand the test of historical criticism if it is confirmed by at least two independent sources or if it occurs in two or more texts belonging to different literary genres. One might think for example of Mark, Q and Paul as independent sources; logia, healing stories and parables are genres or literary forms which differ from one another. On the basis of this criterion, historically it is virtually certain that Jesus announced the coming of God's kingdom, that he held strict views on divorce and that he shared his table with toll-collectors and sinners.[17]

3. The 'criterion of embarrassment' is also a useful one. This implies that the earliest communities and the evangelists have handed down traditions and texts which had an offensive character for them, because they contain statements of and about Jesus which were difficult to reconcile with their own high respect for him. Of course they could also have dropped these statements or adapted them to their own beliefs. They did not do this, at least all along the line. A number of provocative traditions have been preserved. The argument now is that such traditions cannot have been created by Jesus' followers; they must be rooted in Jesus' own activity.

A much-mentioned example is Jesus' baptism by John. This event is provocative in two respects: it suggests that Jesus was subordinate to the Baptist and that he was not free from sin (the ritual was meant for sinners). Texts which speak bluntly about Jesus' human traits also fall under this criterion: he explodes with fury (Mark 1.41), he begs God to be spared a cruel end (Mark 14.36).

4. I think that the criterion of 'contextual credibility' is of great importance.[18] This criterion implies that traditions from the Gospels about sayings, actions and experiences of Jesus are historically trustworthy if they can be plausibly fitted into our knowledge of the socio-political and religious context of Judaism at the beginning of the first century.

The starting point for this rule is that Jesus – like any other historical figure – is embedded in a particular situational context. The Gospels put much emphasis on his interaction with his surroundings. But we must show a healthy mistrust of the information that they offer about relations between Jesus and the Judaism of his time. The picture of this is coloured by later developments, by the tensions between the church and the synagogue that developed markedly towards the end of the first century. For knowledge of Judaism in the time of Jesus we must go primarily to other written sources (like the works of Flavius Josephus, the Dead Sea Scrolls, the early rabbinic literature and Graeco-Roman texts) and to the results of intensive archaeological investigation. On the basis of these written sources and material remains we can develop a quite trustworthy picture of Judaism in Judaea and Galilee in the time of Jesus. In the second instance we can put the Gospels alongside this, not so much because they contain supplementary factual material but in order to check how far they agree with historical facts relating to Judaism known to us from other sources. The greater the correspondence, the more certain we can be that the Gospels indeed contain reminiscences of Jesus' life. Often this operation will prove negative: quite often we shall come upon elements which fit better into the time of the evangelists.[19]

5. It is an indubitable historical fact that Jesus died on a cross under Pontius Pilate. This fact is even mentioned in the Christian creed. Jesus' shameful end cannot be the product of the pious fantasy of his followers. That Jesus endured Roman crucifixion is confirmed by Flavius Josephus and by Tacitus. Now it is important for a reconstruction of Jesus' life to offer an honest explanation for his violent death. With an eye to this, investigators speak of the criterion of rejection and execution: at what points did Jesus provoke opposition, which groups did he fall foul of, and how could tensions rise so high that in the end he was liquidated on the orders of Pontius Pilate?

How these questions are answered largely depends on the results of the application of the other criteria mentioned. If the discontinuity between Jesus and his people is emphasized disproportionately, people will easily take refuge in the old explanation that Jesus was executed because he provoked massive opposition among his contemporaries (and above all the Pharisees) by his divergent teaching about the Torah. This explanation loses its force if Jesus' teaching is put within the pluriform context of Judaism at the beginning of our era and it is emphasized that his standpoints stood within the matrix of the halakhah of his time. Moreover a thorough knowledge of the political and legal situation of the time is required. Did Jesus' message have explosive political connotations? Who had the authority to pronounce a death sentence? The Sanhedrin, or exclusively the Roman governor? Was Jesus crucified after a summary conviction or was his execution the result of an orderly trial? I raise these questions to emphasize that it is not simple to use the criterion of execution in a tidy way.

6. A supplementary criterion is the criterion of coherence. It can be used only when, on the basis of other criteria, facts have been uncovered which we have good grounds to assume to be historical. The argument then is that words and actions of Jesus which fit the data base already developed also have a high historical content. In this case, too, we must work prudently. Agreements in content can also be result of the efforts of the earliest Christian communities to attach new material that they produced as faithfully as possible to the historical activity of Jesus. The new material is then certainly in line with Jesus, but it does not come directly from him. Moreover we must not exaggerate the concept of coherence. Jesus was a colourful figure. He need not have always said the same thing everywhere, and not all his activities are to be brought under a single heading. We cannot turn the criterion of coherence round either; nothing is *per se* unhistorical if it is not connected in a strictly logical way with what is known to us about Jesus from else-where.

A new criterion: 'Where there is smoke there must be fire'

The investigation of Jesus suffers from the law that developments after Jesus' death provide little or no material for a reconstruction of his teaching and life. This idea has been challenged by Graham Stanton.[20] He begins from the experience that the true significance of a political or religious leader comes to light only some years after his death. The influence of a leader can be deduced from the long-term effects of such a person. According to Stanton this can also be applied to Jesus. He chooses as his starting point the 'aftermath' of Jesus' ministry, both in the circle of his supporters and in the circle of his opponents. On the basis of both the positive and the negative effects, statements can be made about the cause, i.e. about the facets of Jesus' activity in which the later response has its origin. The principle formulated here can also be given as follows: nothing comes into being from nothing, and where there is smoke there must be fire. Stanton begins by observing that there is smoke; from there he goes in search of the fire.

In working this out, Stanton first investigates some positive effects of the activity of Jesus. A new and radical development in early Christianity was that Gentiles were accepted into Christian communities without being required to be circumcised. Jesus gave no clear instructions on this point. But the acceptance of Gentiles can be regarded as a response to his own behaviour, since he entered into friendly relations with figures who were regarded as second-class citizens: with toll collectors and prostitutes. So Stanton also tries to relate the post-Easter worship of Jesus as the son of God to sayings of the historical Jesus about his special relationship with God.

Even more fascinating is what he writes about negative reactions to actions and words of Jesus. In this connection he discusses the widespread idea that Jesus was a magician, a deceiver, a false prophet who put his people on the wrong track.[21] Traces of this can still be found in late texts like Justin's *Dialogue with Trypho* (69.7) and in the Babylonian Talmud (bSanhedrin 43a and 107b). However, the accusations mentioned already appear in the canonical Gospels: Jesus drives out demons with the help of Beelzebul (Matthew 9.34; 10.25; 12.24,27; Mark 3.22; Luke 11.15); he is possessed by the devil; he is in the power of an unclean spirit (Mark 3.30; John 7.20; 8.48, 52; 10.20); he is stirring up the people and leading them astray (Luke 23.2, 5, 14; John 7.12, 47); he was himself a deceiver and the movement started by him is a long chain of deception (Matthew 27.63–64).

Over against these texts stand others in which precisely the

opposite is stated: Jesus drives out the demons with the help of the
Spirit of God (Matthew 12.18,28; Luke 11.20); he is a great
prophet (Luke 7.16; John 4.19; 9.17: he also calls himself a
prophet: Mark 6.4; Luke 13.33); the real deceivers are the Jewish
chief priests (Matthew 28.11–15); those who call Jesus possessed
fail to recognize that the Spirit of God is at work in him and so
commit an unforgivable sin (Mark 3.28–29; Matthew 12.31–32;
Luke 12.10); the enemies of Jesus are themselves children of the
devil (John 8.44).

Here we hear the echoes of a sharp debate between two parties
who are at odds with one another. The subject of the discussion is
how Jesus' teachings and his healings and exorcisms must be
interpreted. According to the opposition he speaks and acts under
the influence of the devil. Jesus himself claims that he is driven by
God and the holy Spirit, and in turn he accuses his opponents of
being inspired by Satan. This duel was still extremely topical for
the earliest Christian communities. They were regularly confronted by outsiders with the criticism that Jesus had been a
dangerous dissident. This criticism was particularly offensive to
the communities. Indeed we cannot assume that here we are
hearing only an echo of a conflict which flared up only after Jesus'
death and in which he himself had no part. If that were the case, his
later followers would have spared him all these offensive attacks on
his person. No, there is a very good chance that here the tradition
has prserved scraps of a sharp debate in which Jesus himself was
already caught up.

Stanton thus shows that certain beliefs and rules of the earliest
communities form a distant echo of the ideals and ideas of Jesus.
Just as Jesus himself was deeply rooted in the Judaism of his time,
so early Christianity was firmly anchored in the activity of the one
who inspired it.

Jesus as a historical figure

A global sketch

After these reflections on method I shall venture a global sketch of
Jesus' activity.[22] That Jesus really existed is not open to

serious doubt. At present no one sees him purely as a mythical figure.

He was born around the year 6 before the beginning of our era under the emperor Augustus, in the last years of the reign of King Herod the Great (37–4).[23] According to the sources he was a child of Mary and Joseph, a wood-worker. Probably he saw the light of day in Nazareth and not in Bethlehem.[24]

We know virtually nothing about the first thirty years of his life. The historian faces an enormous gap. This lacuna has been filled in later sources with fantastic material which clearly bears a Christian stamp. In fact we know no more than that Jesus grew up in Nazareth, a small village in Galilee not far from the city of Sepphoris, where many traces have been found indicating a strong influence of Graeco-Roman culture. Jesus had a Jewish upbringing and on attaining adulthood was familiar with the religious heritage of his people.

At the end of 27 or the beginning of 28 an event took place which is seen as a turning point in his life. Before that he had led an un-obtrusive existence; after that he began to appear in public. The beginning of his public career, which was to last around two years, is marked by his baptism by John in the Jordan, on the periphery of the inhabited world. John is to be put within the Jewish renewal movements of that time. It is doubtful whether he had links with the Qumran community, although there are some points of contact. Despite his priestly descent, John put a certain distance between himself and the national cult centre, the Jerusalem temple. He saw himself as the eschatological prophet who was charged with announcing the speedy breakthrough of the kingdom of God. He emphasized that this event would be a catastrophe. Salvation was possible only if one converted and submitted to the ritual which he administered: this brought forgiveness of sins outside the realm of the temple cult. Jesus joined the renewal movement led by John, had himself baptized by John and then presumably remained for some time in the Baptist's company. According to the Gospels, Jesus started his ministry only after John had been arrested by Herod Antipas, the tetrarch of Galilee and Peraea. In this view John is the forerunner of Jesus and both face the same task. It is also possible that Jesus detached himself from John in 28 and began on his own mission. In that case the two preachers would have been active for a while side by side.

Jesus took over from John the idea that God's kingdom is near. At many points he brought a message which resembled that of John, but there were also striking differences. Jesus distanced himself from a one-sided emphasis on the disastrous aspects of the coming of God's kingdom and the apocalyptic idea that it was an event which would take place very soon, ushering in the end of history. Jesus presented God as a good father, who opens a new future to men and women, above all to the poor, the sick and the outcast. He spoke about this new future in simple tales, in parables and similitudes, and he combined his preaching with an urgent call to repentance.

It is not certain whether Jesus went to Jerusalem regularly on the occasion of the great festivals. In John he commutes up and down between Galilee, his homeland, and Jerusalem in Judaea. According to the Synoptics he was for the most part active in Galilee, where during his travels he stayed in villages and small towns. He avoided great urban centres like Sepphoris and Tiberias. He showed a particular preference for the villages on the north side of the Sea of Galilee.

It was not least because of his healings and exorcisms that his fame spread rapidly; there is no doubt that Jesus must have had charismatic gifts which put him in a position to perform such special actions. Within the context of the Judaism of the time and also in the non-Jewish world it was not exceptional for someone to emerge as a healer or an exorcist. On this point there is a similarity between Jesus and well-known Jewish figures like Hanina ben Dosa and Honi the Circle-Drawer. By his own admission his special actions showed that he enjoyed God's favour and was filled with the holy Spirit. This claim was not subscribed to by everyone. Critics accused him of operating under the influence of diabolical power. Initially Jesus was also criticized by his own family; only after his death did his relatives begin to join the circle of his followers.

Right at the beginning of his activity Jesus gathered disciples around him. He referred to his most faithful followers as 'the twelve'. Here he gave expression to his conviction that God's kingdom primarily ushered in a change for the twelve tribes of Israel. His more or less regular companions also included many others, both men and women. This last was quite unusual for a Jewish teacher. Among the women who followed Jesus, Mary of Magdala occupied a special place. The disciples shared in Jesus' mission. They too had to become bearers of the message that he had to preach, and through their activities demonstrate that God's kingdom is a present reality.

Although he did not shun contact with non-Jews, Jesus deliberately limited the sphere of his work to Israel. Pagans could share in God's blessing only if they sought to join the Jewish people. The laborious discussions in early Christianity about the conditions on which non-Jews could enter the community confirm that Jesus did not offer any clear solutions to this question. But later the communities did not stand there with completely empty hands. In seeking a solution they could be inspired by a typical pattern of behaviour on the part of Jesus. He entered into friendly relations with people who occupied a marginal position in the society of the time ('toll collectors and sinners') and shared his table with them. In his teaching he gave a central place to the focal points of the Torah, love of God and neighbour, but he also accentuated the obligations by saying that they also applied to foreigners and enemies and to people who in the light of ritual regulations were regarded as unclean.

Historically we cannot assume that Jesus put the authority of the Torah in question and thus above all fell foul of the Pharisees. On many points he shared their convictions. The Pharisaic current was itself a renewal movement in Judaism which saw the written Torah as an indispensable source of inspiration in seeking solutions to new questions. It is an old-fashioned idea to suppose that the Pharisees turned out to be the arch-enemies of Jesus, who were set on liquidating him. It is difficult to give Jesus a precise position within the discussions about the Torah at that time. We see agreements now with this tendency and now with that. In his time

Judaism was a pluriform whole consisting of various groupings which differed markedly from one another.

This does not alter the fact that Jesus caused provocation at an early stage. I have already pointed out that his activities as a healer and exorcist were open to more than one interpretation. His proclamation of God's kingdom implied a critical attitude to existing power relationships. In his parables he depicted a world which was potentially threatening to creditors and great landowners. In Galilee he thus attracted the attention of Herod Antipas, the local ruler, for whom the maintaining of political stability and the avoidance of conflicts with the Romans had a high priority. John also fell foul of the same Herod. According to Flavius Josephus, political considerations played a decisive role in Antipas' decision to execute John. This event gave a signal to Jesus. Would not his own activity end in a violent death? This sense influenced his self-understanding: he began to interpret himself increasingly in the light of scripture as the righteous sufferer.

By his independent attitude towards the laws of cultic purity it was easy for Jesus to incur the suspicion of bringing the reconciling function of temple worship into discredit. Towards the end of his life (in the year 30?) he aroused this suspicion even further by a demonstrative action in the temple area (the so-called cleansing of the temple). This action had an explosive character because it was accompanied by the announcement that God would build a new temple in place of the old one. For the high priest Caiaphas and his advisers, who were responsible for the orderly performance of worship, this perspective was so threatening that they resolved to do away with Jesus. Here motives of political opportunism also played a role. During his years in office Caiaphas had been consistently able to avoid the simmering hostility against Rome from flaring up and endangering the relative administrative autonomy of Judaea and Samaria.

After a last meal with his disciples at the beginning of 15 Nisan, Jesus was arrested in Gethsemane by night on the orders of the priestly aristocracy of Jerusalem. That same night he was subjected to a brief interrogation. The Synoptics mention a formal session of the Sanhedrin which ended in the joint decision to kill Jesus.

Historically speaking it is extremely doubtful whether the whole Sanhedrin assembled in a nocturnal meeting; nor can we assume that this assembly still had the formal right to condemn someone to death at that time. That right lay in the hands of the Roman governor. The Synoptic account is coloured by developments from a later date. It tries to put responsibility for Jesus' death on the supreme organ of Jewish government and gives quite a mild picture of the role of Pilate in order to exonerate later Christians from a hostile attitude on the part of the Romans.

After the interrogation, which must have been informal, Caiaphas and his companions sent Jesus to Pilate with the suggestion that he was claiming to be king of the Jews. Pilate condemned him to crucifixion without himself making a thorough investigation. The sentence was carried out the same day, just outside the city. When Jesus died he was around thirty-six. He was buried in the immediate vicinity of the place where he was executed.

After Jesus' death, his followers had special experiences on the basis of which they came to believe that Jesus had been raised by God. Mary of Magdala and Peter take it in turn to occupy a prominent place in stories about the risen Jesus. The disciples went to great trouble to find an appropriate interpretation of the fact that Jesus, whom they acknowledged as the Messiah, had had to suffer a shameful death. They found the power to form a community and to draw on it to win others over to their conviction that Jesus was the Messiah and that he abidingly performed a key function in the establishment of God's kingdom.

Is the historical Jesus important for the believer?

The Jesus of history is a pale figure compared with the rich images that Christians have developed of him. The rich formation of images already came about in the New Testament and continued undiminished in the post-biblical tradition. By comparison it is shocking to see how little we (can) really know with certainty about his historical activity. It is even more striking that many elements used in forming the later images are based on a narrow historical foundation. The Jesus of history looks very different in many ways from the Jesus who forms the centre of the faith of his followers.

The facts of Jesus' life which can be established historically are not the object of faith. They are not true for the believer, whereas they would be untrue for the non-believer. What historians say about Jesus is on a different level: they formulate what can be *known* about Jesus in the present state of affairs. Whether their results are reliable or not must be judged by current scientific criteria. Historians are not in a position to restate how the Jesus of believers must look. But their sketches, however diverse they may be, do not leave believers unaffected. They serve as corrections. A simple example can clarify this. Now that historians state almost unanimously that Jesus was deeply rooted in Judaism, it is more difficult for believers to swear by a Jesus who was completely unique and who towered above his Jewish contemporaries.

There is a far deeper reason why faith and history are not two different worlds. At the heart of Christian faith is the conviction that God has revealed himself in history. 'In many and various ways God spoke of old to our fathers by the prophets; but in these last days he has spoken to us by a Son, whom he appointed the heir of all things, through whom also he created the world' (Hebrews 1.1–2). In Jesus of Nazareth, a man of flesh and blood, God has assumed a new face. His life is deeply marked by God. Knowledge of the historical activity of Jesus prevents Christians from making him evaporate into a timeless, mythical figure. Without such knowledge the fantasy of believers easily runs riot. This danger was recognized at an early stage. Already in the Gospels the manifold faith in Jesus is expressed by a narrative about his life. They speak of 'what has occurred among us' (Luke 1.1), and they do so in the conviction that the ultimate truth has come to light here.

Historical investigation is directed to the Jesus of former times, to a time-conditioned figure who is to be put in a specific context. The perspective of believers extends much further: 'Jesus Christ is the same, yesterday and today and to all eternity' (Hebrews 13.8). In their eyes he is not tied to a particular epoch. He is confessed as the Lord who is still present and as the one in whom all of history will come to its consummation. However, this confession must remain anchored in what took place once and for all in a distant past, the precise details of which we do not know.

Notes

Introduction

1. From earliest days the Gospels have been attributed to Matthew, Mark, Luke and John. I also use the names of the four evangelists for their books. The context makes it clear enough whether 'Matthew' etc. refers to the book or the narrator. For example: 'In Matthew Jesus gives five long discourses.' And: 'Matthew concludes these discourses with a stereotyped formula.'

2. Recently the present wealth of methods and approaches has been mapped out clearly by the Papal Biblical Commission in the document *The Interpretation of the Bible in the Church*, English translation in J.L.Houlden (ed.), *The Interpretation of the Bible in the Church*, London 1995. There is an extended commentary on this document in J.A.Fitzmyer (ed.), *The Biblical Commission's Document 'The Interpretation of the Bible in the Church': Text and Commentary*, Subsidia Biblica 18, Rome 1995.

3. The two concepts of synchrony and diachrony were introduced by F.de Saussure (1857–1913) in his lectures given in the University of Geneva in 1906–1911. On the basis of notes taken by students this lecture material was posthumously made into the book *Cours de linguistique générale*, Paris 1916. See also F.de Saussure, *Premier cours de linguistique générale (1907) d'après les cahiers d'Albert Riedlinger*, Oxford 1996; id., *Deuxième cours de linguistique générale (1908–1909)*, Oxford 1996; id., *Troisième cours de linguistique générale (1910–1911) d'après les cahiers d'Emile Constantin*, Oxford 1993.

4. See P.Claes, *Echo's echo's. De kunst van de allusie*, Amsterdam 1988, 28–37.

5. Jaap Zijlstra, in *Lichtgeraakt*, Kampen 1985.

1. The limits of a text

1. Cf. J.Limburg, *Jonah. A Commentary*, Louisville and London 1993, 43.

2. See W.Weren, 'The Lord's Supper. An Inquiry into the Coherence in Lk 22, 14–38', in H.J.Auf der Maur, L.Bakker, A. van de Bunt and J.Waldram (eds), *Fides Sacramenti Sacramentum Fidei. Studies in Honour of Pieter Smulders*, Assen 1981, 9–26.

3. The first group of words includes 'recline at table' (vv.14, 21; cf. v.30, 'at my table'), 'passover' (v.15), 'eat' (vv.15, 16, 30), 'drink' (vv.18, 30), 'cup' (vv.17, 20), and 'serve' (v.27). The second cluster can be recognized from the following terminology: 'suffer' (v.15), 'blood' (v.20), 'betray' (vv.21–22), 'go his predestined way' (v.22), 'trials' (v.28), 'go to prison and death' (v.33), 'deny' (v.34) and 'be reckoned with the transgressors' (v.37).

4. Biblical translators make much use of *The Greek New Testament*, Stuttgart ⁴1993. In this edition of the text the Gospel according to Matthew consists of 149 pericopes.

5. Professional exegetes are by no means agreed on the demarcation of the passage about the Good Shepherd. U.Busse, 'Offene Fragen zu Joh 10', *New Testament Studies* 33, 1987, 516, writes the following about John 10: 'John 10, the chapter on the good shepherd, is beyond dispute an attractive section, but at the same time it is burdened with almost all the problems of Johannine exegesis. Thus there is a dispute about not only the beginning, the form, the internal structure, in part the wording and above all the position in the macrotext, but also the intent of the chapter.' R.Schnackenburg, *Das Johannesevangelium, IV Teil*, Herders theologischer Kommentar zum NT IV/4, Freiburg 1984, 142, asserts on John 10.1–18: 'A precise linguistic analysis of the whole textual unit is greatly to be desired... In some cases it could show a greater textual coherence than many literary critics are willing to assume.'

6. There is the following marginal note on John 10.1–39: 'There is a discussion as to whether the order of the sections has been disturbed (vv.19–29, 1–18, 30–39).'

7. The division into chapters was not made by the original authors. We already find certain divisions in ancient manuscripts of the Bible. The present division into chapters was introduced by Stephen Langton (died 1228). The numbering of verses comes from an even later date. Around 1440 Rabbi Isaac Nathan provided the Hebrew Bible with the

division into verses which is still used. The New Testament was split up into verses by Robert Stephanus for his Greek and Latin edition of the New Testament (1551). See B.M.Metzger and M.D.Coogan (eds), *The Oxford Companion to the Bible*, New York and Oxford 1993, 105–7.

2. Structural analysis

1. According to J.Siebert-Hommes, *Let the Daughters Live! The Literary Architecture of Exodus 1 and 2 as a Key for Interpretation*, Leiden 1998, 18–19, reading the text aloud is the first step in the investigation. In connection with this she formulates five other steps for investigating the literary architecture of narrative biblical texts. Phonology is occupied with the systematic study of speech sounds and their contribution to meaning. Well-known phenomena include alliteration (repetition of the opening sound), assonance (rhyme), paronomasia (word play) and onomatopoeia (a word which is formed from a sound).

2. Cf. H.J.B.Combrink, 'The Macrostructure of the Gospel of Matthew', *Neotestamentica* 16, 1982, 6–10; D.R.Bauer, *The Structure of Matthew's Gospel. A Study in Literary Design*, Journal of the Study of the New Testament Supplement Series 31, Sheffield 1988, 13–20.

3. Some identify him with John the Baptist (cf. 14.2), others say that he is a prophet like the other prophets (cf. 13.57). In 1.1, 16 it was already said that Jesus is the messiah, and in 14.33 that he is the son of God.

4. Cf. F.Breukelman, *Bijbelse theologie. Deel III, afl.2: De Koning als Richter*, Kampen 1996, 173.

5. This proposal largely corresponds with that of O.Schwankl, *Die Sadduzäerfrage (Mk. 12, 18–27 parr.). Eine exegetisch-theologische Studie zur Auferstehungserwartung*, Bonner Biblische Beiträge 66, Frankfurt am Main 1987, 99.

6. See D.M.Cohn-Sherbok, 'Jesus' Defence of the Resurrection of the Dead', *Journal for the Study of the New Testament* 11, 1981, 64–73.

7. F.Schnider and W.Stenger, 'Die offene Tür und die unüberschreitbare Kluft. Strukturanalytische Überlegungen zum Gleichnis vom reichen Mann und armen Lazarus (Lk 16, 19–31)', *New Testament Studies* 26, 1978–1979, 273–83, distinguish three sequences (16.19–21, 22–23, 24–31). P.H.M.Welzen, *Lucas, evangelist van gemeenschap. Een onderzoek naar de pragmatische effecten in Lc 15,*

1–17. 20, Nijmegen 1986, 163–7, mentions 16.19–21 as the opening situation and 16.22–31 as 'the main part'. This last pasage consists of two subdivisions: 16.22–23 (the development of a new situation) and 16.24–31 (a conversation in three stages).

8. This standpoint is expressed by L.Sabourin, *L'Évangile de Luc. Introduction et commentaire*, Rome 1985, 287–8: 'The reversal of fortunes is certainly a central theme of the parable... The story presents in a graphic way the doctrine of the Beatitudes, which promise the gift of the kingdom to the poor and the refreshment of the hungry, while the oracles announce misfortune to the rich and the satisfied (6.20–25).'

3. Narrative analysis

1. See the bibliography at the end of this book under the heading 'literary analysis'.

2. Recent examples are W.Carter, *Matthew. Storyteller, Interpreter, Evangelist*, Peabody, MA 1996; S.H.Smith, *A Lion with Wings. A Narrative-Critical Approach to Mark's Gospel*, The Biblical Seminar 38, Sheffield 1996; R.J.Karris, *Luke. Artist and Theologian*, New York 1985; D.Tovey, *Narrative Art and Act in the Fourth Gospel*, Journal for the Study of the New Testament Supplement Series 151, Sheffield 1997.

3. Here I am incorporating the results of lectures which I gave at the Tilburg Theological Faculty in 1997–1998. Creative contributions to these were made by Jantje Bax, Marie-José Holterman-van der Aa, Salaam Somi and Marleen Verschoren.

4. S.Chatman, *Story and Discourse. Narrative Structure in Fiction and Film*, Ithaca, NJ 1978, 151.

5. Sometimes the narrator makes the later followers of Jesus speak through the mouth of a character from his story, for example in 3.11 ('We speak of what we know, and bear witness to what we have seen; yet you do not receive our testimony'), in 4.22 ('You worship what you do not know; we worship what we know'), and in 9.31 ('We know that God does not listen to sinners').

6. The same choice is made by J.Maas, 'De structuur van de geloofs-communicatie in Johannes 11:1–46', in P.Beentjes, J.Maas and T.Wever (eds), *'Gelukkig is de mens.' Opstellen over Psalmen, semiotiek en exegese aangeboden aan Nico Tromp*, Kampen [1991], 169–181: 169–70.

7. R.Alter, *The Art of Biblical Narrative*, New York 1981, 116–17.

8. For detailed theoretical reflections see M.Bal, *Narratology: Introduction to the Theory of Narrative*, Toronto 1985; J.Darr, *On Character Building. The Reader and the Rhetoric of Characterization in Luke-Acts*, Louisville 1992; also Semeia 63, *Characterization in Biblical Literature*, Atlanta 1993.

9. Cf. A.Marchadour, *Lazare. Histoire d'un récit. Récits d'une histoire*, Lectio Divina 132, Paris 1988, 111–33; C.A.Newsom and S.H.Ringe (eds), *Women's Bible Commentary*, London 1992, ad loc.

10. See also R.E.Brown, 'Roles of Women in the Fourth Gospel', *Theological Studies* 36, 1975, 688–99.

11. Cf. F.Moloney, 'The Faith of Martha and Mary. A Narrative Approach to John 11.17–40,' *Biblica* 75, 1994, 471–93.

12. Martha's name means 'mistress'; *mar(e)ta* is the feminine form of *mare* (= 'master').

13. Jesus' emotions are mentioned in John elsewhere only in 12.27 and 13.21. Cf. R.A.Culpepper, *Anatomy of the Fourth Gospel. A Study in Literary Design*, Philadelphia 1983, 110–11. For the meaning of the verbs in 11.33, 38 see C.Story, 'The Mental Attitude of Jesus at Bethany: John 11.33, 38', *New Testament Studies* 37, 1991, 51–66.

14. J.F.Coakley, 'The Anointing at Bethany and the Priority of John', *Journal of Biblical Literature* 107, 1988, 241–56, mentions some parallels from Graeco-Roman and Jewish texts (here 247–8).

15. The verb 'dry' occurs in John only in 11.2; 13.3; 13.5. Outside John in the New Testament only in Luke 7.38,44.

16. M.Stibbe, 'A Tomb with a View. John 11.1–44 in Narrative-Critical Perspective', *New Testament Studies* 37, 1994, 51, gives the following paraphrase of 11.9–10: 'I can return to Judea because the hour for my death (the hour of darkness) is not quite upon us. I will therefore not be killed ("stumble") at Bethany because I am still ministering in a season of pre-ordained security ("daylight").'

17. M.Ball, *Narratology*, 62–80; Culpepper, *Anatomy*, 53–75.

18. E.van Wolde and J.Sanders, 'Kijken met de ogen van anderen. Perspectief in bijbelteksten', *Tijdschrift voor Theologie* 34, 1994, 221–45. See also J.Sanders, *Perspective in Narrative Discourse*, thesis of the Catholic University of Brabant, Tilburg 1994.

19. We come across such questions in J.Ashton, *Studying John. Approaches to the Fourth Gospel*, Oxford 1994, 140–65: 'Narrative Criticism'.

4. *Meaning in Context*

1. J.Barr, *The Semantics of Biblical Language*, Oxford 1961, reissued London 1983, is a book which has now become a classic. M.Silva, *Biblical Words and Their Meaning. An Introduction to Lexical Semantics*, revised edition Grand Rapids, 1994, is also a good introduction.

2. H.G.Liddell and R.Scott, *A Greek-English Lexicon*, Oxford ¹1843, ⁸1897 = 1928 (reprint). [New edition] Revised and Augmented throughout by H.S.Jones, Oxford ⁹1925–40 = 1983 (reprint). With a supplement [edited by E.A.Barber], Oxford 1968 = 1983 (reprint).

3. F.W.Arndt, W.Gingrich and W.Bauer, *A Greek-English Lexicon of the New Testament and Other Early Christian Literature*, Chicago ²1979; J.H.Moulton and G.Milligan, *The Vocabulary of the Greek Testament Illustrated from the Papyri and Other Non-Literary Sources*, London 1929. The traditional alphabetical arrangement of a lexicon does not show that the lexemes belong to a semantic cluster. This disadvantage is overcome in J.P.Louw and E.A.Nida (eds), *Greek-English Lexicon of the New Testament Based on Semantic Domains, Volume I. Introduction and Domains; Volume II, Indices*, New York 1988.

4. For a concordance to the English text of the New Testament see Clinton Morrison, *An Analytical Concordance to the Revised Standard Version of the New Testament*, London and Philadelphia 1979. The following concordances are indispensable for studying the Greek text of the New Testament: W.F.Moulton and A.S.Geden, *A Concordance to the Greek Testament according to the Texts of Westcott and Hort, Tischendorf and the English Revisers*, Edinburgh ⁵1978 (first edition 1897); K.Aland and H.Riesenfeld, *Vollständige Konkordanz zum griechischen Neuen Testament (Band I, Teil 1 (A–Λ), Teil 2 (M–Ω). Band 2: Spezialübersichten)*, Berlin 1983 and 1978; H.Bachman and W.A.Slaby, *Konkordanz zum Novum Testamentum Graece von Nestle-Aland, 26. Auflage und zum Greek New Testament, 3rd Edition*, Berlin and New York ³1987; A.Schmoller, *Handkonkordanz zum griechischen Neuen Testament. Nach dem Text des Novum Testamentum Graece von Nestle-Aland, 26.Auflage und zum Greek New Testament, Third Edition (Corrected)*, revised by Beate Köster, Stuttgart 1989.

5. See the bibliography at the end of this book, s.v. 'software'.

6. My views on the second line of meaning are inspired by

D.Rensberger, 'The Politics of John. The Trial of Jesus in the Fourth Gospel', *Journal of Biblical Literature* 103, 1984, 395–411. See also W.Weren, '"Het is volbracht." Structuur en betekenis van het lijdensverhaal van Johannes (Joh. 18–19)', *Tijdschrift voor Theologie* 36, 1996, 132–54.

5. Diachronic methods

1. Here I am alluding to the well-known statement by John of Salisbury, *Metalogicus* III,4: 'We are like dwarves sitting on the shoulders of giants, so that we can see more and further than they.'

2. J.H.Greenlee, *An Introduction to New Testament Textual Criticism*, Grand Rapids 1964, 11.

3. According to K.Elliott and I.Moir, *Manuscripts and the Text of the New Testament*, Edinburgh 1995, 14, the total now amounts to 5424 items (97 papyri, 270 majuscules, 2747 minuscules and 2310 lectionaries). Around 60 manuscripts contain the whole New Testament; the rest offer only a particular part of it.

4. C.R.Gregory, *Die griechischen Handschriften des Neuen Testaments*, Versuche und Entwürfe 2, Leipzig 1908.

5. Nestle/Aland, *Novum Testamentum Graece*, Stuttgart[27]1993 (edited by B.Aland, K.Aland, J.Karavidopoulos, C.M.Martini and B.M.Metzger).

6. The most recent edition is *The Greek New Testament*, Stuttgart[4]1993 (edited by B.Aland, K.Aland, J.Karavidopoulos, C.M.Martini and B.M.Metzger).

7. The Codex Sinaiticus contains part of the Old Testament, the New Testament, the Letter of Barnabas and the Shepherd of Hermas. The manuscript comes from the first half of the fourth century. It was discovered by C.von Tischendorf in St Catherine's Monastery on Mount Sinai. In 1859 the manuscript was 'given' to the Tsar of Russia and came to be in St Petersburg. It is now in the British Museum. Codex Vaticanus contains the Old Testament (with gaps) and the New Testament (up to Hebrews 9.14). The manuscript comes from the first half of the fourth century (c.340) and is now in the Vatican Library (catalogued as early as 1475); its origin is obscure.

8. There are twelve basic rules in K. and B. Aland, *Der Text des Neuen Testaments. Einführung in die wissenschaftlichen Ausgaben sowie in Theorie und Praxis der modernen Textkritik*, Stuttgart 1982, 282–3.

9. The Codex Bezae Cantabrigiensis contains the Gospels (in the order

Matthew-John-Luke-Mark), Acts and a fragment of III John, both in the Greek text (left page) and in a Latin translation (right). The Codex dates from the fifth or fourth century and probably comes from Egypt or North Africa. Theodorus Beza gave the manuscript to the Cambridge University Library in 1581, hence the second name, Cantabrigiensis. This manuscript is the most important representative of the Western text, which is characterized by a large number of distinctive choices. A thorough study of D is D.C.Parker, *Codex Bezae: An Early Christian Manuscript and its Text*, Cambridge 1992.

10. For further study – in addition to the book by K. and B. Aland (see n.8) – I would mention the following literature: J.Finegan, *Encountering New Testament Manuscripts. A Working Introduction to Textual Criticism*, Grand Rapids 1974; J.H.Greenlee, *An Introduction to New Testament Textual Criticism*, Grand Rapids 1964 (revised edition, Peabody, Mass. 1995); id., *Scribes, Scrolls and Scripture. A Student's Guide to New Testament Textual Criticism*, Grand Rapids 1985; B.M.Metzger, *The Text of the New Testament. Its Transmission, Corruption and Restoration*, Oxford 1964; id., *A Textual Commentary on the Greek New Testament. A Companion Volume to the United Bible Societies' Greek New Testament*, London and New York 1971 (now in a third edition).

11. Recently exegetes have also been speaking of literary criticism in studies with a synchronic colouring. In R.J.Coggins and J.L.Houlden (eds), *A Dictionary of Biblical Interpretation*, London and Philadelphia 1990, 402, M.Davies proposes that the diachronic branch ('questions of history, reaching behind the texts to their sources, and the events which gave rise to them') should no longer be termed literary criticism, but that the term 'source criticism' should be reserved for it. Literary criticism would then have to refer only to modern forms of investigation of the meaning and influence of texts (of the Bible). I am not adopting this proposal so as not to break with the established terminology.

12. Those who know the Greek text should use K.Aland, *Synopsis quattuor evangeliorum locis parallelis evangeliorum apocryphorum et patrum adhibitis*, Stuttgart 1989, thirteenth revised edition, fourth impression; the Greek text with an English translation is available in K. Aland, *Synopsis of the Four Gospels. Greek-English Edition of the Synopsis Quattuor Evangeliorum*, Stuttgart [10]1993; cf. also A.Huck and H.Greeven, *Synopse der Drei Evangelien mit Beigabe der johanneischen Parallelstellen*, Tübingen [13]1981 (a version with the

English text is available as Burton H.Throckmorton, *Gospel Parallels*, Nashville 1979; cf. also H.F.D.Sparks, *Synopsis of the Gospels*, London 1977).

13. W.Hendriks, *Karakteristiek woordgebruik in de synoptische evangelies*, Band I, Nijmegen 1986, 54–6. A.Barr, *A Diagram of Synoptic Relationships*, Edinburgh ²1995, is a useful book.

14. Hendriks, *Karakteristiek woordgebruik* (n.13), 83.

15. E.Charpentier, *How to Read the New Testament*, London 1982, 16.

16. To explain the agreements within these classes we could also suppose that Mark used Matthew and Luke, but in that case we would have to find a solution for the fact that in writing his Gospel Mark left a tremendous amount of material from his sources unused. Or more precisely, why would he largely have ignored the material from Synoptic classes 3, 5 and 7?

17. A survey of the material usually attributed to Q can be found in R.E.Brown, *An Introduction to the New Testament*, The Anchor Bible Reference Library, New York and London 1997, 118–19.

18. B.H.Streeter, *The Four Gospels. A Study of Origins*, London 1924.

19. K.L.Schmidt, *Der Rahmen der Geschichte Jesu. Literarkritische Untersuchungen zur ältesten Jesusüberlieferung*, Berlin 1919, reprinted Darmstadt ²1969; M.Dibelius, *From Tradition to Gospel*, Cambridge 1971; R.Bultmann, *The History of the Synoptic Tradition* (1921), Oxford ²1968.

20. H.Conzelmann, *The Theology of St Luke*, London 1960; W.Marxsen, *Mark the Evangelist*, Nashville 1969; some studies by G.Bornkamm are included in G.Bornkamm, G.Barth and H.J.Held, *Tradition and Interpretation in the Gospel of Matthew*, London ²1982.

21. Guideline I can also be used for material from Mark which has a parallel only in one of the two other Synoptic Gospels (Mark//Matthew or Mark//Luke). The key questions about Mark's version are the same in this case. The Synoptic survey then has only two columns. After that follow either the key questions under 3 with reference to Matthew's version or the key questions under 4 with reference to Luke.

6. Texts in triplicate

1. F.Lentzen-Deis, *Die Taufe Jesu nach den Synoptikern. Literarkritische und gattungsgeschichtliche Untersuchungen*, Frankfurter Theologische Studien 4, Frankfurt am Main 1970, 195–289.

2. See the division of Mark proposed by B.M.F.van Iersel, *Mark: A Reader-Response Commentary*, Journal for the Study of the New Testament Supplement Series 164, Sheffield 1998, 68–86. Mark 1.1 is the title of the whole book; 1.14–15 forms the transition between the prologue and the following part (1.16–8.21), which is predominantly situated in Galilee.

3. See Chapter 4 of this book.

4. See W.Weren, *Matteüs, Belichting van het bijbelboek*, 's-Hertogenbosch 1994, 34–7.

5. Mark uses it 7 times, Luke 57 times.

6. 'Righteousness' occurs seven times in Matthew (3.15; 5.6, 10, 20; 6.1,33; 21.32). Mark does not know the word and Luke uses it only once (1.75). According to Matthew 3.15 Jesus and John must fulfil all righteousness; this statement resembles 5.17, where Jesus asserts that he comes to fulfil the Law and the Prophets. Matthew also uses 'fulfil' often to indicate that Jesus' career corresponds completely to words of scripture (1.22; 2.15, 17, 23; 4.14; 8.17; 12.17; 13.35; 21.4; 27.9; see also 26.54, 56).

7. In a number of authoritative manuscripts the words which God speaks in Luke 3.22 are 'You are my son, today I have begotten you.' Here Luke's version deviates from the parallel in Mark. See my remarks about this in Chapter 5, under textual criticism.

8. The Fourth Gospel goes one step further and obliterates any trace of the baptism of Jesus. Here John is not referred to by his epithet 'the Baptist'. He is transformed into someone who bears witness to Jesus. In 1.32 he says: 'I saw the Spirit descending from heaven like a dove and resting on him.' The tradition of Jesus' baptism has, however, been preserved in some non-canonical texts (see the Gospel of the Ebionites, fragment 4; the Gospel of the Nazareans, fragment 2; the Gospel of the Hebrews, fragment 3).

9. Such a story also often mentions a reaction on the part of the bystanders (choral conclusion); only that element is missing here.

10. This is indicated by H.J. Held, 'Matthew as Interpreter of the Miracle Stories', in G.Bornkamm, G.Barth and H.J.Held, *Tradition*, 165–299.

11. For an analysis of this quotation see M.J.J.Menken, 'The Source of the Quotation from Isaiah 53:4 in Matthew 8:17', *Novum Testamentum* 39, 1997, 313–27.

12. This thought is expressed by E.M.Wainwright, *Towards a Feminist Critical Reading of the Gospel according to Matthew*, Beihefte zur

Zeitschrift für die neutestamentliche Wissenschaft 60, Berlin and New York 1991, 178–91.

13. See Luke 5.5; 8.24 (twice); 8.45; 9.33, 49; 17.13.

7. *A text in duplicate*

1. More about this in M.Dulaey, 'La parabole de la brebis perdue dans l'Église ancienne: de l'exégèse à l'iconographie', *Revue des Études Augustiniennes* 39, 1993, 3–22.

2. Cf. the presentation of the Greek texts in F.Neirynck, *Q-Synopsis. The Double Tradition in Greek*, Studiorum Novi Testamenti Auxilia 13, Leuven 1988, 54–5.

3. According to J.Jeremias, *The Parables of Jesus*, London [3]1972, 134, this question also includes Luke 15.5–6.

4. The parable itself speaks of one sheep from a flock of one hundred animals. The expression 'one of these little ones' (18.10,14) is connected with 'one of them' in 18.12; here too the number comes first. For those who know the Greek text I would point out that 18.14 contains *hen* (neuter) which is really incorrect; the masculine (*heis*) should stand here. The neuter *hen* shows how much the image of the sheep (in Greek also a noun which is neuter, *to probaton*) has influenced the application.

5. See F.Schnider, *Die verlorenen Söhne. Strukturanalytische und historisch-kritische Untersuchungen zu Lk 15*, Orbis Biblicus et Orientalis 17, Freiburg and Göttingen 1977.

6. Some doubt is called for here, since in some cases 'which of you' is taken from Q: Luke 11.11//Matthew 7.9; Luke 12.25//Matthew 6.27; see also the agreement between Luke 14.5 (*tis humōn* = 'which of you') and Matthew 12.11 (*tis... ex humōn* = 'which among you'). The other cases belong to Luke's special material (11.5; 14.28; 17.7) and therefore do not allow any certain conclusions on the question whether 'which of you' refers to tradition or to redaction.

7. Luke has on some occasions taken 'sinner(s)' from Mark or Q (Luke 5.30–32//Mark 2.16–17; Luke 7.34//Matthew 11.19); however, usually this term is peculiar to the Third Gospel (5.8; 6.32–34; 7.37, 39; 13.2; 18.13; 19.7; 24.7).

8. E.g. J.Lambrecht, *Terwijl hij tot ons sprak. Parabels van Jezus*, Tielt and Amsterdam 1976, 56–67, especially 58–63. His reconstruction of the Q text looks like this:

What man of you who has a hundred sheep and has lost one of them does not leave behind the ninety-nine on the mountains and go after the lost one until he finds it? And when he has found it, he lays it on his shoulders; when he comes home he calls together his friends and neighbours and says to them: Rejoice with me, for I have found my sheep which was lost. I say to you: so too there will be joy in heaven over one sinner... more than over ninety-nine...

9. J.Dupont, 'La parabole de la brebis perdue (Mt 18,12–14; Lc 15,4–7)', *Gregorianum* 49, 1968, 265–78 [= id., *Études sur les évangiles synoptiques*, Bibliotheca Ephemeridum Theologicarum Lovaniensium 70–B, Louvain 1985, 624–46]; J.Dupont, 'Les implications christologiques de la parabole de la brebis perdue', in id. (ed.), *Jésus aux origines de la christologie*, Bibliotheca Ephemeridum Theologicarum Lovaniensium 40, Leuven and Gembloux 1975, 331–50 [= id., *Études*, 647–66).

10. The reconstruction of the Q text offered here resembles logion 107 from the Gospel of Thomas (the agreements are printed in bold) in many points:

Jesus said: 'The kingdom is like **a shepherd who had a hundred sheep. One of them, the largest,** got **lost. He left the ninety-nine behind and looked for the one sheep until he found it.** After he had gone to this trouble he said to the sheep: "I love you **more than the ninety-nine** others."'

The logion from Thomas contains the original fact of the quantitative disproportion (1>99). This fact is given a distinctive colouring here: the lost sheep is the largest in the whole flock, and the shepherd loves this animal more than the other sheep. Probably the largest sheep stands for the Gnostic Christians. This fits with the fact that for a long time the logia collected in Thomas were handed down (and worked on!) by Gnostic followers of Jesus.

8. John and the Synoptics

1. A.Denaux (ed.), *John and the Synoptics*, Bibliotheca Ephemeridum Theologicarum Lovaniensium 101, Leuven 1992, is a fundamental book on this question. From this book it is evident that the hypothesis that John knew the Synoptic Gospels in their final redaction and used them for writing his own Gospel has gained influence. This hypothesis does not exclude the possibility that in addition John also made use of his own oral and written traditions.

2. For a narrative analysis of John 2.13–22 see F.Moloney, 'Reading

John 2.13–22. The Purification of the Temple', *Revue biblique* 97, 1990, 432–52.

3. The quotation follows the formulation of the Septuagint, but by replacing the past tense ('has consumed') with the future tense ('shall consume me') the evangelist has transformed the Old Testament clause into an announcement of the death of Jesus. See M.J.J.Menken, 'Zeal for Your House Will Consume Me' (John 2:17)', in id., *Old Testament Quotations in the Fourth Gospel. Studies in Textual Form*, Contributions to Biblical Exegesis and Theology 15, Kampen 1996, 37–45.

4. R.A.Culpepper, *Anatomy*, 161–2, ranks the following texts among the 'misunderstandings in John': 2.19–21; 3.3–5; 4.10–15, 31–34; 6.32–35, 51–53; 7.33–36; 8.21–22, 31–35, 51–53, 56–58; 11.11–15, 23–26; 12.32–34; 13.36–38; 14.4–6, 7–9; 16.16–19.

5. In seven cases there is no such explanation: 4.10–15; 7.33–36; 8.21–22; 8.51–53; 8.56–58; 12.32–34; 13.36–38.

6. The words of Jesus are addressed to those who sell pigeons, not to all those present. On this point, too, there is an agreement with Matthew.

7. This is also the case in the Gospel of Thomas, where the logion stands completely by itself, detached from any narrative connection.

8. Literature: N.Perrin, *The Resurrection Narratives. A New Approach*, London 1977; P.Perkins, *Resurrection. New Testament Witness and Contemporary Reflection*, London 1984, 113–94.

9. Intertextuality and the Gospels

1. J.Kristeva, *Sémeiotikè. Recherche pour une sémanalyse*, Paris 1969. The formulation of a theory has been markedly advanced by U.Broich and M.Pfister (eds), *Intertextualität. Formen, Funktionen, anglistische Fallstudien*, Tübingen 1985; P.Claes, *Echo's echo's. De kunst van de allusie*, Amsterdam 1988.

2. There are interesting intertextual studies in S.Draisma (ed.), *Intertextuality in Biblical Writings. Essays in Honour of Bas van Iersel*, Kampen 1989; R.B.Hayes, *Echoes of Scripture in the Letters of Paul*, New Haven and London 1989; J.Bastiaens, *Interpretaties van Jesaja 53. Een intertextueel onderzoek naar de lijdende Knecht in Jes 53 (MT/LXX) en in Lk 22:14–38, Hand 3:12–26, Hand 4:23–31 en Hand 8:26–40*, Tilburg 1993; W.Weren, *Intertextualiteit en Bijbel*, Kampen 1993. For criticism of the work of Bastiaens and Weren see

M.Rese, '"Intertextualität" – Ein Beispiel für Sinn und Unsinn "neuer" Methoden', in C.M.Tuckett (ed.), *The Scriptures in the Gospels*, Bibliotheca Ephemeridum Theologicarum Lovaniensium 131, Leuven 1997, 431–9.

3. For a translation of the Septuagint into English see L.C.Brenton, *The Septuagint Version of the Old Testament, with an English Translation and with Various Readings and Critical Notes*, London 1896. In recent years a start has been made on a new French translation under the title *La Bible d'Alexandrie* with extensive introductions and notes. So far the following parts have appeared: Genesis (Paris 1986), Exodus (1989), Leviticus (1988), Numbers (1994), Deuteronomy (1992), Joshua (1997) and I Kingdoms (1997).

4. My commentary on Isa.45.18–19 has been inspired by W.Beuken, *Jesaja. Deel II*, De Prediking van het Oude Testament, Nijkerk 1979, 250–6.

5. The action is described differently in Matthew 5.21b from Exodus 21.12 and Leviticus 24.17. The sanction also differs: in Matthew such a person is liable to judgment, in the two other texts it is said that such   a
person must be put to death.

6. Against W.D.Davies and D.C.Allison, *The Gospel According to Saint Matthew*, Volume 1, International Critical Commentary, Edinburgh 1988, 511: 'This addition to "Thou shalt not kill", although not found in the OT or in extant Jewish literature, is a fair summary of the legislation set forth in Exod. 21.12 = Lev.24.17; Num.35.12; and Deut.17.8–13; it is, therefore, not to be labelled rabbinic interpretation.' U.Luz, *Das Evangelium nach Matthäus (Mt 1–7)*, Evangelisch-Katholischer Kommentar zum Neuen Testament I,1, Zurich, Einsiedeln, Cologne and Neukirchen-Vluyn, also speaks of 'a free rendering of the legal ordinance which is set down in Exod.21.12; Lev.24.16; cf. Num.35.16–18', and adds: 'So Jesus is not alluding to a contemporary halakhic regulation...'

7. See the Wisdom of Sirach (34.25–27), the Qumran Community Rule (1QS 5.25; 6.24–25; 7.3, 4, 5, 9, 14), the Psalms of Solomon (16.10), the Mishnah (m.Avot 2.10) and some texts from the Babylonian Talmud (b.Nedarim 11a; Baba Metsia 58b and 59a). It cannot be said for certain whether all these texts go back to first-century traditions.

8. Cf. the adage of Augustine, *Quaest in Hept*.2, 73, PL 34, 623: 'The New Testament lies hidden in the Old, and in the New the Old is disclosed.'

10. Five women by Jesus' cradle

1. See the bibliography at the end of this book under the heading 'Women's exegetical studies'.
2. The argument which now follows has also been published as W.J.C.Weren, 'The Five Women in Matthew's Genealogy', *Catholic Biblical Quarterly* 59, 1997, 288–305.
3. For example L.Morris, *The Gospel According to Matthew*, Grand Rapids and Leicester 1992, 23.
4. For example, U. Luz, *Das Evangelium nach Matthaus (Mt 1–7)*, Evangelisch-Katholischer Kommentar zum Neuen Testament I/1, Zurich, Einsiedeln, Cologne and Neukirchen-Vluyn 1985, 93–5.
5. R. E. Brown, *The Birth of the Messiah: A Commentary on the Infancy Narratives in Matthew and Luke*, Garden City, NY 1977, 73.
6. F. Schnider and W. Stenger, 'Die Frauen im Stammbaum Jesu nach Mattäus: Strukturale Beobachtungen zu Mt 1,1–17', *Biblische Zeitschrift*, NF 23, 1979, 195.
7. J Schaberg, *The Illegitimacy of Jesus: A Feminist Theological Interpretation of the Infancy Narratives*, San Francisco 1987, 32–3.
8. Here I follow the proposal by R. Laurentin, 'Approche structurale de Matthieu 1–2,' in M.Carrez, J.Doré and P Grelot (eds), *De la Tôrah au Messie: Mélanges Henri Cazelles*, Paris 1981, 382–416, esp. 395–9.
9. My summary of the main lines of the book of Ruth is inspired by E.van Wolde, *Ruth and Naomi*, London 1998. See also ead., 'Text in Dialogue with Texts. Intertextuality in the Ruth and Tamar Narratives', *Biblical Interpertation* 5, 1997, 1–28.
10. M. Garsiel, '"The Story of David and Bathsheba": A Different Approach', *Catholic Biblical Quarterly* 55, 1993, 244–62.
11. For Bathsheba's active role in I Kings 1–2 I follow the analysis by T. Dennis, *Sarah Laughed. Women's Voices in the Old Testament*, London 1994, 140–75.
12. Useful starting points to this common pattern can be found in Schaberg, *Illegitimacy* (n.7), 32–3. We find yet more nuances in E.M.Wainwright, *Towards a Feminist Critical Reading of the Gospel according to Matthew*, Beihefte zur Zeitschrift für die neutestamentliche Wissenschaft 60, Berlin and New York 1991, 60–76 and 155–76.

11. Artistic texts in the light of the Gospels

1. J.Saramago, *O evangelho segundo Jesu Cristo*, Lisbon 1991; German *Das evangelium nach Jesus Christus*, Hamburg 1993; Dutch *Het Evangelie volgens Jezus Christus*, Amsterdam 1993, to which page references are given. There is a brief discussion of the novel in K.-J.Kuschel, 'The Paradox of Jesus in Films and Novels', *Concilium* 1997/1, 10–12.

2. Saramago, *Evangelie*, 303.

3. It is striking that there are no references to narratives about the resurrection of Jesus. An echo of it can be found only at the end of the account of the massacre in Bethlehem. Early in the morning Joseph, Mary and Jesus depart for Nazareth. That same morning Zelomi (a woman!) goes to the cave (a replacement for the tomb) in the expectation that she will find Jesus there dead, but the cave is empty. Zelomi then says to herself, 'He is no longer here… he has been able to escape this first death' (Saramago, *Evangelie*, 106; cf. Mark 16.1–8 and parallels).

4. See E.de Boer, *Mary Magdalene. Beyond the Myth*, London and Valley Forge 1997, 18–41. Mary of Magdala is a popular subject for intertextual studies. From the flood of literature I would mention: S.Haskins, *Mary Magdalen, Myth and Metaphor*, London 1993; M.R.Thompson, *Mary of Magdala. Apostle and Leader*, New York and Mahwah, NJ 1995; A.Marjanen, *The Woman Jesus Loved. Mary Magdalene in the Nag Hammadi Library and Related Documents*, Nag Hammadi and Manichaean Studies 45, Leiden, New York and Cologne 1996.

5. Saramago, *Evangelie*,17.

6. Ed Hoornik, *Verzamelde gedichten*, Amsterdam ²1979, 209.

7. Guillaume van der Graft, *Verzamelde gedichten*, Baarn 1982, Volume 1, 328.

8. The Greek word for fish (*ichtus*) functioned in early Christian art as a monogram containing the initial letters of *Iēsous CHristos THeou Uiou Sotēr* (= Jesus Christ, Son of God, Saviour).

9. Jan Willem Schulte Nordholt, *Verzamelde gedichten*, Baarn 1989, 183–4.

10. Gerrit Achterberg, *Verzamelde gedichten*, Amsterdam ¹⁰1988, 141–3.

11. Ida Gerhardt, *Verzamelde gedichten*, Amsterdam 1980, 535.

12. Northrop Frye, *The Great Code*, London 1984.

13. *Vrij Nederland*, 12 September 1987, book supplement, 13.

12. Jesus as a character and as a historical figure

1. C.Marsh, 'Quests of the Historical Jesus in New Historicist Perspective', *Biblical Interpretation* 5, 1997, 403–37, thinks that at least nine different phases have to be distinguished in the historical investigation of Jesus since 1778.

2. The limits of this period are defined by two pioneering books. In 1778 G.E.Lessing published fragments of the work of H.S.Reimarus, who was the first to make a sharp distinction between the preaching of Jesus and the teaching of the apostles. In 1906 A.Schweitzer sounded the death knell of earlier attempts to rescue the life of Jesus from oblivion (see n.5).

3. D.F.Strauss, *The Life of Jesus Critically Examined* (1835–36), reissued London and Philadelphia 1973.

4. W.Wrede, *The Messianic Secret in the Gospels* (1901), Cambridge 1971.

5. A.Schweitzer, *The Quest of the Historical Jesus*, London ³1950.

6. The lecture was published a year later as E.Käsemann, 'The Problem of the Historical Jesus', English translation in *Essays on New Testament Themes*, London 1964, 15–27.

7. An interim account can be found in R.W.Funk et al., *The Five Gospels. The Search of the Authentic Words of Jesus*, New York 1993.

8. J.D.Crossan, *The Historical Jesus. The Life of a Mediterranean Peasant*, San Francisco and Edinburgh 1991.

9. M.J.Borg, *Jesus. A New Vision*, San Francisco 1987.

10. E.P.Sanders, *Jesus and Judaism*, London and Philadelphia 1985; id., *The Historical Figure of Jesus*, London 1993.

11. G.Theissen, *The Shadow of the Galilean*, London and Philadelphia 1987.

12. G.Theissen and A.Merz, *The Historical Jesus*, London and Minneapolis 1998, 11.

13. F.van Segbroeck, *Het Nieuwe Testament leren lezen*, Leuven and 's Hertogenbosch 1993, 90–1, mentions the following texts: Tacitus, *Annals* 15,44; Suetonius, *Vita Duodecim Caesarum* XXV 4; Flavius Josephus, *Antiquitates Judaicae* 18, 63–64; 20, 200; he also refers to the rabbinic literature and to *Toledoth Jeshu*, a Jewish work from the early Middle Ages.

14. There is a balanced and up-to-date view in G.Vermes, *A Guide to the Complete Dead Sea Scrolls*, London and Minneapolis 1999.

15. D.Aune, *The New Testament in Its Literary Environment*, Philadelphia

1987, 17–76; id., 'Greco-Roman Biography', in D.Aune (ed.), *Greco-Roman Literature and the New Testament*, Society of Biblical Literature Sources of Biblical Literature 21, Atlanta 1988, 107–26. R.A.Burridge, *What Are the Gospels? A Comparison with Graeco-Roman Biography*, Society for New Testament Studies. Monograph Series 70, Cambridge 1992, is a thorough study with comparable results. See also C.Talbert, *What Is a Gospel? The Genre of the Canonical Gospels*, Philadelphia 1977.

16. Reflections on criteria in the investigation of Jesus can be found e.g. in E.Schillebeeckx, *Jesus. An Experiment in Christology*, London and New York 1979, 62–76; J.P.Meier, *A Marginal Jew. Rethinking the Historical Jesus. Volume One*, New York 1991, 167–95.

17. We find Jesus' preaching of the kingdom in both Mark and Q; his prohibition of divorce is attested by Mark 10.11–12, by Q (see Luke 16.16–17//Matthew 11.12–13; 5.18, 32) and by Paul (I Corinthians 7.10–11); for his table fellowship with sinners and toll collectors reference can be made e.g. to Mark 2.16–17 and to Matthew 11.19 or Luke 7.34 (= Q).

18. The term is taken from B.D.Ehrman, *The New Testament. A Historical Introduction to the Early Christian Writings*, New York and Oxford 1997, 195–6. This criterion does not entirely and always coincide with the 'criterion of Palestinian environment' mentioned by J.P.Meier, *Marginal Jew*, I, 180.

19. It may perhaps be unnecessary to observe that the year 30 (the presumed year of Jesus' death) does not form any break in the history of Judaism. There is a great continuity between the years before and after 30. Marked changes take place only in the turbulent 60s and after the destruction of Jerusalem by the Romans in 70.

20. G.Stanton, *Gospel Truth? New Light on Jesus and the Gospels*, London and Valley Forge 1995, 145–55.

21. Ibid., 156–63. Stanton points to the regulation in Deuteronomy 13.5–6 that a prophet who leads the people astray from the way that God has prescribed must be put to death.

22. Cf. E.P.Sanders, *The Historical Figure of Jesus*, London 1993; G.Theissen and A.Merz, *The Historical Jesus*, 569–72.

23. The Christian dating is based on an attempt by Dionysius Exiguus, a sixth-century monk, to calculate the year in which Jesus was born; in all probability he miscalculated.

24. Matthew and Luke put Jesus' birth in Bethlehem; thus they emphasize that Jesus stands in the line of King David. The historian

tends to follow John 7.41–42: 'Is the Messiah to come from Galilee? Has not the scripture said that the Messiah is descended from David, and comes from Bethlehem, the village where David lived?' These lines are put in the mouth of speakers who use the fact that Jesus was not born in Bethlehem as an argument against his messiahship.

Exercises

Structural analysis

Matthew 1.18–25 and the surrounding context (1.1–17; 2.1–23)
The position of Matthew 1.18–25 is disputed. There are two views:
(a) Matthew 1.18–25 forms the sequel to the genealogy from 1.1–17; in this case there is quite a deep break between 1.25 and 2.1.
(b) Matthew 1.18–25 forms a single whole with 2.1–23; in this case there is quite a deep break between 1.17 and 1.18.
Collect arguments for and against these two standpoints by an intensive reading of Matthew 1 and 2. After that balance them out: in other words, do you prefer (a) or (b) or do you see another solution?

Dynamic relations in Luke 14.1–24
Luke 14.1–24 consists of four pericopes: 14. 1–6; 14.7–11; 14.12–14; 14.15–24. Give arguments for and against this division into four. After that, investigate what relationships you can discover between the four parts. Note here the course of action and the interrelationships between narrator text and character text.

Structure of John 20
John 20 is a consecutive narration. Of what sub-units does this narrative consist? Here note the indications of place and time, the characters and motive words (e.g. 'see'). What function do the last two verses (vv.30–31) perform within the whole of John 20?

Semantic analysis

Peter in Matthew
In Matthew Peter is the name of one of Jesus' disciples (sometimes also called Simon): 4.16; 8.14; 10.2; 14.28–29; 15.15; 16.16, 18, 22, 23; 17.1, 4, 24, 25; 18.21; 19.27; 26.33, 35, 37, 40, 58, 69, 73, 75. Try to develop a

reliable character portrait of Peter. First collect his personal details. Then describe his characteristics (his distinctive features, his role in the narrative). Here note what Peter says and does, his relations with other characters and what others say about him. Is Peter purely a representative of the Twelve or the disciples, or does he also have a face of his own?

'Descend' and 'ascend' in John

In John, 'descend' and 'ascend' often relate to a movement which Jesus makes or in which he is involved. 'Descend' (in Greek *katabainō*): 1.32, 33, 51; 2.12, 3.13; 4.47, 49; 6.33, 38, 41, 42, 50, 51, 58. 'Ascend' (in Greek *anabainō*): 1.51; 2.13; 3.13; 5.1; 6.62; 7.8, 10, 14; 20.17. What lines are drawn in the use of these terms? What picture do they give of Jesus?

Form criticism and redaction criticism

A text in triplicate

In this book, at the end of Chapter 5 a reading guide has been made for texts from Matthew with a parallel in Matthew and Luke (Guide 1). If you want get used to form criticism and redaction criticism, the following passages offer excellent possibilities:
– the kinsfolk of Jesus (Mark 3.31–35// Matthew 12.46–50// Luke 8.19–21);
– the storm on the sea (Mark 4.35–41; Matthew 8.18–27; Luke 8.22–25);
– the parable of the tenants (Mark 12.1–12; Matthew 21.33–46//Luke 20.9–19).

A text in duplicate

Guide II at the end of Chapter 5 can fruitfully be applied to the parable of the unwilling guests in Matthew 22.1–14//Luke 14.16–24.

John and the Synoptics

We get a better view of the distinctive colouring of texts from John if we compare them with parallel material from the Synoptics. The Fourth Gospel contains various passages that lend themselves well to this analysis:

1. The three narratives about a miraculous crossing (Matthew 14.23–33; Mark 6.45–52; John 6.16–21);
2. The four versions of the arrest of Jesus (Matthew 24.47–56; Mark 14.43–52; Luke 22.47–53; John 18.1–12).

We do best to start by listing the agreements and differences between the text of John and the Synoptic versions. Here the use of a literal translation (like the Revised Standard Version) is a must; otherwise we see agreements which are not really there. It is worth the trouble to indicate the differences between John and the other authors in your own words. The crucial question each time is how the differences noted can best be explained. Two hypotheses deserve attention: (a) in literary terms John is independent of this Synoptic versions; his text goes back to material from oral tradition which has also been used in the Synoptics; (b) John is directly dependent in literary terms on (one of) the Synoptic versions. The choice of (b) does not imply that John slavishly follows what comes out in the Synoptic text(s). He puts new emphases of his own. Sometimes we even get the impression that he contradicts statements from the Synoptics because they are directly opposed to his own view of Jesus.

Intertextuality

Matthew 19.1–12 in the light of the Old Testament

(a) To which text are the Pharisees referring? Which texts are used by Jesus?
(b) What do the texts quoted mean in their original literary context?
(c) What meaning are these texts given in the debate between Jesus and the Pharisees?
(d) In the Mishnah (Gittin 9,10) we find a discussion about when divorce is allowed. This discussion is carried on on the basis of Deuteronomy 24.1. A translation of the text of the Mishnah runs as follows:

> The School of Shammai say: A man may not divorce his wife unless he has found unchastity in her, for it is written, 'Because he has found in her indecency in anything' (Deuteronomy 24.1). And the School of Hillel say: [He may divorce her] even if she spoiled a dish for him, for it is written, 'Because he has found in her indecency in anything' (Deuteronomy 24.1). Rabbi Akiba says: Even if he found another fairer than she, for it is written, 'And it shall be if she finds no favour in his eyes' (Deuteronomy 24.1).

Three standpoints are expressed in this text. Which view is closest to the statements of Jesus in Matthew 19.1–12?

For further study

Surveys

J.M. Court, *Reading the New Testament*, London and New York 1991

J.A. Fitzmyer (ed.), *The Biblical Commission's Document 'The Interpretation of the Bible in the Church'. Text and Commentary*, Subsidia Biblica 18, Rome 1995

J.B. Green (ed.), *Hearing the New Testament. Strategies for Interpretation*, Grand Rapids, MI and Carlisle 1995

S.R. Haynes and S.L. McKenzie (eds.), *To Each Its Own Meaning. An Introduction to Biblical Criticisms and Their Application*, Louisville, KY 1993

P.J. Hartin and J.H. Petzer (eds.), *Text and Interpretation. New Approaches in the Criticism of the New Testament*, New Testament Tools and Studies 15, Leiden 1991

J.L.Houlden (ed.), *The Interpretation of the Bible in the Church*, London 1995

S. Porter (ed.), *Handbook to Exegesis of the New Testament*, New Testament Tools and Studies 25, Leiden, New York and Cologne 1997

W.R. Tate, *Biblical Interpretation. An Integrated Approach*, Peabody, MA 1991

Literary analysis

R. Alter, *The Art of Biblical Narrative*, New York 1981

M.Bal, *Narratology. Introduction to the Theory of Narrative*, Toronto 1985

S. Bar-Efrat, *Narrative Art in the Bible*, Journal for the Study of the Old Testament Supplement Series 70, Sheffield 1989

J. Barr, *The Semantics of Biblical Language*, London 1961, reissued 1983

D.M. Gunn and D.N. Fewell, *Narrative in the Hebrew Bible*, The Oxford Bible Series, Oxford 1993

F. Kermode and R. Alter (eds), *The Literary Guide to the Bible*, Cambridge MA and London 1987

D. Patte, *What is Structural Exegesis?*, Guides to Biblical Scholarship, Philadelpia 1976

M.A. Powell, *What is Narrative Criticism?*, Guides to Biblical Scholarship, Minneapolis 1990

M. Sternberg, *The Poetics of Biblical Narrative. Ideological Literature and the Drama of Reading*, Indiana Literary Biblical Series, Bloomington 1985

Diachronic analysis

K. Berger, *Exegese des Neuen Testaments. Neue Wege vom Text zur Auslegung*, Uni-Taschenbücher 658, Heidelberg 1977

Margaret Davies and E.P.Sanders, *Studying the Synoptic Gospels*, London and Philadelphia 1989

W. Egger, *Methodenlehre zum Neuen Testament. Einführung in linguistische und historisch-kritische Methoden*, Freiburg, Basel and Vienna 1987

K. Koch, *The Growth of the Biblical Tradition. Form-Critical Method*, London 1969

G. Lohfink, *Jetzt verstehe ich die Bibel. Ein Sachbuch zur Formkritik*, Stuttgart 1973

N. Perrin, *What is Redaction Criticism?*,Guides to Biblical Scholarship, Philadelphia [4]1973

H. Zimmermann, *Neutestamentliche Methodenlehre. Darstellung der historisch-kritischen Methode*, 7. Auflage, neubearbeitet von Klaus Kliesch, Stuttgart 1982

Exegetical women's studies

R.E. Brown, 'Roles of Women in the Fourth Gospel', *Theological Studies* 36, 1975, 688–99

M. Fander, *Die Stellung der Frau im Markusevangelium, unter besonderer Berücksichtung kultur- und religionsgeschichtliche Hintergründe*, Munsteraner theologische Abhandlungen 8, Altenberge [3]1992

R.J. Karris, 'Women and Discipleship in Luke', *Catholic Biblical Quarterly* 56, 1994, 1–20

C.A. Newsom and S.H. Ringe (eds), *Women's Bible Commentary*, Louisville and London 1992

E. Schüssler Fiorenza, *In Memory of Her. A Feminist Theological Reconstruction of Christian Origins*, New York and London 1983

E. Schüssler Fiorenza, *Bread Not Stone. The Challenge of Feminist Biblical Interpretation*, Boston and Edinburgh 1984

E. Schüssler Fiorenza (ed.), *Searching the Scriptures. Volume 1. A Feminist Introduction. Volume II. A Feminist Commentary*, New York 1993 and 1994

E.M. Wainwright, *Towards a Feminist Critical Reading of the Gospel According to Matthew*, Beihefte zur Zeitschrift für die neutesta-mentliche Wissenschaft 60, Berlin and New York 1991

Intertextuality

S. Draisma (ed.), *Intertextuality in Biblical Writings. Essays in Honour of Bas van Iersel*, Kampen 1989

W.Weren, *Intertextualiteit en Bijbel*, Kampen 1993

The historical Jesus

M.J.Borg, *Jesus. A New Vision*, San Francisco 1987

—, *Meeting Jesus for the First Time. The Historical Jesus and the Heart of Contemporary Faith*, San Francisco 1994

B.Chilton and C.A.Evans (eds.), *Studying the Historical Jesus. Evaluations of the State of Current Research*, New Testament Tools and Studies 19, Leiden, New York and Cologne 1994

J.D.Crossan, *The Historical Jesus. The Life of a Mediterranean Jewish Peasant*, Edinburgh 1993

C.A.Evans, *Life of Jesus Research. An Annotated Bibliography*, New Testament Tools and Studies 13, Leiden, New York and Cologne 1994

R.W.Funk et al., *The Five Gospels. The Search for the Authentic Words of Jesus*, New York 1993

– , *The Acts of Jesus. The Search for the Authentic Deeds of Jesus*, San Francisco 1998

J.Gnilka, *Jesus von Nazaret. Botschaft und Geschichte*, Herders theo-logischer Kommentar zum Neuen Testament, Supplementband 3, Freiburg, Basel and Vienna 1990

C.J.den Heyer, *Jesus Matters*, London and Valley Forge 1996

J.P.Meier, *A Marginal Jew. Rethinking the Historical Jesus. Volume One: The Roots of the Problem and the Person*, Anchor Bible Reference Library, New York and London 1991

– , *A Marginal Jew. Rethinking the Historical Jesus. Volume Two: Mentor, Message, Miracles*, Anchor Bible Reference Library, New York and London 1994

J.Rousseau and Rami Arav, *Jesus and his World. An Archaeological and Cultural Dictionary*, Minneapolis and London 1996

E.P.Sanders, *Jesus and Judaism*, London and Philadelphia 1985

—, *The Historical Figure of Jesus*, London 1993

G.Stanton, *Gospel Truth? New light on Jesus and the Gospels*, London and Valley Forge 1995

G.Theissen and A.Merz, *The Historical Jesus*, London and Minneapolis 1998

B.Witherington III, *The Jesus Quest. The Third Search for the Jew of Nazareth*, Downers Grove, IL 1995

Software

Bible Works for Windows
Logos Bible Software
Thesaurus Linguae Graecae